THEY CAME BUT COULD NOT CONQUER

The Struggle for Environmental Justice
in Alaska Native Communities

DIANE J. PURVIS

UNIVERSITY OF NEBRASKA PRESS   LINCOLN

The University of Nebraska Press is part of a land-
grant institution with campuses and programs on the
past, present, and future homelands of the Pawnee,
Ponca, Otoe-Missouria, Omaha, Dakota, Lakota, Kaw,
Cheyenne, and Arapaho Peoples, as well as those of the
relocated Ho-Chunk, Sac and Fox, and Iowa Peoples.

Library of Congress Cataloging-in-Publication Data
Names: Purvis, Diane J., author.
Title: They came but could not conquer: the
struggle for environmental justice in Alaska
Native communities / Diane J. Purvis.
Other titles: Struggle for environmental
justice in Alaska Native communities
Description: Lincoln: University of Nebraska Press,
[2024] | Includes bibliographical references and index.
Identifiers: LCCN 2023031758
ISBN 9781496237576 (paperback)
ISBN 9781496239211 (epub)
ISBN 9781496239228 (pdf)
Subjects: LCSH: Alaska Natives—Government
relations. | Environmental justice—Alaska. | Alaska
Natives—Violence against. | BISAC: SOCIAL
SCIENCE / Ethnic Studies / American / Native
American Studies | NATURE / Natural Resources
Classification: LCC E99.E7 P88 2024 | DDC
304.2/809798—dc23/eng/20231024
LC record available at https://lccn.loc.gov/2023031758

Set and designed in Arno by N. Putens.

Thank you Fred John Jr., Mike Williams Sr., and Ilarion "Larry" Merculieff

CONTENTS

ILLUSTRATIONS

PHOTOGRAPHS

Following page 116

Following page 172

THEY CAME BUT COULD NOT CONQUER

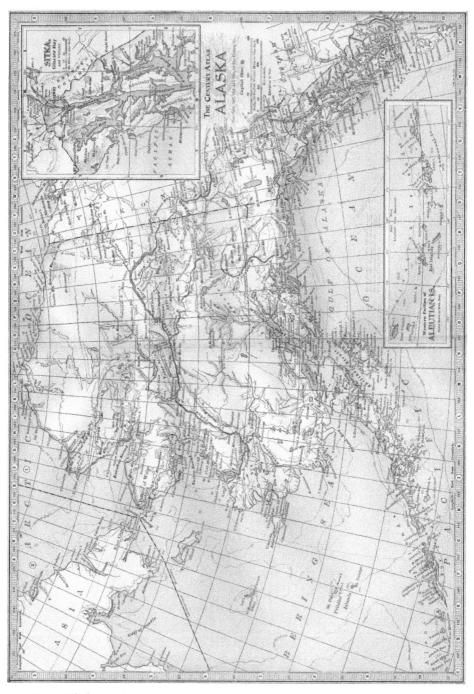

Map 1. Alaska, 1906.

Introduction

Imagine you find out that the Atomic Energy Commission is making plans to explode a thermonuclear bomb on the edge of your coastal village, or you read in the newspaper that politicians, including the current president, are scheming to build a mammoth dam that would flood your village. What would you do if suddenly, after years of harvesting salmon for your family, a fish cop pulls up to your boat and declares you are breaking the law and seizes your nets and gear? These were real-life events that played out for rural Alaska residents as they pursued daily activities, much like their ancestors. When confronted with these issues, they found ways to counter the tide. The following chapters offer examples of historical environmental crises that Alaska Natives faced and fought to prevent imminent disaster to their villages.

In the most fundamental terms, America's march of progress and technological innovation has come at the cost of defying natural laws and situational ethics while ignoring Indigenous science, all for economic gain. One side had lived with the landscape or seascape for thousands of years with reverence, stemming from the knowledge of the trees, the berry patches, the stream where one's uncle taught him to fish or an old grassy knoll where a young girl learned the art of basketry passed down from her aunt. Each day revealed a balance between humans and the environment based on guidelines from ancient oral narratives. In contrast, the newcomers were filled with conquest fever and a drive to seize nature's bounty for pecuniary prosperity. The cries for expansion and advancement, with its roots in European ethos, had traveled across the Atlantic Ocean to a land new to them, where these migrants declared ownership of the territory based on the Bible and bullets, initiating a violent subjugation of the plains, forests, rivers, and original inhabitants. Yet it took decades for the American outward expansion to reach the Pacific Northwest and then turn north to Alaska, with its massive coastline, previously but only rudimentarily explored by the Spanish, English, French, German, and, most important, the Russians. Alaska Natives found avenues for coping and seeking justice while they sought to reestablish a partnership with the landscape and waterways despite language and cultural barriers.[1] In the process they developed tools ranging from civil disobedience to an understanding of the Western courts system to counter the theft of their legacy. The following twelve Alaska Native sociocultural and ecological cases demonstrate how federal and state schemes to advance Alaska's standing in the world, regardless of the ultimate expense, were halted by Alaska Native villages and their allies.

TO FULLY UNDERSTAND the historical predicaments that occurred in Native villages, there is a need to clarify terms, beginning with *subsistence*, a word with no translation in Native languages. The neologism was created by the government to quantify a way of life. Often it is assumed that people in rural Alaska are eking out an existence in utter poverty, but nothing could be further from the truth. Conversely, gathering food and hunting are holistic processes that require great skill and planning, and these lessons are passed down from generation to generation while underscoring the special relationship with land and waters that is held sacred through rituals and in didactic stories. As Axel Johnson from the southwest Alaska village of Emmonak explains, "We, the Native people . . . are very proud of one thing, that is our culture and our Native way of life, to live off the land, because we know culture and our tradition and way of life cannot be bought," while Gwich'in activist Jonathon Solomon concludes, "You cannot break out subsistence or the meaning of subsistence or try to identify it, and you can't break it out of the culture. The culture and the life of my Native people are subsistence way of life."[2] Nonetheless, it is important to be aware of the term since it was (and is) frequently used in natural resource management and congressional decisions that had a great impact in the Alaska territory.

WHO ARE THE Alaska Natives? For one thing the people are not a monolith—there is a wide spectrum of attitudes and opinions within a single village, let alone regions. There are, however, broad cultural groups that can be geographically identified by their name, often the same as their language. In the north above the Arctic Circle, the Iñupiat live on fragile permafrost covered by an abundant tundra carpet that offers rich lichen and mosses. Villages were permanently settled along the coast to take advantage of the sea-mammal hunting until it was interrupted in the mid-nineteenth century by the Boston Men, or Yankees, as they plied the waters for the whaling trade. Below this northern region, in southwest Alaska, Yup'ik villages are located either along the coast to hunt seals or in the delta area, where fishers set their nets in the Kuskokwim and Yukon Rivers.[3]

To the more extreme southwest, toward Russia, the Aleutian Chain extends over nine hundred miles. The Unangan, often referred to as Aleut, lived well without climate extremes, except for wind, which made it impossible for trees to grow. The Unangan adapted driftwood and grasses for their needs, including sod-house roofs and utilitarian baskets so tightly crafted they could be used for cooking, while the maritime environment encouraged kayak building suitable for both the unforgiving northern Pacific Ocean and the Bering Sea. In 1741 this was the lifestyle encountered by the first Russian explorers who briefly stopped at one of the islands, a historical event that would change Alaska Native cultures forever. Not only were the Unangan enslaved by the Russians to hunt sea otters and other marine animals, but some men were moved to the previously uninhabited Pribilof Islands, about two hundred miles north of Unalaska, to hunt fur seals.

In the interior the Dene, or Athabascan, made their homes in the boreal forest, where they developed innovative ways of using birch-tree bark for everything from medicines to carefully crafted canoes. Hunters and fishers relied on moose and caribou migrations and put up salmon at their traditional summer camps. When the newcomers arrived, these activities were threatened politically and ecologically by business concerns and governmental entities aiming to develop the region as they saw fit. If the Athabascan were in the way, they were pushed aside, but not without a fight.

The Athabascan also built villages in south-central Alaska, which hosts Alaska's largest city, Anchorage. Unfortunately, these settlements were abandoned due to the construction of the Alaska railroad in 1915. Their neighbors, the Alutiiq and Eyak, two distinctive Alaska Native groups with separate languages and customs, were located in the more easterly portion of south-central Alaska. The Alutiiq language is a dialect of Central Yup'ik, but their environmental adaptation was much different from the southwest delta area, largely because of their dependence on a coastal harvest, while the Eyak, a proto-Athabascan people, occupied the Prince William Sound (specifically Cordova).[4] From the Alaska Peninsula to Yakutat, the small Native villages experienced continual natural disasters, from earthquakes to tsunamis to volcanic eruptions, but one of the most infamous tragedies occurred in 1989, when the *Exxon Valdez* ran aground, spilling millions of gallons of crude oil.

The Tlingit have made their homes in southeast Alaska, or the Alexander Archipelago, for more than ten thousand years. Their social organization was based on an intricate clan structure that differs from the political designation of tribes, particularly in the rules of inheritance and stewardship.[5] The Haida, originally from Canada, share the same laws, customs, resource-stewardship expertise, art styles, and cosmology as the Tlingit, but the language distinctions indicate different places of origin. The Tlingit and Haida had an advantage over other Alaska Native groups from harsher environments. The abundant Tongass rainforest and fisheries allowed more free time to build and support a complex sociopolitical system and intricate art forms, such as the characteristic totem poles, pieces of carved history.

Southeast Alaska Natives' economic system mirrored Western transaction strategies, leading to complex trade agreements, but the relationship was not without friction.[6] Trader journals, dating back to Russian times, describe the southeast Alaska Natives as superior bargainers and not easily dominated, based on the demand for their trade items and a superior military organization. The ownership concept, however, differed between the individualistic European or American. Tlingit and Haida clans held stewardship responsibilities for certain streams, tidal pools, land areas, and other resources in a form of Indigenous title. Attempts to disrupt this balance were viewed as theft and a vulgar lack of reverence for the land, water, or people, resulting in a simmering anger that often boiled over to revolt. For example, in 1802 Tlingit resistance fueled an uprising against Russian domination that was not resolved until 1821, and even then it was not with genuine justice for Native interests.

Over time Alaska Native groups strengthened their traditional village power and worked within the U.S. sociolegal framework, although with great difficulty. Federal Indian Law, with roots in English common law, was modified by Chief Justice John Marshall in the 1820s and 1830s without an understanding or respect for Indigenous lifeways. Within this context the outcomes favored governmental pursuits and corporate stakes in a combined drive to conquer the frontier, veiled in the theme of progress and paternalism. Legal historian Sid Harring acknowledges this perplexity and finds that "Indian law reflected this imagery as much as it did economic and political interests, as whites destroyed the tribes because their sovereignty rejected universal Anglo-American cultural values."[7] Moreover, Harring continues to explain that legal decisions in Native American cases are decided politically, not doctrinally. For Native Americans, however, the judicial system was often the only method for seeking redress.

ENVIRONMENTAL JUSTICE HAS been a buzz phrase in the popular vernacular for a while, along with numerous interpretations. In the Alaska Native example, the quest for fair dealings extends beyond pollutants or bad water. The loss of homelands left a cultural and physical trauma in its wake, while others were forced to adjust to a new ecosystem without any knowledge or guideposts, often resulting in hardship and death. Beyond outright dispossession there were other uninvited ecological modifications, emanating largely from outside forces. In the early 1900s, Alaska Natives were already observing ominous terrain and forest changes, such as dead trees, flooding, fewer birds, and other ecological warning signs. When similar issues, like fewer fish runs or dangerously melting permafrost, were reported, they were ignored.[8] It was the media, fed by various conservation groups, that brought the problems to the surface. Yet to this day, the damage that has already occurred is denied and dangerous situations are covered up by powerful groups who politically dominate the public forum. Dreams of expansion were manufactured at the expense of Native American communities and the results often left adverse conditions without consideration for the unseen consequences, imminent hazards, or long-term effects. When a people's ecosystem was destroyed and they were displaced, it became more than immoral; it was a struggle for survival.

For years Indigenous stewardship has centered on protecting the lands and waters, and in the past century, Native leaders have stepped up to disrupt proposed projects that could endanger the environment and put the inhabitants at risk. As Peter Wenz succinctly and reasonably argues, the need for environmental justice arises when people want to take more from the land than what is feasible for the health of the region.[9] What do these powerful companies or governmental agencies do when something stands in the way? They seize it without consequence, despite the fact that Indigenous communities have occupied the same ground for thousands of years. These companies or prodevelopers act with impunity motivated by avarice and hubris, often legally supported by what Walter Echo-Hawk refers to as the "courts of the conqueror."[10] Further, politicians and rule-makers assume they inherently hold a higher status than Native dwellers based on their position (and other markers), validating a right to take over whatever appears desirable—all done in the name of theoretical improvement, regardless of realties.

At the core of these conflicts we can find sharply contrasting values. In mainstream America if one uses the word *rich*, it conjures up a picture of money or what it might buy, but for Alaska Native villages wealth is measured by a healthy family, the elder's wisdom, the fish coming back every year, the stories told during ceremonies that still exist after so many years, and young people learning the cultural ways. The Western view of land centers on profit, whether that is timber harvesting, selling fur seal skins, or even providing recreational sites for tourists. Conversely, Alaska Native cultures embrace a place-based outlook, reinforced by ancient legends, passed down from generation to generation, relating the origin of mountains, streams, berry-picking patches, and the proper relationship between humans, animals, and resources. Since these are cherished sites, they must be treated with veneration to sustain life and maintain cultural mores for generations to come. In the words of noted anthropologist, Frederica de Laguna, the associations between land and dwellers are "conveyed by the names given to places, sometimes descriptive of the locality, sometimes referring to historical or legendary events . . . intermeshed through anecdote and shared experience . . . and has human significance for what it offers" in food sources, material necessities, and identity.[11] To receive monetary gains from one's home is adverse to Native cosmology, and when these ancient patterns were damaged by outsiders, not only were physiological needs in peril but also a sense of one's place in a holistic world. In the midst of this chaos, fragile ecosystems were put at risk when the original stewards were cast aside.

Why did Euro-American forces believe they were entitled to the land and resources? That answer lies with the first colonists to the eastern shores of North America. Visions, assumptions, and intellectual thinking about these lands and inhabitants were mythologized by the first bold adventurer merchants, who created a false image of Indigenous peoples as primitive and childlike. In some cases, to borrow a term from the Age of Enlightenment, they were deemed "noble savages" or those allegedly untainted by the baser aspects of civil society. The original inhabitants were considered backward in their development, and it was assumed that, through exposure to the finer points of European culture, starting with Christian indoctrination, these men and women might be uplifted from the depths of their primal nature. Such "teachings" would cut out the brutish elements, leaving a compliant person, although unequal to even the lowliest of Europeans. Coupled with these societal divisions, Native Americans were at a further disadvantage without firearms, fortifying a lopsided balance of power and enabling some of the worst abuses ever recorded (and hidden) in history.

In the fifteenth century, the church had been concerned about the treatment of any "aboriginals" the explorers might meet in the course of their travels, and to presumably ease guilt, a papal bull was decreed to act as law in these matters, mandated by the European God.[12] As this document grew in importance, it became known as the "Doctrine of Discovery," and over the years the dogma was interpreted to provide Europeans the best advantage in dealing with Natives and their resources, often based on the exigencies of the moment. As these principles were secularized, the concept of aboriginal title was added, which was not only subject to European-American definition, but any tribe, clan, or band must prove their claim. In common practice land acquisition could be consummated through a consent process and an agreeable purchase, and this strategy led to the colonization of the first inhabitants across the world, as their lands and waters were seized, and they were pushed back to undesirable and unknown environments or subjugated into menial labor.[13]

Eventually, sociopolitical refugees, escaping Europe's stratified society and with nothing to lose, risked voyaging to the prophesied haven they had heard about in taverns. The rigid class system in Europe had vanquished any notions of egalitarianism, but in America, through hard work, they dreamed of elevating their status by way of property acquisition, an impossible aspiration in their homeland. If the "Indians" must be vilified in the process, so be it. Even before leaving their shores, these expatriates already held preconceived attitudes toward the Indigenous people that oscillated between condescension and fear. Above all, they believed they were protected by their God, but they had underestimated the Indigenous peoples.

Alan Taylor argues the "European Christians insisted that humanity had a divine charge to dominate and exploit the natural world" after the biblical orders to "subdue the earth and have dominion over every living thing that moves on the earth." But the persistence of the first dwellers endured, and the tribes, bands, and clans would not allow the title of their land to be forfeited so that the intruders could "exploit lands and animals to their fullest potential" to draw a profit. As the colonists cleared the land, the wild animals escaped out of sight and "water did not seep as easily into the soil, so there were new runoff patterns, increased flooding and erratic shifts" in waterways. Often these transformations exacerbated the cyclical droughts and naked, untethered loam could not provide a barrier against massive mudslides, destroying everything in their path. Essentially, while the "settler's plows ripped into the earth, destroying native plants in favor of cultivated ones," the soil wore out.[14] This was the first sign of environmental damage. Native Americans, living in permanent villages, were forced to become nomadic, seeking fish and game to survive, drastically altering their ancient lifestyle. In the early 1820s, the Supreme Court cited this "roaming nature" as evidence for forfeiting their rights and land possession.[15]

In Native American cultures, trespassing is a matter of disrespecting another people's legends. Oral narrative retains the instructions and remembrances of a place-based culture, where each site is revered through didactic stories of origin and maintenance. As long as the land, waters, and animals are cared for and a hunter does not take more than is necessary for his family or community, territories need not be rigidly quantified since they are defined by the natural landscape from a time before memory. A stone formation might be part of an origin story, while the carvings in a mountain tell the story of the great flood. Indeed, physical objects reinforce the long term relationship between the people and their home and hold them sacred for future generations. This pattern was greatly upset by the newcomers.

MUCH OF WHAT transpired between the first Americans and the colonists can be captured in the words of those contemporary statesmen who influenced sociopolitical life. Thomas Jefferson held conflicting ideals concerning Native Americans, shifting between quixotic or practical terms. When he looked through his self-acclaimed naturalist lens, his vision imagined the American noble savages living close to the land but malleable to an agrarian life where they might cease their nomadic way of life, although he admitted the difficulties that would be encountered in the process. In "Notes on the State of Virginia," he denied any accusations that the Indigenous were weak and instead "wrote and spoke of his expectation that American Indians would assimilate into American society."[16] They would survive if they would shun their tribal cultures, religions, economics, and ways of life. In essence Jefferson was asking Natives to give up everything he admired about them, and he was not alone in his inconsistencies.

Jefferson also expressed the way to get more land was to play a ruse, resulting in "Indian debt" so complete they would be forced to sell whatever they had at a low price. What appeared to be an underhanded ploy was not shared by other statesmen. John Adams, a rival of Jefferson, carried a disdain for the Native Americans, believing they stood in the way of societal advancement, but his legal ethics turned his thinking in another direction. As a lawyer, Adams assumed the land could be purchased rather than appropriated, and this could be managed by moving villages to the south or the unseen West.[17] Later his son, John Quincy Adams, the sixth president, believed in one nation, one religion, and one people, not including any tribes, bands, or clans.[18] Regardless of who was calling for expansion, it was justified by any convenient law, whether upheld by European conquest or biblical verse.

To round out but a few examples of the thinking in this period, Alexander Hamilton, with an eye to the national treasury, was not only anxious to pay the debt incurred by the Revolutionary War but was intent on finding a legal way to wrest this so-called wasted land from Native communities. To support his strategy, he relied on the "Doctrine of Discovery" by a European power and took his case before the colonists to convince them how the acquisition of this land would elevate their position. With his knowledge of "European title, Indian title, and tribal limited sovereign and commercial rights," he advocated for the swift withdrawal of former Indian hunting lands that he believed would be better utilized in the hands of settlers.[19] This legal framework convinced those in power to take action, although it was never grounded in common law.[20]

These views were melded together in the pressure cooker of the 1787 Constitutional Convention, heavily influenced by James Madison, another iconic Founding Father, who professed the same intermix of frontier progress coupled with the presumed secondary status of the "Indian" that had been carried in the collective consciousness from generation to generation. This new American nobility believed their government was superior to all others, and it was their duty to protect the Indians from the brutish class, thereby coining the idioms "Great White Father" and "God's Indian children" to describe the paternalistic nature of the relationship. They would make decisions in the settler's interests while simultaneously attempting to convince the Native population that this was also best for them.

Madison, a practical man, believed the sale of "Indian lands" would pay for federal and local debts and fund government operations. In fact, Alexander Hamilton and James Madison "supported the new Constitution exactly because the federal government would assume the debts of the states." Once this premise and policy were established, the land grabs escalated and were sanctioned by the only existing and recognized formal government in the growing, land-voracious country. As for the Indigenous tribes, they were once again forced to move farther and farther out, while this government insisted it was safeguarding the Indian—erudite logicians saw no imminent quandary with these actions. "It was easy to conclude, salve one's conscience, that what civilization and progress was going to do to Indians" was not their fault nor problem, and this washed away all guilt or "moral responsibility for the dispossession and displacement of indigenous people."[21] These understandings, legal precedents, and approaches were all present when the Founding Fathers signed the U.S. Constitution, which remains a guiding principle to this day. Conveniently, the Indians were not citizens nor entitled to the protections of the Constitution.

As Jefferson organized his schemes, the Supreme Court gained potency through its mandated authority to interpret the Constitution. At first the executive branch was the most powerful body for making public policy and law, including Indian containment strategies, but this changed under Chief Justice John Marshall, who grew up on the "hardscrabble frontier of Virginia." His "only formal education consisted of one year of grade school and six weeks of law school," and from there he went from military officer to statesman to chief justice of the Supreme Court.[22] From this humble background, Marshall was able to uplift the status of the court in *Marbury v. Madison* (1803), winning the right of judicial review.[23] This meant the court could evaluate all laws or statutes to determine if they complied with the Constitution. Consequently, Chief Justice Marshall and the court gained respect as a separate and equal branch of government, authorized to decide the most pressing matters of the day. One of those urgencies was the Indian problem.

The Marshall Supreme Court crafted decisions about the "Indian title" that influenced Native American policy, but before that time it was established that the tribes were inferior people without privileges or the notion of individual property. The source of property rights relied on discovery, originally vested in the British Crown before being passed down to the colonies.[24] In the end Marshall determined the tribes were domestic nations and dependent people, an inconsistency in implication from the onset. The term *domestic* indicated the tribes were wards of the government, while *nations* implied a degree of sovereignty, although self-rule was never the intent. They were only independent in their own villages or when it was necessary to sell off land or resources in their jurisdiction. Treaties had been signed, some in return for reservation land, but in many cases Native leaders had no idea of the hidden implications or outright traps in these papers.[25] The dire situation was exemplified in the words of Andrew Jackson, who prided himself on being "benevolent" because, after all, he could have exterminated them all: "Humanity has often wept over the fate of the aborigines in this country, but its progress has never for a moment been arrested, and one by one have many powerful tribes disappeared from the earth."[26] Eventually, Jacksonian policy played out in the tragic Trail of Tears, an act of genocide.

NOTHING WAS MORE destructive than the concept of Manifest Destiny. The cry was "Go West, Young Man," in what Frederick Jackson Turner has encapsulated as the "Frontier Thesis," believing it was these young men who built the West by wrestling geography and fierce Indians, declaring the untamed wilderness had shaped the American character—that this rugged individualism was preeminent over all obstacles. By the late 1800s, the country's general climate of overspreading and dominating allegedly vacant lands was incorporated within "the political agenda with a vengeance."[27] Historian Richard White contends that Manifest Destiny was the "sanction for expansionists who retained Jefferson's old vision of an 'empire of liberty' for the imperial republic . . . of white freeman who made their living farming the land and trading agricultural products." In this hypernationalistic atmosphere, the Euro-American dream would be sustained, while the "Indians" could be mowed down one way or the other until the ultimate solution was confinement in reservations, hidden out of sight and mind. In essence Manifest Destiny provided "the key to economic stability and prosperity while simultaneously cooling sectional conflict" that was raging not merely because of the Indian problem but also because of the intense and complex slavery controversy occurring simultaneously.[28] And the settlers kept moving West until stopped by the Pacific Ocean, leaving the "Last Frontier" the only wilderness to subdue.

President Abraham Lincoln's secretary of state, William Seward, envisioned a land so mysterious that hidden treasures must abound—that was Alaska. In 1867 Seward was instrumental in the sales transaction between Russia and the United States, yet to this day the Alaska Natives dispute the agreement that resulted in the Treaty of Cession. When the first U.S. military troops entered Sitka, the Russian, then American, capital, located on Alaska's Panhandle and bordering Canada, they brought decades of governmental and settler bias against the continent's aboriginal inhabitants and a deeply entrenched belief in their own privilege, exerting full authority over Alaska's land and seascape.

Regardless of the immediate Tlingit protests, the U.S. government assumed jurisdiction over the population, although its influence was often thwarted by the sheer immensity of the landscape, the inability to manage an inhospitable terrain, and the inborn autonomy of all Alaska Natives. The Treaty of Cession, the bill of sale between Russia and the United States, had divided Alaska Natives into arbitrary and artificial divisions of civilized and uncivilized tribes; presumably, the civilized Natives had been under Russian control, while the uncivilized were the independent clans similar to the Tlingit. Although murky, these categories were used to decide future legislation and other legal matters.

WITH THIS BRIEF background, the following twelve environmental cases demonstrate the historical crises that occurred when isolated villages were threatened by the governmental monolith or big business. In defense they rallied together to protect their land, waters, resources, and a way of life against the bulldozer of unwanted, often dangerous, alterations labeled as progress. Since the Age of Discovery the Indigenous had been placed in inferior positions without basic human rights. In defying these attitudes, Alaska Natives faced challenges against "the harsh edges of settlerism that drove the conquest and colonization of the continent during the era of Manifest Destiny," with the hopes that the "legal system, whose function it is to serve the society, should evolve along the way and support the quest for a just culture."[29] The aggression from outside forces strengthened the innate resolve to fight for their destiny.

Yes, there is a thread of environmental justice that runs through all these case histories, but as Dina Gilio-Whitaker explains, the issues are more than the poisoning of communities—they are about "regaining access to and protection of their sacred sites and ancient territories" as a means of confronting "capitalism, colonialism and white supremacy." Further, the Norman yoke, held by the Bureau of Indian Affairs, perpetuated the administration of people without respect for self-determination, while the "domination paradigm" supported the power structure and kept "tribal governments disempowered," impeding actions to protect against risks to life and livelihood. Kivalina elder Enoch Adams believes this was a human right issue. "There is racism involved. There is class warfare. This is that rural versus urban Alaska thing. The time for talking is way past—action is demanded now."[30] The clarion sounded, and Alaska Native villages worked together to overcome decades of unwarranted bias, never settling for victim status. These are their stories.

1   Fish Camp to Picnic Bench in Áak'w Land

In October 1867 the Russian flag was lowered in Sitka, Alaska's first capital, and replaced by the U.S. flag, signaling the end of the Russian mercantile era in Alaska. The southeast Alaska Natives, the Tlingit and Haida, had undergone cultural changes when the Russians set up trading posts in the 1700s, but the pace elevated under U.S. rule, requiring major adaptations. Southeast Alaska, or the Alexander Archipelago, consists of heavily forested islands and salmon-filled waters in such abundance that the Tlingit were released from the heavy burdens of making a living and instead had the time and energy to develop an elaborate social, economic, legal, and spiritual culture. The Natives' regional dominance and sovereignty were marred, however, when their traditional socioeconomic system and environmental patterns were undermined upon the arrival of the interlopers, who staked a claim on land already occupied by those who had made it their home for thousands of years. To fully engage with this historical legal case, it is helpful to further understand traditional Tlingit sociocultural foundations, the importance of seasonal and winter camps, and the events that preceded this family's day in court.

BEFORE THE EUROPEANS or Americans arrived on the shores of southeast Alaska in the late 1700s, the Tlingit had resided on the archipelago for over ten thousand years, establishing numerous villages from what is currently known as Ketchikan to Yakutat. Their traditional social organization was divided by moieties, the Eagle (Wolf) and Raven, and further divided by matrilineal clans, all occupying large regions designated as Ḵwáans.[1] Each matrilineal clan possessed certain land sectors, tidal pools, fishing areas, berry-picking plots, or forest areas, to name a few natural sites, with oversight also extending to customary regalia and intellectual property, all managed by a clan head, *hit.sati*, and guided by an ancient spiritual foundation. In this particular legal case, the defendants were of the Áak'w Ḵwáan regional designation and specifically the Wooshkeetaan (Shark) clan. This Indigenous system was unlike the Western lineage structure. All property was passed down through the matriclan, and children followed their mother's line, although they carried prescribed duties to their father's clan as well. This intricately networked social system further shaped the political arena and social positions.

Each Tlingit village was composed of several clans in residence, as was the situation at Aanchgaltsóow, or the Town That Moved, the village in question. Tlingit historian Philip Joseph documented that at one time these clans were highly mobile until they formed a village, and they continued to fish at other locales in the spring, depending on the runs.[2] According to Joseph, the Áak'w clan leader had told the people to establish their village at this location, which provided a sandy beach for the canoes and a sheltered boat harbor, specifically for their use and occupation during the late fall and winter months. Joseph explained that "the 'Auquwon' claimed the lands from Berner's Bay (Daxanáak) down to Point Bishop. . . . The Auk Village should be four hundred years old and finally settled with clan houses by 1564," two hundred years before the Russians came.[3] The Yaxteitaan (Dipper People), originally from closer to the Stikine River in present-day Wrangell, were important neighbors, with their own property claims. The clans fought for this new territory and won, which in Tlingit law marks a customary acquisition, and to punctuate their claims they built a fort to defend their possession, Áak'w Nu, or Noow, and erected a totem pole to designate their physical and cultural title.

IN THE 1790S English explorer George Vancouver navigated through the Lynn Canal and by the Áak'w village. His men noted they saw smoke coming from the numerous beach campfires, but they recorded only the date and approximate location.[4] Later, in 1835, the Russian Orthodox priest Ivan Veniaminov estimated the number of Native residents at this site to be about seven hundred and believed the number could have been much higher at one time if not reduced by the prevalent epidemics.[5] Despite these few occasional visitors, outside contact was rare until gold fever hit southeast Alaska and forever altered the lives of all Alaska Natives.

In 1880 a notable Áak'w leader, Kowee (sometimes spelled Cowee), guided the prospectors Joe Juneau and his partner, Richard Harris, to the prized ore at what is now called Gold Creek (Dzantik'í Héeni) at the head of Gastineau Channel, and from that moment on a social revolution exploded in Alaska.[6] Early ethnologists, such as the German Aurel Krause, documented the gradual residential shift on Admiralty Island after the gold strike, stating that by the late 1880s the Tlingit lived in three villages in the vicinity of the channel, with an additional seasonal fish camp near Gold Creek. Anthropologist John Swanton recorded that the old "Auk" village, Aanchgaltsóow, remained inhabited at the turn of the century, but the Tlingit residents maintained a dual residency at the new Juneau "Indian" village due to their employment at the gold mine.[7] For many years the Natives outnumbered the prospectors, merchants, and settlers combined as more Tlingit families gravitated toward the town that would eventually be called Juneau (from the initial Rockwell) to work in the mines and other related jobs, including supplying wood, coal, or water.

In the intermixing of multiple ethnic groups, the Tlingit were influenced by diverse lifestyles, American culture, and the wage and cash economy with employment opportunities that might pay up to two dollars a day, a grand sum for those times.[8] These adjustments did not render the subsistence life unimportant, yet there was no mistake that Tlingit were lured by a paycheck and the ability to obtain Western goods.[9] The mines constantly needed more workers, and the Tlingit were hired in large numbers, but the long hours meant that returning to the village (about fifteen to eighteen miles away) after a shift was impossible.[10] As a temporary solution, Tlingit families pitched tents near the mine. During their days off or on approved leave, the Tlingit returned to the home village to take care of matters, such as putting up fish and game, drying seaweed, picking berries, and other traditional tasks.

BEFORE CIVIL GOVERNMENT was instituted through the 1884 Alaska Organic Act, and even some years afterward, peacekeeping responsibilities fell to the military, particularly the navy. Capt. Henry Glass foresaw the potential for trouble between the boisterous miners and the Tlingit and encouraged the Tlingit to relocate north to the mouth of Gold Creek.[11] Without realizing it, by complying with this order, the Tlingit had unintentionally abandoned all rights to their initial Juneau community, even though the authorities had "urged" them to do so for their own safety. Despite the disruption, another Native enclave was built and known as the "Indian Village." By 1885 traveler and journalist Eliza Scidmore observed that Juneau was populated by about fifty houses with "the Auk and Taku camp on either side."[12]

Eventually the provisional tents gave way to permanent dwellings and smokehouses, while canoes lined the beach, although the Tlingit workers never relinquished their seasonal homes or related claims. Meanwhile, the settlers and miners moved in by the droves, and the Tlingit were afforded little legal protection for their property. With the general lawlessness in the region, there was a cry out from the settlers and merchants for more governmental protection. Some demanded the fulfillment of promises made in the 1884 Organic Act, a loosely worded document establishing a governor, courts, and judges. Within the document there was also a clause stipulating "Indians or other persons in said district were not to be disturbed in the possession of any lands actually in their use or occupation or now claimed by them."[13] The wording left much to interpretation, and the growing business and governmental interests ignored Native land tenure or any other complaints. Gold acquisition was a priority, and the only messages heard came from prospectors or the owners of the Alaska-Juneau Mining Company. The Tlingit were incrementally nudged out of their usual and accustomed sites, while the fledging territorial government grappled with a need to fill its coffers. Naturally, Alaska's abundant timber stands, fisheries, mineral sites, and tourist lures were most alluring.

AN IMPORTANT ENVIRONMENTAL development occurred in the early 1900s that would greatly affect Tlingit possessory claims to the Tongass Forest, which covers almost all the Alexander Archipelago with its lush growth of spruce, hemlock, and pine. In 1902 retired naval captain George Thornton Emmons wrote a pamphlet titled *Woodlands in Alaska* for President Theodore Roosevelt. Emmons had been involved in southeast Alaska affairs for many years and was particularly integral in the affairs of the Chilkat Tlingit and Chief Chartrich in the Klukwan village. He was often called on to keep the peace between the Russians, Americans, English, and other Tlingit clans. With this experience he was well suited to be a liaison between Alaska and Washington DC. Emmons advised that the forest should be protected as a reserve and suggested that the president might take actions along those lines. Roosevelt agreed with his assessment, announcing, "The Alaska Forest reservation strikes me favorably. Let us look into it and if it is proper have it done."[14]

The other crusader was the famed naturalist John Muir. Like Emmons, he had visited the Áak'w village in 1890 but barely mentioned it in his writings. His larger goal was to defend the forests and mountains of California and the Pacific Northwest, but he too had the president's ear on the matter of preserving natural areas.[15] Roosevelt, often referred to as the conservation president, signed a series of protective measures, resulting in the Tongass National Forest reserve, and by 1909 a third proclamation extended the boundaries even farther to include Auke Bay. Although Emmons and Muir had wanted the Tongass Forest to remain unaffected by industry, President Roosevelt eventually revealed ambitious plans for development, coupled with his pervasive disdain for any Natives who might get in the way. He considered Native Americans as mere obstacles and illegal squatters. In fact, Roosevelt carried such contempt for "Indians" that he referred to them as primitives without rights, a sentiment that had been an integral part of Americanism for decades.[16]

TOURISM WAS A priority for the newly created forest, and this aspiration was supported by a growing market of well-to-do travelers, whose imaginations were sparked by notions of massive ice caps and roaming polar bears. Alaska, forever deemed a natural treasure, was a favored destination for steamer travel. Passengers were allowed to wander through Native villages, collecting the substance of grand tales for their return home, highlighted by curios to share.[17] In 1884 Alaskan tourism was extended when the Pacific Coast Steamship Company initiated summer excursions through the Inside Passage.[18] The territorial government saw the potential and requested increased funds from the federal government to build recreational sites to entice more tourists.

In response the Department of Agriculture and its Forestry Division, the agencies responsible for the oversight of the Tongass National Forest, sent out survey parties to several locations, including the waters and lands surrounding Auke Bay. Their 1923 report concluded that the region appeared to be uninhabited and would make a suitable recreational area. The plan was to clear the land of the few remaining structures and replace them with picnic benches and firepits.[19] Subsequently, the old Tlingit seasonal camp was destroyed, enraging the family who believed they "owned" the site. They were determined to seek justice. Their first defiant act was to rebuild structures that had been destroyed, and for their efforts they were issued a restraining order and told to keep out of the entire area.[20] That ultimatum set the stage for a skirmish between contradictory values and the ancient cultural meaning of ownership.

The tug-of-war went on for several years before the Department of Agriculture brought William Murphy, a miner, and his Tlingit family before the Alaska District Court for violating the restraining order, citing his dismantlement of government property. Murphy was the leading defendant and a natural representative for his family because he was male, familiar with American ways, and spoke English. According to his testimony, he had been born in 1859 to immigrant Irish parents and grew up in Minnesota. When he heard about Alaska gold, he crossed the United States and then took a coastal steamer to Juneau. By 1888 he had married the Tlingit woman referred to in Murphy's statement as "Cal-hough," and they settled into a traditional clan house, which would later become one of the structures referred to as evidence of occupation. Murphy, as was the Tlingit custom, had been adopted by the opposite clan of his wife. Since she was an Eagle, he became of the Raven moiety, while their subsequent five children were of their mother's Wooshkeetaan clan. Murphy, now following the Tlingit socioeconomic code, had a duty to fight for his children's legacy, Yet, on a broader level, he also represented Áak'w Ḵwáan because all other Crow/Raven (his adopted clan) were considered siblings with certain loyalties and duties.[21]

Given these factors, Murphy understood the obligations and challenges when he appeared in the Juneau court, wearing his ever-present Irish tam, and began his testimony, knowing he lacked public experience and fancy words. Nonetheless, he remained undaunted and claimed that in 1926 or 1927 his wife had asked him to rebuild a house at the village site for their children, because in 1910 the original house had burned down and they only had tents during the fishing season. He had taken her request to heart and started the project, but Murphy explained that once the authorities saw the buildings, he was charged with trespassing on federal land and was served a restraining order. Appealing to traditional Tlingit law, Murphy was convinced the Tongass Forest Reserve did not include their piece of land since it had been in his wife's family for generations.

Originally, Murphy and his wife had joined forces in this fight, but in February 1931 Mrs. Murphy passed away before the case went to the district court. Though obviously the underdog, Murphy forged ahead, with encouragement from his deceased wife's clan. In turn the plaintiff, the United States of America, specifically the Department of Agriculture, claimed full possession of the land based on President Theodore Roosevelt's 1909 executive order reserving large parts of the Tongass Forest. The Murphy family had a tough hill to climb since not only would they need to contest a presidential order but also prove continuous use of the site, as the Organic Act, one of the few legal precedents, required in these situations.[22]

The Organic Act was a problematic document. Although it stated the original inhabitants should not be disturbed on the land they occupied or otherwise claimed, the legislation also included a phrase indicating that final property "ownership" would be decided by congressional ruling. This left the question in abeyance, since Congress could ignore the issues and by default maintain the existing conditions in the government's favor. Up to this point, courts had consistently determined that "legal" land usage meant verified occupation and improvements for twelve months out of the year parallel to the Homestead Act.[23] In legal terms Murphy had everything stacked against him.

TO PUNCTUATE THE importance of Western-defined occupation and how it applied to all parties, regardless of ethnic background, the plaintiff's attorney, George Folta, emphasized that in the past even non-Native homesteaders had lost their land if they abandoned their claim for more than six months.[24]

Folta had recently passed the bar and was filled with vigor. He represented the Department of Agriculture, an agency that had never shown sympathy for the Native cause and instead desired to develop Alaska's resources to the maximum with the goal of advancing Alaska's position in the nation.[25] The judge, Justin W. Harding, a former Ohioan and World War I veteran, had been appointed district judge in 1927. He was a hard man to read. One of his first cases involved a Ketchikan desegregation case, and he had favored the plaintiff, a Tlingit student—quite ahead of the times.[26] On the other end of the scale, he had ruled harshly in Native fishing disputes.

This was a question of principles and ethics between those who saw the highest objective as developing former Native land for camping grounds versus the Tlingit ideal of stewardship of ancient lands, regardless of their actual physical presence. In addition, the proceedings were complicated by language difficulties. Murphy, the chief defendant, spoke both English and Tlingit, but his wife's family did not, which drew questions about their dictated affidavits and what they had actually attested to—there were rebuttals from the defendant's witnesses claiming their words had been misconstrued, while attorney Folta accused Murphy of falsehoods.[27] This was a common scene in court cases involving Native Americans. Historian Patricia Nelson Limerick explains, "Conquest also involved a struggle over languages, cultures, and the pursuit of legitimacy in way of life and point of view."[28] So it was left to Murphy to argue for the inherent ownership of his wife's land based on the fact the Tlingit were the first to leave footprints on what their opponents claimed was vacant land, or *terra nullius*.[29]

Murphy began his testimony by referring to the time he first saw his wife's village and how many acres they were using for gardens and putting up fish. He recalled that when the "young people" started working at the Treadwell mine, "the old folks kept the fires burning" until his wife's father died in 1910. Still, they returned every summer to fish and hunt, maintain gardens, and occasionally add on to existing dwellings. To Murphy and the Tlingit, these lands and waters had always been clan-owned, but the court had a different interpretation of "occupied" and gave full credence to the subpoenaed non-Native witnesses, many who stated they had merely glanced over at the island as they sailed by.

Murphy was required to give detailed explanations for the family absences, even when his wife was a child. He stated that she periodically left the home to attend school, as the missionaries demanded, and the distance required overnight stays. Beyond this point, Murphy added, his wife liked school, and it was important to her, but she always returned to the village to help her mother smoke fish, store food for the winter, and cultivate a garden, as was the custom. The garden was a key cultural symbol of possessory rights, later reinforced in a significant 1940s government study.[30] Murphy stressed that gardens were as common as fish camps even before the Russians' arrival in the late 1700s, but his arguments could not find fertile soil. The legal definition of ownership remained continual occupation spanning over all four seasons, perhaps an irony considering those wealthy tourists who visited Auke Bay often owned their own summer homes used only on a part-time basis. Nevertheless, in the eyes of the law, unoccupied land was a resource ripe for "progress."[31]

IN 1931, after numerous civil showdowns between Murphy and government agents, the matter was brought before the Alaska District Court in *United States v. Murphy et al.*, with charges filed against William Murphy and his children for trespassing on federal land and purportedly destroying structures and equipment. On the defense Murphy declared the government was wrong to think their village had been abandoned, while attorney Folta cast suspicion on the defendant's motives, accusing him of deliberately restarting a garden at the site in question only after hearing the news that the government was going to build a recreational park. In his attempt to discount Murphy's testimony, Folta refused to hear any other explanations.

Amid language difficulties and conflicting descriptions, the Murphy family maintained their right to the land, held by the clan from a time before the written word. The most detailed testimony came from Shawn-Sook, often referred to as Salmon Creek Jim or Auk Jim.[32] He remembered the Murphy family because he was also living there at the same time. Auk Jim went on to explain that, when Mrs. Murphy was alive, there was a house on the site, and so many relatives wanted to live there that the house had to be expanded, possibly referring to the traditional long clan houses of the Tlingit. For some baffling reason, the court questioned the fact that the house had been enlarged and mentioned this tended to "muddy the waters" yet offered no reasoning why they felt this way. In retrospect questions may have stemmed from the court's lack of knowledge concerning Tlingit culture. Clan houses were occupied by lineages with ties to a specific clan or subclan, and when a particular clan house (hít) became too crowded, another clan house was built or the original extended to accommodate all the kin. The Western view, however, could conceive only of single, nuclear family housing and consequently adjudicated without an understanding of the cultural context.[33]

The testimony took an unsuspecting turn when Susie (Cropley) Michaelson testified that she had been born in the original village, and the site had been an active and vital place with numerous clan houses. As a charter member of the Juneau Alaska Native Sisterhood, a Native civil rights group organized in 1915, she had experience interacting with Western society, unlike many of the others, and this background proved beneficial in the foreign environment of a courtroom. Her affidavit explained she knew the Murphys, but not from the old village at Auke Bay. Instead she had met them at the Juneau "Indian" village that had been built when naval commander, Capt. Henry Glass, ordered the Tlingit to change their location in relation to the Alaska-Juneau mine in the 1880s.[34]

Would-be homesteader John Macwilliam rebutted the Native statements, saying there may have been residence in 1886, but there was "no life" when he went by there in 1906, 1914, and 1915. In contrast, Gudmund Jensen testified he stayed in a "common house" when he was traveling through at about the same time.[35] Yet it was unequivocally the garden that was at the center of the debate. William Murphy maintained that he and his family had always grown vegetables and herbs at the old village, but that claim was countered by witnesses, including Lance Hendrickson, who was at the village in August 1922 with the survey party, plotting out the future recreational park. Hendrickson documented there were two gardens, but he said none of them belonged to the Murphys. He offered no evidence or map to back up the statement, relying solely on his personal recollection.

Beyond the significance of the gardens, there was a question concerning the cemetery, a sacred place for the Tlingit, as it is for many cultures. The defendants fought vehemently for these ancestral gravesites, and they feared the grounds might be dug up and destroyed. Harold Smith, also a member of this survey party, had reviewed the area to determine the appropriateness for a recreational park, and he verified there were "some graves" in the area. As off-handed as his testimony appeared, his observation eventually became a critical factor for the Forest Service, forcing the agency to reevaluate its land policy several years later for this area, resulting in the preservation of the cemetery site.

Charles H. Flory was the associate regional forester and responsible for maintaining the Tongass Forest and the Chugach Forest (in south-central Alaska), in addition to upholding President Theodore Roosevelt's early 1900s reserve orders. As a Yale graduate with a degree in forestry and with political ambitions, he was called on to satisfy two opposing groups: the prodevelopment investors, anxious to hasten Alaska's industrialization through resource exploitation, and the Alaska Natives, determined to protect their ancient village. Flory felt an allegiance to his government job, but simultaneously he could not disregard the Tlingit claims. At the hearing he described several ancient relics, petroglyphs, and a totem board at this site and indicated they should be preserved as part of the long Native heritage.[36]

The evidence of long occupation was dashed, however, when Flory cast aspersions on William Murphy's version of the events by claiming, as others had, that Murphy's garden did not reappear until 1924, after word had reached the people that the government planned to develop the area into a recreation center. Flory's testimony was corroborated by Forester M. L. Merritt, who had been in charge of the original survey party tasked to determine if the land was suitable for a camping area. Merritt contended the trespassing issue could not be ignored because, if the Murphy family was not stopped, it might encourage others to do the same thing. Then, for an unspecified reason, he mentioned Auk Jim as an illustration of someone who might attempt to start such a protest. This argument was coupled with the assertion that the Tlingit had probably "walked" over many areas in southeast Alaska, and if they could lay claim based on this history, chaos would ensue. Attorney George Folta agreed with this assessment and noted the same in his final decision.[37]

During the proceedings Folta cited several previous cases to prove that the court needed to demand that Native use and occupation of the site in question be proven beyond doubt, while Murphy and his family clung to the one fragile clause within Organic Act that guaranteed their family "were not to be disturbed" in their home. Looking back at the many ways the Organic Act had been previously used reinforced its shaky legal basis. Previous legal cases, such as *Sutter v. Heckman* (1901), *United States v. Berrigan* (1905), and *United States v. Cadzow* (1914), all revolved around the right of non-Natives to acquire Alaska Native land based on the stipulations within the 1884 Organic Act. The legislation had been evaluated under the premise that aboriginal titles may exist, but since American Natives were wards of the federal government, title and use of the land remained under congressional control. Yet, in a later case, *Worthen Lumber Mills v. Alaska-Juneau Mining Company* (1916), the title and ownership issue was confused by the ruling that the Organic Act "made no distinction between the rights of the white settlers and the rights of the Indians," and Congress could not deprive either of former rights to possession. This would suggest that everyone, regardless of ethnic origin or U.S. citizenship status, was on a level playing field.[38]

Apparently, Judge Harding did not consider this 1916 case, because he concluded the Murphy clan had not sufficiently proven their occupation had been "notorious and shown to the world."[39] The court was looking for fences and markers to define ownership, but the Native definition did not see the land and waters in a tightly quantified manner—their worldview was less restrained and defied plat maps.[40] Tlingit oral narrative recounts how Lingít Aaní, Tlingit land, existed centuries before Europeans reached Alaska. This was their territory, and no further requisites were necessary. Disregarding these Tlingit beliefs, the Western courts questioned, What did the "Indian" own? Was it all the land they roamed on while seeking game? As stated outright, it would be illogical to give all these resources to the Indigenous people. As with many Alaska Native cases, the absurd seemed to find its way into testimony, as when Folta claimed that it was actually Murphy who owed the federal government for educating his children and offering them a future just like the "white man."[41]

The labored testimonies of Murphy's sisters-in-law served up the final blow. These women, unfamiliar with English, were called before the judge and asked what they knew, and their only reply was they knew nothing. The record indicates that Murphy encouraged them to speak up, but they appeared intimidated by the judge and the setting. One of the deceased wife's sisters volunteered she was happy with her home and husband in Juneau, and that was it.[42] These women had gone through a Western school system that had punished them for speaking their Native language and practicing Tlingit customs—they were not about to rock the boat now, especially on what looked like a lost cause.

Against all odds Murphy did not give up what he believed was the good fight and stood up against the charge that the Tlingit, by pursuing the wage and cash economy and U.S. education, had been transformed into white men. They continued to be barred from full citizenship and therefore qualified for protective status under the federal government's trust relationship. Murphy was convinced this ruling was wrong and again contended that George Vancouver had "discovered" their village in 1790 and reported the area was fully populated. This point was so important to him that he made sure it was part of the record in his deposition and that his attorney reminded the court of the historical information in his closing arguments. In Murphy's view nothing had changed since that time, and the genuine trespassers were the forestry department.

Murphy went on to demand relief and the sum of $1,000 plus attorney fees. In the matter of fees, however, his attorneys, George B. Grigsby and Frank Foster, probably were not expecting any recompense, considering Murphy's financial situation, but that did not halt their vigorous representation of the clan's cause. Grigsby, a well-known political figure and criminal lawyer, had been the Alaska territorial delegate from 1919 to 1921, giving him an understanding of both Alaskan provincialism and the more metropolitan world of Washington DC—both were brought to the defense. Perhaps Grisby or Foster, who had traveled from Cordova in the Prince William Sound region to represent Murphy, thought this case might offer them a different sort of notoriety as keepers of the moral compass. They argued that the Organic Act applied in this case because the descendants were living on the soil in 1884 and should not be "begrudged" the right to their traditional village, particularly given that the Forestry Department was currently the oversight agency for over two thousand miles of forest, and this was such a small piece of land. Why should there be this grandstanding for so little? In their final plea, Grisby and Foster brought up the Federal Indian Law standard: in legal cases of this nature, the final conclusion ought to be calculated toward the Natives' advantage.[43]

What should have been a turning point in the case occurred when Grigsby cited a specific clause from the February 16, 1909, extension of the Tongass National Forest Act, which denoted that nothing in the legislation could be construed to "deprive any person" of the lands they occupied at that time. Although this proviso most likely referred to non-Native settlers, that distinction could not be made without blatant bias. Nonetheless, Folta found a way around it through the wording "the occupier had to have a valid right," supported by an act of Congress.[44] This brought up a whole new discussion of what constituted a valid right, and the vagueness in language did not favor the Tlingit cause, which, coupled with the Organic Act, merely preserved the status quo until such time that Congress should take up the matter. Murphy was unaware of these precedents and what they meant—to him, this was his wife's land, and he was fighting for justice.

In the ninety pages of testimony, including pictures of the family and maps, the defendant's lawyers used everything in their arsenal to contest the 1909 presidential mandate and the Department of Agriculture's position, but it was for naught. In the end the Murphy family claimed no victory, and the restraining order was sustained. Not only did William Murphy not receive the $1,000 he had requested, but he was charged $294.85 for court fees and witness transportation costs. In a most bitter irony, he was forced to reimburse those who had testified against him. The sting must have been painful. By now Murphy was in his early seventies and an anomaly, not only in his unlikely longevity for that era but in the fact he continued to labor in the Alaska-Juneau mine. This scenario, however, drew little compassion—his wages were garnished just the same.

THE FINAL 1932 judgment concluded that Murphy's wife's clan had abandoned their village location, and "the continuous possession by the Murphys is denied by a number of individuals who passed the old village or camped there a few days" and by Flory's report that, among the old "ridges of earth," no recent garden was located.[45] The recreation center was restored and welcomed tourists while the Murphy's story faded out of notice. A couple of years after the legal decision, in an apparent stab of conscience, a small plot of land and the cemetery were awarded back to the Tlingit descendants by the Forestry Division.[46]

Nonetheless, the clash between what was considered appropriate land use versus inherent, perpetual Indigenous stewardship of the resources continued for decades to come. In the Tlingit worldview, the land and waters were there for the people as long as they showed respect for the resources, a law carried in the oral narrative and marked by totem poles. Titles and deeds did not carry weight in this ancient culture. Conversely, the courts defined land tenure on the basis of single-family dwellings in finite terms rather than the wider, unrestricted Native view of extended clan houses and villages. In essence Murphy's family had been required to defend their position based on an alien legal code and a malleable 1884 Organic Act, offering no relief, since to do so would impede territorial expansion.

William Murphy can be considered a hero: first for taking on the Western legal system against all odds and, second, for fighting the cause for his children at his advanced age, only to forfeit his wages for court expenses. When two cultures meet, there will be troubles because of diversity and contradictory philosophies, as each faction faithfully clenches to their foundations based on their brand of logic. Murphy was lacking one component that might have made a difference—community involvement and outside allies with political muscle. Further, the cultural event was fraught with miscommunication and verbal misunderstandings between Native testifiers and the court, including Murphy's sisters-in-law, who undoubtedly remembered years of enforced assimilation and were afraid to speak up. Like so many Native missionary students before them, they had never forgotten the punishment they received for speaking their language or displaying traditional customs. The missionary influence conditioned Alaska Natives to remain in the background, accepting a contrived second-class status that had first taken root in the original European colonies and then spread over the continent.

This would not always be the case. In time these internalized handicaps were discarded, as Native communities built village power. From there they developed strategies to combat the loss of social or environmental rights, resulting in much different outcomes. Unbeknownst to Murphy and his family, they had kicked major boulders off the path, and in the next millennium this court testimony was resurrected and used as basis for reclaiming Auke Bay as a sacred and historical site for the Tlingit clans. The struggle required continued persistence.

The area, now called Auke Recreation Picnic Area, encompasses the former site of the Auke (Áak'w) people, and the clans have never forgotten the significance of this place in their oral narrative. The boundaries and traditional ownership privileges were recorded for posterity in a 1940s government report by agents who had scoured southeast Alaska to document Indigenous possessory rights.[47] Decades later these collected findings assisted in launching a concerted effort to reclaim the former clan locations that the descendants believed had been taken unjustly and without compensation. Their guide was the Murphy's trial transcript, and in an initial triumph Indian Point (X'unáxi), which spans seventy-eight acres, has been returned, an area likened to Plymouth Rock for the Tlingit.[48] A marker has been placed at Indian Point to designate the site as federally recognized cultural property.[49] The activists have not stopped working, and currently several other nearby areas are also under investigation as well.

2 Aleutian Shores to Scorched Earth

Dutch Harbor, located on Unalaska Island, one of many Aleutian islands on the chain, was bombed in June 1942, a matter of months after Pearl Harbor in Hawaii. In the face of imminent threat and without planning or logistics, the Native inhabitants of the Aleutian Chain were rounded up and taken onboard the *Delarof*, without a hint of their future. The ship sailed from the home islands to southeast Alaska, where the passengers were let off on various islands to live without proper food supplies, medical necessities, or infrastructure. The dwellings consisted of mostly dilapidated canneries, old gold mines, or abandoned Civilian Conservation Corps camps, and this was to be "home" for the duration of the war. Nine villages on six islands north and west of Unimak Island were evacuated, including Akutan, Atka, Umnak (Nikolski), and Saint George and Saint Paul in the Pribilofs, and the 881 refugees were told this was for their protection.[1] When the Unangan protested the deplorable conditions and lack of necessities, they were ignored, increasing their confusion over why they were treated as the enemy and confined in a geographic region they did not understand, creating an environmental crisis.

Thousands of years in the past, the Unangan had made an adaptation to the Aleutian Islands, a "treeless, windswept, foggy, and volcanic" place that appears barren to outsiders.[2] With a lack of trees, the people were dependent on driftwood and the abundant grasses, which were used in several ways, from roofs for dwellings to cooking containers. Tools were made from marine animal bones, including sewing needles used to assemble the airtight seal-intestine rain gear that was so important for keeping dry in inclement weather. Villages were situated in areas near freshwater, but oceans were just as vital to the culture. From an early age, a boy's maternal uncle would teach him how to make a *qayaq*, the specialized vessel that was strong enough to withstand both the turbulent North Pacific Ocean and the Bering Sea. As part of the social system, the boy was trained under his uncle's tutelage, guaranteeing a cultural continuity for generations to come. One individual could not survive alone. When the Unangan were forcibly removed to a foreign environment—that is from the Aleutian Chain to the southeast Alaska rainforest—they were lost without these tools, implements, and social stability. To survive they forged new kinship relationships and bonds, and these newly created communities built the essential strength to break through adversity.

This was not the first time the Unangan had faced tough times. In the eighteenth century, Russian explorers discovered the wealth that could be made in this region through the fur trade. The Aleutian Islands and Kodiak Island became outposts for mercantile interests, and international powers assumed the lands and waters were theirs for the taking by right of first discovery, regardless of the original inhabitants.[3] Word spread about the magnificent bounty, motivating *promshylenniki* (free traders) to venture to this unknown continent. The initial capital outlays were financed by Russian companies, but there were no skilled hunters. To overcome this critical obstacle, the Russians enslaved Unangan men to harvest sea otters and other marine mammals, quickly resulting in the devastation of Native communities and the sea otter population. The cruelty the Aleutian Natives suffered resulted in numerous deaths, broken families, and the shattering of the Indigenous social and environmental world.[4]

This grave situation lasted for many years, until the Russians had to admit they could no longer keep their heads above water. The trade situation had waned, hastened by sea otter overkill, and even the fur seal colony on the Pribilof Islands was not without its problems.[5] Faced with financial ruination, Russia looked for ways to offload its American acquisition, eventually leading to the transfer of power from Russia to the United States in 1867. Although the

Unangan were freed from Russian hegemony, their troubles and adjustments were not over. They had to make concessions to American oversight, including resource management, a cash and wage economy, and an unfamiliar political structure, all resulting in the further erosion of sovereignty on their own land.

For a while the Aleutian Island dwellers were sheltered from mainstream activities because of their remote, inaccessible location and lack of perceived wealth found in gold, silver, and timber, but this was not true for the Pribilof Islanders. In the 1830s the Russians had removed Unangan hunters from their original homes on the Aleutian Chain to hunt fur seals on these islands, about 250 miles north of the Aleutian Islands. After the 1867 transfer of power, these same sealers came under U.S. jurisdiction, and this was yet another form of enslavement. The status quo was maintained for several decades until global tensions fired up and threatened peace between nations.

For Alaska the big shake up occurred in 1942, when Alaska was bombed by the Japanese, and suddenly there was a war on the Aleutian Chain. The U.S. military forces and intelligence had speculated that Alaska might be vulnerable to attack, but unfortunately doubt and confusion blocked preventive actions.[6] Suddenly, one of the most crucial questions centered on what to do about the resident population and the Aleut (Unangan) villages. At once, without adequate planning, there was an urgency to remove the innocent bystanders from the islands to relocation facilities. Elders and children alike were gathered up and boarded on a ship without provisions or clothing. There was fear and a forlorn wonder as they sailed away, watching the villages ablaze in the distance.[7]

Since the evacuees had not been permitted to take many possessions, necessities were in short supply. In the case of the Pribilof Islanders, each person was allowed one suitcase, but since many did not own luggage, they packed their belongings in empty seal-skin barrels left over from the commercial trade. Aboard the ship, conditions were terrible, and sickness ravaged the young and old, especially cases of "ship's cough," and at least one baby was committed to the sea. The villagers had not been told where they were going, and some thought maybe California or even Seattle, but when the ship finally anchored, the people were dismayed and astounded. Instead of simple accommodations that might have offered basic comfort to offset the isolation and unexpected removal, the Unangan were housed in decaying, weather-beaten, canneries or similar structures on various southeast Alaska islands. For instance, at the encampment near Angoon, the only shelter was an abandoned mine. An immediate cry was heard: "When are we going home?"[8]

Families, existing in the wretched conditions, were advised to make do without medical help, adequate food sources, or decent and protective shelter against the elements. More than 850 residents from the Pribilof Islands and the Aleutian Chain were left in these makeshift camps, while the general public had no idea what was going on, nor did the refugees have access to news media that might inform them of how the Japanese had taken over two Aleutian islands, Kiska and Attu. In dilapidated buildings that had been forsaken years ago, families were separated by only a sheet with no bath or toilet facilities. The women, trying to keep their families together, were the first to speak out against the injustice and to organize, but their first priority was to keep everyone safe.[9]

These were common conditions in the southeast Alaska relocation sites, but if there was a yardstick of comparison, it was the Pribilof Islanders who experienced a harsher reality, and they had not forgotten how the Russians had exploited their ancestors for the fur seal trade. It was easy to recall, since they continued to be under contract with the government to slaughter and process fur seals. This temporary refugee status did not change the fact the sealers and their families were managed under the auspices of the U.S. Fish and Wildlife Service. Even so, resignation was not an option, and they dealt with this displacement through readaptation and faith. It took both qualities to gather food without knowledge of the rainforest flora and fauna, a potentially fatal pursuit. These evacuees occupied Funter Bay, one of the most notorious camps, located at the former site of the Thlinget Packing Company, a salmon cannery that had weathered to the bare bones in the rainforest environment. To bring back the feeling of home, they divided the camp into two sections: Saint Paul and Saint George. After organizing, the women tried to find someone in authority to listen to their pleas, even if it were only the fish and wildlife agents assigned to watch this particular camp because the valuable sealers were housed here. They pleaded, "We the people of this place want a better place . . . to live. This . . . is no place for a living creature. We drink impure water and then get sick the children get skin disease even the grown ups are sick from cold. . . . Do we have to see our children suffer? We all have rights to speak for ourselves." Complaints were carried off into the wind, never to be acknowledged by those in the government who might make a difference.[10] Unfortunately, there was no way to coordinate with other evacuees who were in the same situation, because they were not allowed to leave their camps, blotting out any efforts to form a solid political bloc in the early days. At other relocation centers the complaints were similar. Alice Petrivelli, culture bearer from Atka, related the conditions that were found in her camp:

> We got to Killisnoo [Admiralty Island] and most of the houses were in disrepair. The only decent house there they gave to Mr. and Mrs. Magie [Magee], the teachers, the only ones that had the stove. . . . Later on, the men were able to repair the homes and eventually everybody had their own little apartment. Like we lived in a two room place which was—well, summertime, it was all right, but wintertime it was icy cold and I remember being hungry. Some days were okay because we were able to get clams and crabs and fish, but a lot of time we had nothing. Well we did not have guns. We were not able to go out and get our own food.[11]

The Unangan (referred to as Aleut in documents) had no idea they would need to tolerate these conditions for up to three years, long after the Japanese had left their islands.

Alice Petrivelli yearned for the horizon of her native island, recalling how she often climbed to the top of a local hill and could see all over, but in southeast Alaska she was surrounded by trees, and it gave her a claustrophobic feeling. She did not understand the dense forest and had no history or stories to educate her about the different plants and animals and whether they were good for cooking or were poisonous. When there was sickness, she did not know where to look for the healing plants. She was saddened when she saw hungry children, yet there was so little to hunt with at that time. Years later, when she told her story, she remarked on how grateful they had been when the Tlingit from nearby Angoon had supplied their camp village with fresh salmon. She believed that was a large reason for their survival, and her story was matched by others.[12]

AT THE END of the war, those who had not succumbed to tuberculosis, malnutrition, or starvation were returned to the Aleutian Islands; others were permanently interned in camp cemeteries.[13] As repatriates, they were left to rebuild their lives from scratch as marginal U.S. citizens with few resources or funds. Unfounded enemy stigma festered just below the surface, leaving gossip and newspaper editorials doubting they were full U.S. citizens, which stung not only for its inaccuracies but also because several Native men had served in the war effort and earned commendations.[14] Nonetheless, their citizenship was questioned while civil liberties and constitutional rights were ignored, spurring a desire for equity. For a time, however, energies were directed toward recouping their lives and health.

After enduring grueling conditions in southeast Alaska, they returned to their villages in 1945 to find the structures either burned out or grossly modified for the purposes of billeting U.S. soldiers—some houses were gutted out to be nothing more than carports for military vehicles. Amid the destruction and chaos, they also found their precious Russian Orthodox icons had been stolen, apparently as wartime mementos. How could this theft have helped the war effort? The people started doubting more things as well, such as if this process had been "for their own good" and the maxim that the "government knew best." They also questioned if all this had been necessary, as they viewed the devastation war brings to the innocent.

For instance, Atka Island was nothing but a shell of former houses; the lumber had been appropriated for other purposes or demolished as part of a scorch-and-burn policy. On Nikolski Island, one of the oldest continuously occupied places in the world, homes with family pictures still on the wall had been converted into storage barns to stock army equipment. There are other similar stories, but what posed the gravest environmental danger was the wartime paraphernalia left behind, including loaded arms, grenades, and other unexploded ordnance. Accounts abounded of young boys playing with these explosives, a dangerous business that cried out for rectification.[15]

THE EFFECTS OF military vandalism were rampant across the islands, as the Unangan sought to regain a sense of normalcy. Although the people were stoic, grumblings slipped out, and there was anger over how they had been treated in southeast Alaska and the conditions of their home village upon their return. The Natives felt their plight was largely overlooked, despite a few investigations back at the relocation camps, when journalists and agency officials, even Governor Ernest Gruening, had made brief appearances. Back on the Aleutian Chain, no one outside of the military or the federal government visited in person—the story remained untold, although a governmental memorandum titled "Aleut and Pribilof Islanders" did document the southeast Alaska situation, stating, "They suffered in the camps from lack of adequate shelter, lack of medical care, lack of proper sanitation facilities, and lack of potable water supplies." The survivors knew the deaths were inexcusable and compensation was due.[16]

For a while, the survivors dealt with the immediate urgencies and left the matter of reparations on hold, but gradually the Unangan realized there was strength in numbers. The next move was to band together to make future plans and strike out for justice. Previously, councils had formed in the southeast Alaska camps, but a full politicization took several years before they could demand the government's acknowledgement of the hardships, including recognition of those who had died in southeast Alaska. Meanwhile, repairing villages fortified community unity, enhancing future political mobilization despite being hampered by a lack of supplies and government assistance. The Aleutian Island dwellers were able to make more progress on these issues as compared to those on the Pribilof Islands, who had been sent back even before the war was over to continue sealing for the government. The intense labor and lack of freedom dampened the energy needed to organize against what they believed were oppressors, but the time would come. Meanwhile, they did not forget, and they were gaining allies.

The Pribilof Islanders endured some of the worst conditions out of all the evacuees, as authors like Dorothy Jones documented in *A Century of Servitude*.[17] The sealers did not believe this was the best the powerful U.S. government could do, as they eked out an existence amid rotting walls, where all cooking was accomplished on two rudimentary stoves that served over two hundred people.[18] They recalled how space was so limited, the people slept in shifts and watched over the children so they would not slip between the floorboards. The circumstances were bad enough that the few agents who had visited the sites quit their post in disgust.[19]

Yet what price is human suffering when there is a profit to be made in fur seals? When the Pribilovians were sent to evacuation camps, the fur seal trade suffered to the point where Unangan sealers were sent back, though the war was still in full action. The 1942 return, facilitated by a forced conscription under the Selective Service, meant they were GIS (Government Issue), a commodity in every sense of the word. Yet they were also under the Bureau of Indian Affairs authority. In 1943 the secretary of the interior, Harold Ickes, had pleaded for Department of War approval to send the Pribilof Islanders back to the fur seal operation, so as not to incur further losses to the federal government coffers or the war effort. Ickes, who had been a champion of Native American rights and had met with Native leaders in the 1930s, appeared to be reversing his former stance in an uncharacteristic fashion, but this might have been part of his strategy. As secretary of the interior, he was also the overseer of the Bureau of Indian Affairs, and as such he may have reasoned that this was the best way for the people and community to be protected, and at the least it would get them away from the dreadful Funter Bay camp. Under political pressure Secretary of War Henry Stimson agreed to repatriate the "Aleut" due to what he termed a great financial duress to the United States.[20]

Upon returning to the islands, the repatriates found there was no place to stay. Any available housing was taken up by the military, leaving them to make tents and sleep outside. Regardless of conditions, the sealers were ordered to produce seal skins packed in barrels that could be used by soldiers in cold weather conditions—at least that was the government story.[21] There were reports the men were paid very little at this time, not a living wage, and their subsistence practices were curtailed because of the long hours.

Not all the Pribilof Island sealers returned to the island, as ordered in 1944. Some hid in nearby towns, while the younger boys went to school to avoid capture. The Unangan who remained until the war ended in 1945 found methods to get around scrutiny and enjoyed a bit of freedom. Some even managed to land jobs and consequently develop a taste for the wage economy—so much so that officials felt it necessary to threaten the Natives by telling them and their families that, if they chose this type of employment, they would never see their homes again. But the Natives would not be intimidated: "The native gang here at Funter wish for me to notify you that they do not want to make the trip to the Islands until the war is over. Some here and one I know in Juneau say they will not return while the war lasts. Others say they will go only if ordered to do so." They were answered with the reply that they would never be returned at all if this was their attitude, and this included their immediate family as well.[22]

Nonetheless, those who found jobs were taught skills they could take back to the islands. In addition to commercial fishing, several men found openings in construction, particularly for the army base at Metlakatla and the Tsimshian reservation on Annette Island. Also, "some were in Alaska Sea Scouts, and during the summers of 1943 and 1944, several went up to work for the Aleutian Livestock Company, a sheep ranch near Nikolski."[23] The wages had to be sustainable because once the men found work, they were no longer eligible for government-distributed food and supplies (such as it was). For others there were no jobs. They waited out the war not knowing what was going on in the world or how to better their situation. It became one dismal day after another, trying to survive.

There are various stories of how an individual made it through this period, and it was often through the kindness of others. For instance, one man recounts, "I only had about $15 in my pocket and I went to Juneau. . . . [His friend] took him down to the USED [Engineering Department]. We were building government docks." He wanted his wife to join him and became concerned when she did not arrive on one of the ships. "I didn't have nothing—no supplies." But he was able to finally get provisions from a store owner who was convinced that since he was working he would pay up.[24] Still the man and his family were in Juneau illegally and faced the threat of expulsion, or worse, on a daily basis. These once-thriving people had been lured into a world not of their making and left with no civil liberties.

NATIVE AMERICANS DID not gain full citizenship until 1924, and then even those rights were under question. In the U.S. Constitution, we know that the Indigenous, women, and African American slaves were initially ignored until addressed through several amendments. These minorities were tainted by second-class status that could not be overcome to gain full civil rights.[25] In the Unangan case, the Third Amendment, concerning the quartering of soldiers in civilian homes, should have applied in their case. Yes, this was wartime, but the soldiers stayed in these homes way after the threat was gone, and there was no reason to deliberately destroy personal property and steal precious religious icons. There is much to be said for the moral argument.

The Fifth Amendment can be combined with certain stipulations within the Fourteenth Amendment, guaranteeing that all persons born or naturalized in the United States are citizens with identical privileges, which cannot be altered without due process of law. Despite the requirement for a fair application of rights, Alaska Natives continued to live in a marginalized reality. In referencing the Bill of Rights, the Aleutian Pribilof Islands Association (APIA) later made a compelling argument that "the naked and unilateral act of billeting the troops in their homes, without legal authority or contractual right, constituted a direct and unequivocal violation of the Third Amendment." The report went on to conclude that the "Aleut" had been falsely imprisoned based on the fact that movements were restricted, similar to prisoners of war, and that this historical episode was motivated according to the government's convenience. It was easier to segregate the Native population and limit their personal freedom while they were in the camps, managing them "as a herd of animals."[26]

By unveiling the list of injustices, including lack of medical care, housing, fresh water, and sanitation facilities, combined with the loss of life, Native activists alleged they had a solid case on constitutional grounds. They stood by the stipulations within the Thirteenth Amendment, which states that there shall be no slavery or involuntary servitude. In essence and even beyond the Constitution, there had been a disregard for fundamental human rights. There was even speculation that the segregation had been motivated by the rumor that they might side with the Japanese. Although this particular theory lingers, a review of the period indicates that the panic and shock after the invasion led the government to make reckless decisions based on the exigencies of the moment. Direct ethnic bias is difficult to prove.[27]

We can get a sense of the urgency through the following eyewitness account that expresses the sheer terror upon seeing Japanese planes overhead: "When we were coming up here they was being invaded at Attu. Invasion starts and we sat off from the dock-anchored right in Unalaska Bay there, three or four transports. We didn't know what was going on. . . . The Army was here and didn't allow us—over 100 men were here. But they all scattered all over the island. At North Hill, Rush Hill, and all around fox holes . . . everything was disconnected. No running water, no beddings, nothing. And here you are—no grub."[28]

Years later, common threads ran through testimony describing the terror, lack of planning, and confusion that led to the deplorable conditions in southeast Alaska and finally the grave disappointment upon returning to the islands and finding homes demolished or converted into garages for military vehicles. Whether rebuilding their communities or planning action from a bunkhouse, the repatriates remained stoic in the face of continuing hardship. The first summer the sealers were returned, 117,164 seals were harvested for their oil and skins, and afterward the men were told to remain for the fox harvest. The Aleutian Campaign did not end until August 1943, and the returned sealers were forced to hide out because of nearby combat. One of the sealers recalled, "We come up in '43 to do sealing. Army was here. We pretty near get stuck here. . . . We hear the machine guns going off. I thought they might make a mistake on us and shoot us out."[29]

A DEPARTMENT OF the Interior report stated, "There is still evidently resentment and bitterness of the abrupt and disastrous removal. . . . The sufferings, deprivations and uncertainties that resulted from the war-time tragedy have not been forgotten."[30] One of these misfortunes was that children had missed out on months of schoolwork. Although there were attempts to bring an educational experience to the young people, no schools were available except for the Wrangell Institute. For more on that story, we once again turn to Alice Petrivelli's recollections, as she described how Mr. Barrett, the Wrangell Institute principal, came to their class one day and asked if there were any boys and girls of high school age who would like to attend his school. "As soon as I heard this I wanted to go," Alice recalled. She loved the idea of school even in this alien environment, although she thought the girls may have had it easier than the boys. In 1944 she said some of the boys were not allowed to continue in school because "the Government Services of Fishing and Wild Life puts them to work." The boys begged to stay there instead of going back to enforced federal government service, but their protests were not acted on. The boat destined to transport the young boys back to the Pribilof was known to come in the middle of the night and kidnap the boys as they slept.[31] Ironically, the shelter of Wrangell Institute may have kept the students and their parents from some of the worst abuses of the wartime years.[32]

Before I close this chapter on the Aleut Relocation, it is instrumental to relate another little known historical episode concerning the forty-two Attuan who were taken hostage by the Japanese navy and shipped to Otaru, Hokkaido, as prisoners of war. We have one recounting of this time through the eyes of a young boy, who survived this experience by his wits and naivete. Young Nick Golodoff was probably expecting to go fishing that Sunday after church or take some friends down to the beach and look for creatures in the tidal pools, but that was not to be on this June 1942 day. In the early morning, the six-year-old and his family were woken up by explosions in the air that later turned out to be Japanese warplanes strafing his small island of Attu on the Aleutian Chain. In the end everyone in his village became Japanese prisoners of war, under the watchful eyes of foreign soldiers. No one knew the future, but if they had, they would have been more scared than they already were at the time.

Two non-Native teachers, Etta Jones and her husband, Foster, who also ran the ham radio station, their only mode of communication, were also on the island. When Foster refused to enable the radio so the Japanese could get messages out, he was killed. After almost two months of occupation, forty-five Attuan were taken across the ocean to Hokkaido, Japan. Their first prison location was a vacant railroad-employee dorm. Etta Jones, however, was housed in Yokohama, where she spent thirty-nine months in the nurse's quarters under harsh physical and psychological conditions.

The Attuan prisoners of war were kept in squalid circumstances without the ability to clean or cook. They existed on rice or grasslike mixtures with occasional "spiny fish." It was never enough. Nick, more than others, often made friends, possibly because of his age and naive outlook on life. One such friend was a Japanese police officer, who supplied his family with goat meat from time to time. The women were forced to dig "clay" each day, which turned out to be dolomite for use in brick factories. Nick did not remember hearing complaints, but he often heard excited Japanese voices and planes overhead. He later learned they had been U.S. planes. He recalls also being asked if Americans were good people and who their gods were.[33] One of the most taxing burdens for the people was finding a way to bury their dead. People were dying of tuberculosis or starvation.

These innocent Attuan were held for the duration of the war, until finally permitted to sail back to the Philippines, where a military ship was waiting to transport them back to the United States. The women had been paid the equivalent of $700 in scrip for digging clay, but the money was confiscated by military authorities. Etta Jones returned by another route on September 1, 1945, and was eventually paid $7,371 for her back pay as a Bureau of Indian Affairs teacher. For all involved, the trauma was never forgotten.[34]

NOT ALL THE former evacuees sought restitution for property or psychological damage. Instead, they wanted to suppress the experience. Many were reluctant to talk to their children or grandchildren about the events they had endured, but there was a cadre that would not let these abuses go unnoticed. Before they could be effective, however, there was a need for innovative political organizations with stable leadership, inspiring others to come together to fight for both tangible and intangible losses. Meanwhile, the rebuilding efforts were overwhelming. The government helped with some of the material costs, but it was nowhere near enough. The U.S. and Japanese military had left debris, some of it hazardous, including leaked oil, chemical drums, diesel engines, weapons, and live munitions. On Atka, for instance, "children used to entertain themselves by placing powder from unused 50-caliber machinegun shells in empty beer cans and igniting them."[35] Initially, the Unangan were told it would cost too much money to move these deadly items from the islands, but they would not be deterred in their quest for environmental justice.

Despite promises and agreements, the rebuilding of several villages was deemed impossible, and the original inhabitants were forced to relocate to other locations, creating the need for massive social adjustments.[36] There was no forgetting that oppressive era or the high mortality rate in the camps, where "substandard, unsanitary and crowded living conditions deepened the psychological trauma of losing all their possessions after a sudden uprooting and voyage in the holds of ships." The ecological adjustment and the "loss of a generation of village elders had a cultural impact far beyond the grief and pain to their own families." The collective events obliterated a way of life and the wisdom of the ancestors.[37] In retrospect the chaos and death could have been avoided, but the government merely blamed these tragedies as the usual fallout from war, while the Unangan were left with the repercussions.

DESPITE THE BLATANT discrimination and disregard for basic human rights, those from the Aleutian Chain and the Pribilof Islands eventually joined forces to work for equity, a story more closely analyzed in the following chapter. In conclusion it is of interest to note what markers were left to designate these historical events. After several decades monuments and cemeteries were created to memorialize the war efforts on these islands. In 2008 President George Bush named the Pacific National Monument on the Aleutian Islands as a remembrance for an overlooked part of World War II. In more Native-centric efforts, the Funter Bay State Park was developed, preserving the Unangan cemetery located there, as well as other protected sites. In a bitter irony, in 2021 arguments against this legislation came from those in the Alaska House and Senate, who objected to closing off an area with the possibility of natural resource extraction.

3   Sealers to Slaves on the Pribilof Islands

After depleting the otter species along the Aleutian Chain, the Russians traveled southward to hunt in other parts of Alaska, until those waters were exhausted all the way down to northern California. Besides the otter, however, there was another source of furs, motivating Russian traders to establish a base on the Pribilof Islands to exploit seal rookeries. The labor was dependent on enslaved Unangan men, who were threatened with loss of life or that of their families if they attempted to escape. Avarice provoked indiscriminate harvesting, immediately taking a toll on the seal population, much as it had with the sea otter. The mounting crisis was ignored by the Russian slave masters, who instead demanded more skins to be readied for export, in what Barbara Torrey analogized as the era of "Russian serfs on an Arctic plantation."[1]

The plight of the Pribilof sealers has been obscured in history, and these stoic Alaska Natives rarely spoke of their experiences. In the early years, protests, if they existed, went unrecorded in this remote geographic location, and later generations were astounded when the saga was finally made public.[2] There would be no remedy without action, and political meetings began in earnest after the sealers returned to the Pribilof Islands from the southeast Alaska relocation camps. Under furtive cover, plans were developed in the hope of ending this oppressed existence and the fishery managers reign—the sealers vowed to shed the chains of servitude.

After years of Russian subjugation, the Pribilof sealers' fate was altered when the United States assumed control in 1867. Their masters had changed hands. The fur seal–skin market was lucrative, and the federal government wanted to be the recipient of the immense profits, preferably without competition. As other nations started sealing, however, the monopoly was impossible to maintain, as harvesters from several other countries competed on the northern seas, all with ruthless methods of killing the animals, coupled with terrible wastage. In a short time, it was apparent that conservation methods were necessary, or the entire seal population would be decimated. To preserve peaceful international relations, the first of many fur seal treaties was established to bring parity to the haphazard circumstance. The North Pacific Sealing Convention (1911) with Great Britain (standing in for Canada), Japan, and Russia was an agreement to abolish pelagic sealing on the high seas for fifteen years, and in exchange for this moratorium Japan and Canada received 15 percent of the Russian and U.S. fur seal harvest. To make this quota, the Pribilof Island managers had to increase an already overburdened workload on the Unangan sealers, who received no genuine wages and hardly had time to carry on subsistence practices. Instead, the Natives were paid in scrip that could be used at the company store, and because they were captive consumers, the government managers controlled the goods and prices.

The convention had been an unusual move and the first of its kind by involving several countries and employing rudimentary conservation principles, including a ban on pelagic sealing or open ocean harvesting. These efforts, however, did not discount the idea of profit, and efforts were not necessarily for the good of the animal, but rather to safeguard the U.S. Treasury. In the 1870s the Alaska Commercial Company, which leased the islands, objected to outside sealers, while the Department of the Treasury claimed that the United States had exclusive jurisdiction over the Bering Sea, establishing a legal basis "for restricting the killing of fur bearing animals by pelagic sealers." Congress upheld these restrictions until it was shown that it applied only to waters within three miles of the land. Tensions were not eased, and in 1886 the Revenue Marine Service seized vessels, many flying the Union Jack, causing an international clamor, but the greater debate surrounded the need to keep the fur seals from extinction without completely halting the harvesting and subsequent profits.[3]

Overharvesting continued to threaten the overall seal population. A 1913 congressional committee investigating the conditions of Alaska's fur seal industry found a great deal of piracy and numerous violations of the lessee rules, which were addressed while ignoring the condition of the sealers, a pattern that continued for decades.[4] Like so many other infractions, however, this matter faded away because Congress was far away and cared little about any issues in Icebergia. The only threats that moved the political compass centered on international conflict or a threat to business interests.

When the international focus turned to the sealers, Congress reviewed the situation and allowed, at least on paper, a legal right for the Unangan to be the sole harvesters of seal and to establish legal right of residence. This might have absolved the conscience of Congress, but did not change a thing on the islands, let alone rectify inequities. The Unangan were already the sole harvesters because of their expertise, and the government officials treated them as second-class individuals and afforded only a paltry salary. As historian Barbara Torrey explains, the U.S. government gave "with its right hand while its left land was consolidating control over the Pribilof people." She went on to conclude that, even though the "Aleuts" were integral to the commercial venture, they were in no way equal. They were not treated as citizens with basic constitutional rights.[5]

THE FUR SEAL slaughter was out of control. In the early years, the number of seals killed was estimated to be fewer than 3,500 per year, but in 1918, when the sealing business took off again, company owners were determined to make up for lost time by taking 34,890 skins that year, all harvested by Unangan, who were now considered government employees. Until 1913 the raw seal skins had been shipped to London for processing, but that was changed when skilled laborers and skins were sent to the Fouke Company in Saint Louis, Missouri, which carried the sole contract with the government to accept the skins and sell them at auction each year.[6] One can only imagine the culture shock these men went through and the level of biased treatment, as witnessed through a memo that stated the "Indians" had to be segregated from the rest of the work population.[7] These series of events solidified the colonial status of the Pribilof Islands into the 1920s and 1930s. The domesticated workforce was commanded to follow strict rules or encounter severe consequences, while continuing to be paid a pittance.

In a sardonic twist of the imagination, at one point authorities deemed the sealers might be buying luxuries, so their pay was reduced further. This was haphazardly balanced by bonuses earned by those individuals who hauled in an exceptional number of seals. Conversely, if a sealer was perceived to be out of line, his rank and pay were lowered. For the Sealing and Foxing Division, this procedure was "valuable from the standpoint of administration and maintaining control over the natives."[8] In addition to this coercion, a school was started for younger children with a strict assimilative agenda aimed to train more sealers. These efforts were disorganized, since the managers were in "the business of harvesting seals, not running schools," despite orders from the federal government officials, who reminded the overseers that schools guaranteed "a continual supply of labor on the Islands to do the sealing jobs because the students were not given other options for their futures."[9] Boys left school to become sealers at a young age, and the cycle continued until World War II shook up the convenient system, and the Fish and Wildlife Service scrambled to preserve their domain.

WITH THE SEALERS' status of government ward, the Fisheries Department thought it could make a case for keeping them out of the war so they could continue their harvesting activities. The rationale was that the Unangan were not citizens of the United States, despite the 1924 Indian Citizenship Act.[10] This assumption intensified the chattel existence, until a Washington DC court declared that the Unangan were citizens for the purposes of military service. Would they go off to battle like so many other Alaska Natives at this time? In figuring out what this all meant, the Pribilof Islanders received their military assignment—to be sealers. Nothing changed after all, except the highlighting of their apparent alien status. As Ilarion "Larry" Merculieff confirms, the law did not recognize them as genuine citizens, and instead the government treated them "like wayward children, to be pushed into becoming like the white man." But they were not like the "white man," because basic rights, such as voting, were denied.[11] The bondage was real, yet the sealers had some leverage, based on their expertise in seal-skin preparation, increasing the government's dependence on their labor until World War II.

After the Dutch Harbor attack in June 1942, the sealers were rounded up and sent to Funter Bay to live in deplorable conditions, but unlike the other Unangan evacuees, the sealers remained valuable to U.S. financial interests and so were sent back to the Pribilof Islands earlier than the rest of the evacuees to restart the seal harvest. On August 7, 1944, President Franklin D. Roosevelt approved an allocation of $200,000 from a national-defense emergency fund, to be used by the Department of the Interior for the restoration, repair, reconstruction, and equipment for the Pribilof Island operation. These funds were woefully inadequate, and the sealers continued to work backbreaking twelve-hour shifts, often forced to cook and sleep outside. These circumstances added to the previous trauma suffered in relocation camps and further separated the Unangan from their cultural bearings. Meanwhile, there was little monetary support to improve conditions, even though Congress had approved increased funding to be sent to the islands. Mysteriously, the monies and supplies had disappeared without a trace.[12]

At the time of repatriation, few families had been allowed to accompany the men back to the islands, which created more social instability. Several reasons were offered for this decision, including the lack of usable housing. Being uprooted from their homes and forced to live in squalid conditions had poorly affected the elders, whose only wish was to see their homeland again before they died—a genuine concern given the high mortality rate in the relocation camps—but officials decided that elders must stay put and not attempt the challenges of an ocean voyage. In the end "the loss of a generation of village elders had a cultural impact" that left a gap for years to come.[13] What does this mean? In many cases there was no grandfather to pass on fishing techniques and no grandma to tell the stories of the ancient ones. There were no longer women who could show younger women the best places to gather grasses to make the exquisite Aleut baskets and no men who could show young boys how to make a *qayaq* that could withstand the temperamental waters of the North Pacific Ocean.

On the Pribilof Islands, the government's resettlement policies eroded sociocultural foundations and any semblance of autonomy—not only because of the sealing managers' actions but also because of the repressive military presence as the soldiers stayed on even after the war had ended, presumably to guard the workforce. The poor conditions were exacerbated by the indiscriminate shooting of seals for sport by the soldiers, which greatly cut into the Natives' main food source. Fox farming had been introduced to the islands during the Russian period as an additional source of income, but once again it was reported, "Foxes, a cash crop and subsistence animals such as seals and caribou, were slaughtered in great numbers as a pastime by bored servicemen and ship crews" in an enormous waste of animal life for target practice.[14] These were only a few of the injustices suffered upon their return back to the islands, but the sealers did not give in and instead held a vision for their future.

AS LARRY MERCULIEFF emphasizes, the sealers might not have been Russian slaves anymore, but they were prisoners in an autocratic system and in a "state of servitude and seals were still the first class citizens."[15] In reality, he believes he was born into slavery. Because of the lack of food and long strenuous hours of sealing, the average life expectancy dropped to thirty-five years old.[16] It was not sensationalism to say that the Unangan were in the middle of a social and environmental crisis that was escalating without an endpoint. To address these ills, the Natives recognized they must organize their ranks to be effective. In fact, a camp council had begun back at Funter Bay, while they were still in southeast Alaska, and it was resurrected upon their return. The council dynamics, based largely on ancient traditions, were modified for the existential threats with an ambition to chart their destiny. The first order of business was to build effective communication channels to counter the enforced silence. The sealers and their families were not allowed outside contact: no sending letters out unless they were approved, no traveling off the island, no setting up unauthorized households, and no holding meetings unless they were related to the church or island improvements.

They were dominated but not conquered. Brave leaders looked for ways to contact others on the outside, and to do so they turned every new event into an opportunity.[17] For instance, when the sealing managers allowed a council to plan rebuilding houses and infrastructure, the meetings became a forum for action, and all methods of trickery were used, including the use of the Indigenous language or Russian to disguise conversations. Simultaneously, the Unangan on the Aleutian Chain were also forming political action groups and would become aware of the Pribilof Island situation. Once those forces joined ranks, they were indomitable.

THERE WERE SO many men and women who played significant leadership roles in those early days. Unfortunately, there is room enough to portray only a few of the champions. One of these men was Elary Gromoff Sr., who had started the move for justice back in the relocation camps, where he met with William Paul Sr., the famous and infamous Tlingit attorney and civil rights activist. By 1929 Paul had already made a name for himself by winning impossible legal cases such as the Ketchikan school-desegregation suit, years before the 1954 *Brown v. Board of Education* case. He had also politicized the Alaska Native Brotherhood, a civil rights organization, to make it more effective as a tool to fight for Indigenous citizenship throughout Alaska. Paul encouraged Gromoff to start his own chapter on the islands when he returned home, and in 1948 Gromoff persuaded the Pribilof people to do just that, with the help of well-known authority on Federal Indian Law, Felix Cohen, who advised the Pribilovians how to coordinate their efforts and take advantage of favorable legislation. Cohen had a long history of working with Native American rights, and history demonstrates he was selfless in his efforts. While working in the solicitor's office in the Department of the Interior, he was the architect of the 1934 Indian Reorganization Act (IRA), which assisted Native Americans in starting their own businesses, thereby bolstering sovereignty. When Delegate Tony Dimond and attorney William L. Paul Sr. noted that the IRA would not work for Alaska Natives, Cohen assisted on changes that led to the 1936 Alaska Reorganization Act, still an integral part of tribal governments today. In addition, Cohen was the author of *The Handbook of Federal Indian Law*, published in 1941, which is still referred to today and has become a standard. All in all, this was the expertise the Pribilof Island people needed.

The Native activists were ready to do the hard work that was necessary despite doomsayers who professed it could not be done. Aggey Galaktionoff recalled that the agent in charge of the islands did not want them "to put up an organization," because it might cause dangerous waves, but that warning would not deter them. They fooled the agent with the ruse they were meeting to discuss village self-improvement, but meanwhile they slipped out a petition to Juneau, the territorial capital, in the hopes they would garner support from territorial lawmakers and eventually Washington DC.[18] Most of all, they needed to get the word out about their situation to a world that knew nothing about them.

The islands were receiving some attention from outsiders, but it was not helpful to the Unangan cause. In the 1940s Walt Disney, a self-professed naturalist and conservationist, became enthralled with the northern fur seal population and decided to make a documentary about the seals so others might be aware they were a threatened species, according to his calculations. During the course of filmmaking, as clearly seen in the end product, he anthropomorphized the animals until they appeared to be frolicking children. He enjoyed his fantasy and was adamant that no "Eskimos" should be part of the feature film. *Seal Island* was widely viewed and won awards, while the nation assumed the Pribilof Islands were home to cute little animals, remaining clueless to the people's plight.[19]

AFTER MEETING WITH William Paul Sr. and establishing the Saint Paul chapter of the Alaska Native Brotherhood, Elary Gromoff Sr. and Gabe Stepetin Sr. secured the services of Curry, Cohen, and Bingham, who, beginning in 1949, became the first lawyers to represent the Pribilof Island cause. Together they petitioned the Department of the Interior to inspect the conditions on the islands, and a government survey crew was sent out to document the seal industry. The work must have been superficial because their report concluded that the Pribilof Island people were healthy and had not picked up any debilitating diseases—even that the housing was adequate. The lack of disease was probably due to the enforced quarantine on the islands, and the housing left much to be desired, but beyond this initial whitewashing of the conditions, the survey crew recommended a raise in wages and more benefits. It was no secret the sealers worked for a pittance, especially considering the strenuous labor and long hours, and the small raise (when they found out the amount) was not near enough, nor had their initial grievances been addressed in a satisfactory manner.

Initially, the Alaska Native Brotherhood local chapter (also called camp) had been helpful in fine-tuning political skills, but it could not take the place of the local council, which was patterned more on Unangan ways of conflict resolution. Yet there was a need for more tactical pressure to escape governmental oppression. Back in 1932 there had been an initial attempt to form a council, but the fisheries official had selected the foreman of the sealing operation as the "chief" of the council, a good company man who obeyed the orders of the operation managers and was limited to settling local disputes and planning social events in conjunction with the church. Later a fisheries agents allowed a committee to be formed to allegedly discuss the issues, but it did not take long to realize the meetings were supervised by the managers.[20] Although these attempts appear to be failures, there was no disguising the building community's unity.

The Pribilof Island leaders were masters at turning federal legislation into their own benefit as soon as they learned about it. During the Great Depression, President Franklin Roosevelt created the New Deal, and one of the corollaries was the Indian Reorganization Act, often dubbed the Indian New Deal. This legislation included the right for Native villages to author their own constitution and to organize local IRA councils backed by the federal government. Felix Cohen instructed Pribilof Islanders on how to organize their efforts through the IRA council using U.S. laws to take "forceful legal action to correct injustices." These efforts led to a major lawsuit against the U.S. government, bringing significant attention to the plight, although little changed.[21]

By the late 1940s, Congress had superficially heard the Pribilof Island case, but officials failed to admit there were any abuses by the Fish and Wildlife Service, and wages could not be raised because of budget constraints. They concluded that the claims were "unjust, unwarranted, and without foundation." When Felix Cohen read what he judged as a mockery, he wrote a missive to the government condemning the domination held over the sealers, including ownership of land; what churches should be built; "who may trade, visit, or meet with the natives"; the rights of local government; and the continuing state of serfdom. When comparing these oppressive circumstances to a "white community," Cohen was adamant that *peonage* would be the mildest term appropriate in this case. His words provoked the Department of the Interior to take action, and in 1950 a corporate charter was approved that allowed a consulting arrangement with significant government officials to allow the sealers to be on more equal footing and to address possessory rights.[22] A document, however, means nothing without implementation.

A revamped IRA council was formed in the early 1950s on Saint Paul Island, and Gabriel Stepetin was chosen president. Stepetin had never forgotten the sealers' treatment in southeast Alaska camps, declaring "they did not want us to get too smart. Only to learn how to say 'yes sir, no sir' and that was it." This memory formed the core of the movement. The IRA guaranteed the Unangan a government-to-government relationship and the ability to manage their own economic affairs, which was a major step out of servitude. Stepetin was determined to hold the government to that agreement. In 1951 Pribilof Island sealers filed a land rights and civil liberties claim, citing mistreatment as wards of the government through the Indian Claims Court (ICC), but the case never saw the light of day.[23] It was, however, recorded in the *Federal Register* along with the comprehensive history from the Russian era to the Americanization of the islands.[24] At the very least, the crisis and background were in print.

Obviously, the Pribilof Islanders were not a federal priority, as the nation faced rebuilding the economy after the war. The national atmosphere was besieged by waves of xenophobia and anticommunist sentiments.[25] Even the Alaska Natives were carefully watched for any ties to Siberia or the Chukchi Peninsula beyond the Ice Curtain.[26] In this atmosphere the Pribilof Islanders accomplished only incremental progress, hampered by their inability to leave the island, along with other restrictions.[27] It was unfortunate that the sealers could not join forces with other Alaska Native groups to fight for sovereignty at that time, but isolation remained a problem. Yet an innovative answer was on the horizon. A Point Hope man, Howard Rock, saw the need to report Alaska Native news throughout the territory and created the *Tundra Times*, which immediately acted as conduit to disseminate village events and rally Alaska Natives in common cause. In short order the Pribilof Islanders found a way to slip out news about their struggles.

Meanwhile, after a long battle, Alaska achieved statehood in 1959, but that fact had little consequence for the Pribilof Islands. The newly created Alaska Department of Fish and Game had taken over many of the tasks and responsibilities of the old federal Fish and Wildlife Service, but not the fur seal industry. In the interim the nascent agency attempted to get on its feet, generating a tussle between state and federal officials, including the inevitable turf wars. These factors were multiplied when Alaska started selecting the 104 million acres the federal government had legislatively permitted under the Alaska Statehood Act to build an economic base to support the state. In the haste to find lands that promised development opportunities and revenue, little research was conducted concerning former land use or aboriginal rights, which caused an uproar among Native communities. And where would the Pribilof Islands fit into the equation? The Pribilofs, after all, were a federal government reserve whose administration was controlled by an international treaty that continued to be updated every couple of years. After several heated discussions, the State of Alaska was allowed to keep the Pribilof Islands and would receive 70 percent of the fur seal profit, which cut into the federal take on the harvest, prolonging the territorial disputes.

Nevertheless, the quarrels were left in abeyance while alleged management inefficiencies were resolved. Sealing was mandated to become a seasonal operation with strict control and budget limitations in an attempt to con- solidate the industry. Again the government acted without considering the people, their homes, or their traditional way of life, which had all about been lost. For efficiency the Saint George residents were ordered to pick up and move to Saint Paul. In other words, they were displaced once again, while the authorities rationalized the move through a promise of better jobs. Even early on the sealers knew this was a false assurance. Stealthy measures were needed, and according to Larry Merculieff, a note was slipped out to Howard Rock, the editor of the *Tundra Times*, which was by now acting as a lifeline between Alaska Native villages. In turn Rock wrote a searing article that drew the attention of Governor William Egan, who engaged the State Human Rights Commission to investigate matters. Within days the ban on outsiders traveling to the islands was lifted, but there needed to be more.[28]

The Natives' quest for civil rights was aided by the pan-Indian movement that started in the 1960s and the discovery of oil on the North Slope, which made Alaska Native land claims an imperative. The *Tundra Times* picked up on that energy, and in 1964 not only printed articles about traditional Native land but also began a relentless campaign centered on the injustices the Pribilof

Island people had suffered, claiming, "Most people think slavery in the US was abolished with the Civil War and the Emancipation Proclamation," referring to the Thirteenth and Fourteenth Amendments. The article went on to argue that slavery still existed in Alaska: "The Aleuts of the Pribilof Islands are today living in servitude to the U.S. Fish and Wildlife Service," and there was a cry for justice.[29] This editorial was followed by a letter to government officials from the Russian Orthodox priest Father Baranof, explaining that there were real troubles on the islands, even though people were not speaking out for fear of losing their jobs—all they had to keep body and soul together. The Human Rights Commission published these atrocities, and word reached the U.S. Congress and to someone who could make a real difference: Edward "Bob" Bartlett.

Before heading to the islands, Bartlett understood the situation was under scrutiny, though managers had created a facade to make it appear as if everything was aboveboard. It was all for show, as Larry Merculieff wrote in his memoir: the Pribilof Unangan were allowed "the rights of other citizens of the United States" on paper, yet their economic base did not change because they were still dependent on the government for jobs, set wages, and the overall management of the fur seal harvesting programs. To undo the damage would take an enormous effort, yet for now there was a rigorous protest against the government's forced relocation—the people were tired of being disrespected, and that was just as true for their landscape, waters, and animals. Merculieff likened this Indigenous removal to a new-fashioned "Trail of Tears."[30] On that score a Russian Orthodox priest and a well-respected member of the community, Father Michael Lestenkof, met with a congressional delegation to explain that the people did not want to move—that this was their home: "I can tell you the most meaning of the people trying to make a move from St. George to here; that is their own place their birthplace."[31] He made it clear no other place could replace what they knew as home.

Senator Bartlett, the leader of the congressional party, was known for getting results, particularly as regards Alaska Native issues. Through the *Tundra Times*, he learned of this uprooting and relocation proposal and was appalled by the cavalier attitude. Further, he was angry about the plan to deliberately burn down the remaining houses based on the rationale that the federal government could not allow anyone to live there beyond their jurisdiction. In essence Unangan residents were treated as squatters in their own homes, and to many this was a reenactment of the wartime hardships.

Bartlett spoke with Susie Merculieff, who confirmed that the government had destroyed the homes in an act of vengeful control so that no one could settle into the vacated houses. Witnesses agreed that Senator Bartlett was visibly disturbed when he asked a member of the Bureau of Commercial Fisheries if this was true and if it had been planned. He received the answer that it was the "feeling that from the standpoint of the fur seal industry this was adequate."[32] Infuriated, Bartlett halted all further measures to destroy homes, and the residents were spared from a trauma that had already been repeated numerous times in other places and times. But there was more work to be done before solid legislation could start to resolve the inequities and heal the open wounds.

When change occurred, it was due largely to priority adjustments and the national mood. In the 1950s sealing operations were concerned about protecting fur seals based on conservation guidelines, including the abolishment of pelagic sealing. The United States continued to be earnest in seeking profits and became more aggressive in its operations, exerting concerted pressure to gain complete dominion over their designated territory. This competition took a toll on the sealers. Government agents policed their every move, and protests were suppressed by threatening to "deport" them or "kick them out of their homes, limit their rations of food, clothing, or housing or take away their jobs."[33] While the seals were monitored, and international negotiations continued, the sealers were left to grow more irate. In 1957 the United States entered into yet another convention prohibiting pelagic hunting, except by Natives, which was meant to limit the harvests of the United States, Japan, Russia, and Canada. Yet, in the Pribilof Islands case, this put more pressure on the Unangan sealers, and what was meant to relieve the problems actually made things worse. The North Pacific Fur Seal Commission acted as an "interim treaty" and was subject to revision should the conditions change to align the harvest with the "development of a stable diversified and enduring economy for the Aleut residents," and this ostensibly included Native control, but the federal government could not let this lucrative enterprise out of their grasp. Further, it was assumed that conservation requirements were met by the seasonal nature of harvesting, but this also meant there were no wages for a large part of the year. For further job training, men were sent to Anchorage to take advantage of programs there, but the instruction was not culturally or environmentally appropriate for their needs.[34] It became increasingly obvious that something else must be done on the Pribilof Islands for the human population and the fur seals.

YEARS OF MEETINGS, fighting with authorities, newspaper editorials, and the help of Delegate Bartlett finally led to the 1966 Fur Seal Act, which was complex and multilayered but did promise Native sovereignty and established that the sealers had first priority over the harvest for domestic needs if they followed the traditional manner or cultural use and were not wasteful.[35] Although this appeared to be a breakthrough, in reality the tie with the federal government was not completely severed, and the Unangan remained wards of the federal government and subject to its rules, including when to work and scrutiny over personal freedoms. Yet there was no denying the fact that the Fur Seal Act of 1966, sometimes called the Bartlett Act, facilitated equality, self-sufficiency, and self-government. "The act provided for the transfer of government land and houses to Aleuts, large steps for township incorporation under Alaska law."[36] The transition, after years of servitude, was difficult, but a new dawn had arisen, politically and economically. The Pribilof Islanders caught up to the outside world and found ways to run their own government while joining other Alaska Native groups in seeking equity.

The Alaska Native land claims issues were front and center during the 1960s, while those on the Pribilof Islands believed their individual and specific causes had been ignored, slowing down progress. In the late 1960s, Iliodor "Eddie" Merculieff, the president of the Saint Paul Community Council, testified before the Senate Committee on Commerce Hearings and complained the sealers had never been paid fair compensation. Gabe Stepetin added that they "were not allowed to speak for ourselves. Everything we did we had to get authorization through the management of the Island."[37] Other Unangan spoke out and stated they did not believe they truly had unencumbered subsistence hunting. There was sound reason for their dismay. Even after the 1966 act, the Department of the Interior retained control, based on what it called "scientific research" aligned with the ongoing conservation of both the seal and sea otter. The islands were administered as a special reservation, including Native facilities, services, and equipment. With this intense government presence, the Unangan were not allowed full decision making over their own resources, and government agents continued to control fur seal harvesting, proving that power is addictive and not easily given up. The 1966 Seal Act had sounded like the path to self-determination, but as Larry Merculieff argues, "it changed very little."[38] Yet without these Native organizations and committees, they may never have achieved that status in 1966, and there were hopes that things would get better. After all the people had endured, they had made progress and inroads to sovereignty. It was time for spiritual healing.

AFTER RETURNING TO the islands after the war, the Unangan had stayed vigilant, finding strength in the old community organizations, which relied on cultural principles for conducting discussions and reaching consensus for future actions. Meetings were (and are) conducted by first discarding all notions of mirroring the Western approach. In the past the organizations that had formed "had their own ideas about what should be done and they had their own interests to protect." This had not been a bad strategy, even as they looked toward new ideas. Tradition was restored when the wisdom keepers were consulted and had an equal voice in matters, and an air of respect was reestablished as "deliberations went as long as was necessary. . . . During this period the Unangan leadership went to unprecedented lengths to keep the community informed of the daily process."[39] Ad hoc groups had come full circle and built undeniable political sway from an agreed-on platform. As they gained solid footing, they were able to compete in a rapidly changing world and with the harsh realities of environmental crisis. Village power had stood up to meet the demands. In this way the communities were able to put the elders back in their rightful place and restore a holistic way of living.

Although the 1966 Seal Act remained in effect, at least in name, amendments were added over time. In 1976 and 1980, supplementary wording emphasized the federal interest in the economic benefits of the fur seal harvest, but there was also a provision requiring the Fur Seal Commission to give consideration to the Native needs. By 1980 a Senate extension went beyond supporting purely subsistence needs to consider the overall community economic status and growth, which included increased Native control, and by 1983 Congress terminated federal management and created a trust fund to be used by the residents to build a stable socioeconomic base. The Pribilof Islanders, with other federal and state funding, have since built harbors and other infrastructure needs, yet the Unangan continue to deal with uncertainty surrounding their political and ecological world. The latter is often centered on extreme erosion—not an uncommon problem in western Alaska.[40]

WHAT ABOUT A settlement for the treatment of the Unangan during World War II? In the 1980s, through the urgings of Alaskan senator Ted Stevens, the Unangan (referred to as Aleut) joined formerly interned Japanese Americans, including Alaskan citizens of Japanese ethnicity, to seek reparations. After volumes of testimony, they met with a modicum of success through congressional actions, and the 1988 Civil Liberties Bill was signed into law, allowing 450 Unangan to collect $12,000 a piece. An additional $6.4 million was put into trust for community relief and development, and in 1993 more was added to cover church damage.[41]

The Aleut–Pribilof Islands Association, an outgrowth of the 1966 Aleut League, developed a strong relationship with the federal government on their own terms, but this has done little to improve the financial situation. Many continue to struggle, and this has worsened from the accelerating rate of climate change. According to Larry Merculieff, who grew up on the Pribilof Islands, the residents reported these issues in the 1970s, particularly the case of fewer birds occupying the high cliffs surrounding the islands, but government wildlife agents ignored these warnings. The problem became worse, and Merculieff attributes this to the loss of habitat and nutritional sources, lamenting that nobody listens to the hunters.[42]

That the federal government was heavily involved in thoroughly colonizing the people and resources for profit was scandalous. "Racism and segregation are bedrocks of a colonial system . . . keeping the oppressed demoralized and without spirit, rewarding managers with symbols of superiority." For decades Alaska was a colony, and the trajectory of dehumanization followed from the Russian mercantile era to missionary assimilation and finally to the U.S. oversight period. Native labor was a cheap commodity. The overriding theme, however, is that the Alaska Natives refused to be victims and used every tool available to gain their self-determination. They would not, as one Saint Paul agent put it, "be tamed into compliance."[43] Instead, the sealers and their families developed strategies to not only cope with the initial circumstances but set up barricades against the federal government, the once impervious monolith. Persistence and local wisdom turned out to be the most effective devices for lifting the Pribilof Island sealers out of these restraints "because you feel it is in harmony with the Earth, and without judgment of those who do otherwise. . . . The focus must be on the vision, the dream of what we want the world to be."[44]

4 Hunters to Reindeer Herders

In *The Siberians* Farley Mowat remarks that "it seems incredible that a free-enterprise, competitive society such as ours should not have turned the Christmas reindeer-in-the-sky into a going industry. The truth is that we tried—or rather, a pair of perceptive young men in Alaska did. They were the Lomen brothers and they saw what the Soviets and Scandinavians were seeing and acted on a vision." This was what occurred in the early 1900s, until the tables were turned in a story about truth, partnerships, adaptation to change, and the Native reindeer herder facing the monolith of corporations and government on the tundra plains.[1]

DOMESTICATED REINDEER WERE not indigenous to Alaska, although wild caribou had been hunted for centuries. In the 1890s these reindeer were brought over from Siberia and later northern Europe for the Iñupiat, an Indigenous people of northwest Alaska, who have occupied the frozen northern landscape for more than ten thousand years.[2] The reindeer project, designed and initially funded by the Presbyterian Mission Society and federal government, received an initial impetus from Capt. Michael Healy of the Revenue Cutter Service, who reported the "Eskimos" were in poor condition due to exhausted food supplies. He believed this predicament could be rectified through the importation of reindeer, accompanied by lessons in herding. In that way the Indigenous people would have a permanent food source and a beneficial livelihood.[3] It was true that years of outside encroachment had led to the demise of several animal species the Alaska Natives had depended on from a time before memory, particularly the bowhead whales. Those great animals had been the center of the Native socioeconomic and spiritual system for centuries, and during the 1800s whaling era, the "Boston Men" or "Yankees" had severely depleted the resource.[4] Yet, for the Arctic Northwest Iñupiat, the extent of their relative poverty could have been exaggerated or misunderstood. Alaska Native oral narrative chronicles times of want and starvation followed by prosperity in a natural cycle, though there could be no denying that Indigenous life suffered after the entrance of non-Natives into Alaska.[5]

The few missionaries who ventured north to set up churches and schools believed their Western values, including the Christian religion, would ultimately bring salvation to Alaska Natives.[6] With characteristic zeal the missionaries attempted to change the Iñupiat ways—a people who had carved out an existence against incredible ecological odds. The most influential church organizer was Sheldon Jackson, the founder of the Alaskan Presbyterian mission. Beginning in southeast Alaska, he set up mission districts across Alaska, but religious instruction alone could not deter frontier lawlessness. In hopes of order and stability, Jackson petitioned Congress for a civil government, and his efforts were rewarded in 1884, when the Alaska Organic Act was passed by Congress. By 1890 Jackson had finagled a political appointment as general agent for education—a newly created position with far-reaching tentacles into every aspect of Alaska, particularly Native communities.

Jackson's newly created duties included mission-school inspections across the vast territorial expanse, and when he arrived on the Arctic coast, he agreed with Captain Healy's assessment that the "Eskimos" were in a depressed state. To effect a solution, he and Healy devised a plan to bring reindeer and expert trainers from Siberia to the Arctic coast.[7] Naturally, shipping reindeer across the Bering Sea was a daunting task, but after several mishaps the first successful cargo of reindeer were brought to Port Clarence, and in 1892 a makeshift reindeer station was established after a possession ceremony under the auspices of the church. Within a few years, Jackson and Healy had brought over 726 reindeer to Alaska and hired Chukchi herders to teach the Alaska Native hunters how to be reindeer herders.[8]

Unfortunately, the Chukchi trainers did not work out. Although the Chukchi and the Iñupiat were traditional trading partners, they were also bitter rivals, which led to violent fights. In one instance the Siberians were accused of cruelly lassoing the animals like cattle ranchers of the Old West.[9] These presumed abuses led to the decision to send the Chukchi back home. Jackson had to figure out what to do next and reviewed his correspondence with Norway concerning their northern reindeer herders and the Sámi (also referred to as Lapps). From there he formed a new plan, resulting in an invitation for six Sámi to set up an apprentice program for the Iñupiat. In recompense the European reindeer herders were loaned reindeer and promised complete ownership within a set time, usually about a year.[10]

In 1894 the Norwegian Reverend T. Brevig, who had accompanied an early group of Sámi reindeer herders to Alaska, built a mission, school, and station at Port Clarence with 118 reindeer. This was the site that Sheldon Jackson had initially named the Teller Reindeer Reserve to honor Henry Moore Teller, the secretary of the interior who had convinced Congress to invest in Alaska schools. It was renamed the Brevig Mission and stood as the first reserve on the western coast of the Seward Peninsula. This project held the promise of launching an Alaskan industry and training the Iñupiat as a further step in the assimilation process.[11] The reindeer station was financed by charitable donations from the Presbyterian Mission Society, whose monies were coaxed by Jackson to help the "poor Eskimo." This stereotype also influenced the Arctic social hierarchy. Since Alaska Natives were assumed to be in a dependent state, the foreign Scandinavians were more respected by the federal government in contrast to the local Natives, generating a pattern of rivalry and competition.[12] The Iñupiat did not accept this subordinate designation and accepted nothing less than their customary independence, initiating a complicated relationship between the two ethnic herders, which ranged from supporting intermarriage and blended families to Natives poking fun at the Scandinavians for their customs and three-pronged hats.

ALTHOUGH THE IÑUPIAT were promised their own reindeer after completing the training program, the actual transference never seemed to take place, and the would-be herders grew resentful. To keep the peace, Sheldon Jackson realized he had to head off this problem, but the only Native reindeer herder he marginally trusted was Charlie Antisarlook from Cape Nome, located on the Seward Peninsula on the northern shores of Norton Sound. Consequentially, in early 1895 Antisarlook was allowed to select 115 deer from the Teller Reserve, with the agreement that after five years he would return 100 deer and 75 would be the valuable females, which were strictly regulated for breeding purposes.[13] During the winter of 1895–96, Antisarlook lost a dozen deer in a snow slide, but 200 were spared, and the following winter he kept his herd even closer to the coast for safety. It was a tough winter. The reindeer moss, the main source of food, was scarce, while the herders also struggled to feed themselves. Since the reindeer could not be eaten, the herders relied on fish to stay alive.[14]

Since Antisarlook was not an autonomous herd owner, but merely a lessee, he was at the beck and call of the project's mastermind. This ambivalent status was reinforced when Sheldon Jackson asked him to lend his reindeer to feed starving miners. Charlie felt an obligation to do so, relying on Jackson's word that the reindeer would be returned to him within two years. Unfortunately, Antisarlook died in 1900 from one of the epidemics brought to the northern region by the gold miners during the time of the "Great Sickness."[15] Before his death the deer loan had been restored, but the deer were not in the same healthy condition as the original animals. When Charlie fell ill, his wife, Mary, attended the herd and kept them alive.

Mary, whose Russian name was Palasha Makrikoff, expected to be the sole owner of the herd, but there were several legal obstacles based on her social status, gender, and Native traditions. She was a tough one and fought the legal matter at the frontier court in Nome—a court more accustomed to hearing mining disputes. During the proceedings it came to light that not only was Mary attempting to hold on to her reindeer, but she also had problems with two men who accused her of nonpayment for services rendered when they had driven her herd to Unalakleet, located on Norton Sound. Mary countered that she had satisfied the debt through the payment of three reindeer, as agreed, but the parties pressed her for more, believing they could take advantage of a woman.[16]

Mary was a formidable match, with her sharp wit, multilingualism, and experience with Americans. Previously, she had been an interpreter in English, Russian, and Native languages and was quite capable of arguing her case. Although the exact testimony will never be known since the court case was not transcribed, allegedly for "the protection of Mary," in the end she was granted sole ownership of her herd, one of the few Natives who owned reindeer outright without government interference or oversight.[17] This was unprecedented and set the stage for others to also have ownership papers for their reindeer. In retrospect it was remarkable that a Western court had made this decision in the case of a Native woman, but she still had to fight off the Native legal system.

After the trial her tribulations were not over. Charlie's extended family claimed ownership of the herd, stating that under Native law a man's inheritance went to the brothers or other male kin, not the widow.[18] Although this was traditional Iñupiat law, Mary successfully argued her position within the Native community and won favor. She was never challenged again and stood as a model on many levels. During the next years she achieved legendary status as "Sinrock Mary" or the "Reindeer Queen," but beyond notions of wealth she maintained Native values of community generosity, even adopting several orphaned children. Her story was an anomaly in a rapidly changing Arctic landscape, where socioeconomic relationships were becoming more complex, and Alaska Natives were determined to maintain their way of life and ethics. Despite the odds, she managed a large and healthy reindeer herd until old age.[19]

IN THE SUMMER of 1898, more reindeer arrived at Unalakleet on Norton Sound, greatly expanding the number of reindeer and herders to "more than 600 Inupiaq and Yup'ik apprentices." By 1910 the number of reindeer "grew from a few hundred to 27,000."[20] In this decade the reindeer business diversified to value-added products, such as reindeer parkas and boots. The reindeer were also used as work animals to, for instance, pull sleds for mail delivery. As the number of animals increased, there was a greater taxation on environmental resources. The tundra could support only so many animals, and the carrying capacity, the amount of biota that can be successfully fed, was overstretched, leading to a serious competition for deer grass between the imported reindeer and the native caribou.

Sheldon Jackson also found that his monetary deficit made it difficult to sustain the expanding number of reindeer stations, motivating him to search for outside investors. To acquire funding he pledged herd owner-ship.[21] Although his worries over the demise of the reindeer experiment were justified, his grasp of Native realities was off-center—they would no longer be patronized. In plain terms, the Iñupiat had made the adjustment to com-mercial enterprise and would not settle for a dependent position. Further trouble was engendered when the disgruntled Sámi grew angrier when they were not granted the promised autonomous herds. Yes, there were a few Scandinavian trainers who had increased their assets by accumulating fully owned reindeer offspring, but it was not enough to be competitive in the marketplace. Collectively, these factors intensified the rivalry between the Iñupiat and the Sámi, as both groups tried to adapt to adverse environmental conditions, including the loss of deer fodder.[22]

THERE IS NO doubt the reindeer industry transformed Iñupiat founda-tions, economically, politically, and culturally, which, of course, had always been the intent of the missionaries. If Natives chose to have herds, they were supervised by the church missions, which had regulatory power over every aspect of their daily routine, including the initial "reindeer school." Because of this paternalistic attitude, the Natives were never fully trusted with the deer.[23] Regardless, the herders worked to be good stewards while wrestling with the idea of Western property ownership, often resulting in a cultural dissonance and a need to rationalize all these transformations, including a capitalistic economy. In effect, traditional communalism was modified along with the tundra landscape, but this did not go unnoticed, and Native village leaders met to discuss the cultural disruptions, especially to the seasonal hunting practices, which were more and more neglected, to the detriment of the villages.[24]

Within the Iñupiat socioeconomic framework, decisions were often made through group consensus, and in this relatively egalitarian society, leadership positions were assumed based on charisma, charity, and hunting expertise.[25] The missionaries and later government agents did not understand these traditions, and as Dorothy Jean Ray summarized, "The role of a hunter was not lower or less profitable than that of a herder; indeed, in an Eskimo's own culture it was higher and more rewarding."[26] The mention of profit draws another assumption that the Alaska Natives embraced the Western economy as superior to their own system of sharing and bartering. That was untrue for the majority, although the lure of Western goods was profound.

BY THE EARLY 1900s, the class division among the Arctic reindeer herders was readily apparent. There were the Sámi, often living a nomadic lifestyle with their animals; the government-managed herds attached to the missionary reserves; and a few quasi-independent Native owners, still subjected to governmental dictates as wards.[27] In the midst of this atmosphere, non-Native entrepreneurs had migrated to the region, who were not held back by second-class status or anything else. Consequently, it was not long before big business was in the picture, and the Alaska Natives were faced with additional challenges. Little by little missionary reindeer reserves were usurped by profit-seeking outsiders in tandem with Alaska slipping deeper into a colonial existence. The missionaries fought to maintain their authority, but it was hopeless against the industrial conglomerates as they eclipsed Native operations. And then there was gold.

The 1900 Nome gold rush was like a social earthquake, and eager miners came by the droves, trampling the ground already suffering from overgrazing.[28] The meeting between two distinct cultures was fraught with troubles. In addition to devastating diseases, of which the Indigenous population had no immunity, the criminal element was introduced, and there was outright theft of reindeer by starving outlaws. One of Reverend Brevig's journal entries read, "Everyone did as he pleased because there was no government. No one made an attempt to maintain law and order. Saloons and gambling houses with their customary set-up and loose population of both sexes flourished. Robbery, assaults, and murder occurred quite frequently. But no one felt under obligation to do anything toward establishing order, except in cases where the lynch law was evoked."[29]

By June 1900 six thousand people lined the beaches of Nome, forcing the Iñupiat to coexist with much more diversity than the initial foreign Scandinavians. Roughshod miners took over with rules of their own, and the Natives moved farther out for safety. As ethnohistorian Hugh Beach described, "[Sheldon] Jackson was no longer the orchestrator of development in the North. Gold took it out of his hands."[30] As an added bitter note, during the Nome gold rush, Alaska Natives could "own" reindeer under the discretionary view of the missions or educational authorities, but they could not stake a gold claim. Eventually, Sheldon Jackson was dismissed from the reindeer business, and the federal government took over the operations. The industry was secularized for efficiency, but the Native reindeer herders were no more autonomous in the process.[31]

William T. Lopp, former Cape Prince of Wales missionary turned bureaucrat, advocated for the Native interests without flaunting Western superiority. In his capacity as head of the reindeer project, he learned Native languages and the ancient ways of the north through a blend of "piety and pragmatism."[32] He pressed government authorities for Native-run companies and suggested "the natives be permitted to own herds on the corporation plan, each owning a fractional share of the entire herd . . . and receive from time to time a pro rata share of the profits in the form of dividends."[33] This was a radical idea, but nonetheless Native reindeer herders received instructions in Western business practices before being whisked into a quasi-corporation world. Lopp was convinced this scheme would allow Natives to be self-sufficient reindeer herders, but after a five-year apprenticeship through the Bureau of Education, the Native herd remained "under the supervision of the government, mission station, or Lapp owners for a period of twenty years."[34] In truth the Scandinavians, who had been imported by Sheldon Jackson and were foreigners, had more rights than their Native employees. Lopp disagreed with a system that left the Native herders defenseless against the rising number of outsiders, and he included the Sámi in his contention. Lopp published the annual *Eskimo Bulletin*, and in one editorial he made his point clear: "What the U.S. Bureau of Education expects to accomplish by bringing in so many Laplanders to Arctic Alaska, is an enigma to all who are personally acquainted with the destitution, need, and possibilities of the Eskimo race."[35]

Relentless and stubborn, Lopp recommended that Native reindeer herders form their own companies to counter those who were taking the reindeer industry out of their hands, but the political atmosphere was not conducive to this transformation.[36] The belief persisted that Natives could not be trusted with their own reindeer, and the situation turned worse when the government stopped protecting Native herds. Suddenly, without preparation, the Iñupiat were thrown into full-blown competition with large companies outside of Alaska. One can imagine the contrast between a lone Native herder pitted against unregulated international markets with massive capital.

IN 1914 TWO Norwegian American businessmen, Carl and Albert Lomen from Saint Paul, Minnesota, formed the Lomen Company, based in Nome. They had first arrived in 1900 for the Nome gold rush, but when that venture did not work out, they looked toward the reindeer industry as a path to riches. At first they bought reindeer from Teller, Golovin, and a Kotzebue Sámi herder, Alfred Nilima, whose contract was up, allowing him to sell 1,200 reindeer, including females, indicative of the loosening restrictions.[37] As the Lomen business expanded, they built cold storage plants and secured shipping vessels that could carry cargo to Seattle and beyond. On the day the Lomens were listed on the New York Stock Exchange, there could be no doubt about their financial standing and how it translated into economic power.[38]

The Lomens had no trouble building their reindeer monopoly, even though approximately thirty-seven thousand animals were "owned" or otherwise managed by the individual Native families. These smaller herds usually numbered only about fifty head, which was financially inefficient, and when it looked like a losing proposition, the Lomens swooped in, promising they could reduce their burdens by selling the deer at a quick profit. This was in addition to the "company store" that tempted Native herders to put up their deer as credit for goods.[39] A few Native herders realized they were essentially being swindled, but the Lomens' enticements were difficult to resist, and the government was too far away to help. The few courts that existed seemed feckless and bent on improvised frontier justice. For instance, in 1920 Gudbrand Lomen, Carl Lomen's father and an attorney, was charged with illegally purchasing Teller

Mission reindeer, but there was no one to hear the case, enforce a sentence, or provide any equity in the matter.[40]

Carl Lomen, ultimately dubbed "The Reindeer King," expanded the operation without impediments. The government attempted to extend its fiduciary responsibly by consolidating Native herds into larger units as cooperatives and issuing stock to Native owners (one share for each deer), but this strategy failed, largely because the herders were merely government employees.[41] If the plan had been backed by trusted Native leaders, strategic alliances might have built, but without this foundation and a reliance on Native values, it was doomed to failure. Alternatively, a situation developed where no one took responsibility for herd maintenance.[42] Amid the chaos and dismal failure, there was hope that the Reindeer Service might come up with a solid plan.

The Alaska Reindeer Service (ARS) had begun in 1893 to be a watch dog on federal appropriations for the reindeer herds and to ostensibly protect the Natives from outsiders. The ARS, under the U.S. Bureau of Education, was based in Seattle and included seven local agents with a mission to educate (another word for assimilate) the Natives through the reindeer business, yet no amount of government sponsorship afforded equity.[43] By 1909 the program had enjoyed little "success, reportedly due to the lack of funds and trained Eskimo herdsmen."[44] The ARS had aimed to gradually extinguish federal ties and allow outright Native ownership, yet too many factors blocked that goal. Rules were made, particularly concerning the valuable female deer, through a Reindeer Council, where it was hoped the Iñupiat interests would be represented, but the Native herders were without a mandate to implement decisions. The ARS also had no knowledge of the terrain or way of life, plus they carried a disdain for Sámi herders, increasing the discord between herding groups, particularly since there were several mixed marriages.[45] In sum troubles were not eased, and communities became even more divided, leading to a stalemate.

Enlightened governmental officials were convinced that Indigenous rights must be addressed, and to do so required influential Native spokespeople to act as cultural brokers. Traditionally, villages had relied on a loosely organized structure, and now they had to contend with a mystical place called Washington DC. Their only hope was to rely on Office of Indian Affairs agents to act as a liaison between Alaska and the people who were making the policy, particularly Congress. In the meantime the agents advised the Natives to form "ownership clubs" in conjunction with the reindeer fairs, grand gatherings still talked about today.

The reindeer fairs brought communities together to socialize, share tips, trade animals, discuss issues, and incidentally bolster informal political bodies. In some cases these fairs were more effective than the more official reindeer councils because they were structured in a manner that paralleled the old trade gatherings before the arrival of missionaries. The first fair was held in the village of Igloo, forty miles from Teller, and was organized by Walter C. Shields, the superintendent of education for northwest Alaska. Although representatives from the missions, government agencies, and even Carl Lomen were in attendance, the proceedings were controlled by the Natives.

These meetings took on the atmosphere of the traditional regional ceremonies with displays of handicrafts, story sharing, and competitive games of skill.[46] Business was also conducted, including discussions concerning the importance of deer markings used to define animal ownership. An understanding of a herder's marks, similar to cattle brands, went a long way to mitigate the confusion over loose animals who could not be recognized, creating a question of who owned the deer when they merged into other herds out on the tundra.[47] As more reindeer wandered from the herd and mixed in with the caribou, these markings became essential and prevented potential disputes. In spite of these precautions, however, some animals wandered so far in their search for food sources that they were permanently lost.

A 1918 Bureau of Education bulletin confirmed the fairs were important and tended to support the Natives over the intrusions of the "white man." At these fairs the superintendent described the "reindeer men" as highly regarded leaders, capable of bringing unity and "brotherhood" to their communities to achieve "native rights."[48] Further, it was documented that "the fairs were a great success insofar as they attracted leading Eskimo personalities . . . and stimulated interest in reindeer through competitive events stressing deer strength and herder dexterity and imagination."[49] Regardless of sprouting Indigenous political groups, the Lomen influence and hubris prevailed, and the Lomens thought nothing of interfering in Native business. Untethered, they secured deer with only a promise to pay—no one questioned the reindeer monarchy. Later it became known that they were secretly suffering financially and did not have the means to pay. In this unsettled atmosphere, the protective arm of Bureau of Education urged Native owners to "band together in reindeer associations" for their own protection.[50]

Shielded or not, the Native herders learned how to navigate within governmental agencies, though their naivete often forced them to rely on outsider expertise and take their chances. For instance, the Biological Survey (forerunner of the Fish and Wildlife Service) recommended open herding to the Native ranchers, deeming it would be healthier for the reindeer. The herders reluctantly accepted this drastic change, but it turned out to be of no benefit to the animals or recordkeeping: "While the corporations boast of millions of dollars invested, the natives have done remarkably well until the heresy of open herding was introduced. . . . He has accomplished much for a man only one lifetime removed from a hunter on the sea."[51] The fact was that, without borders, the herds strayed farther from base operations, entering into caribou herds and becoming indistinguishable.

DURING THE 1920S and early 1930s, the reindeer industry continued to be neglected by the government, but that does not mean that individual Native herders were not doing well. For a moment it is of interest to review how the descendants remember the events of the time. Dan Karman, the former director for the northwest Alaska Reindeer Herders Association, shares that "Teller was selected as the site to administer the growing industry to get herders involved," and that was when the Sámi were introduced to the Natives as those who would train them. Clifford Weyiouanna from Shishmaref recalls how his grandfather, Will Malaklak, earned two bulls upon the completion of his "education," while his wife, who cooked for all the reindeer herders, "earned seven females and started a herd."[52] That was the way many spontaneous herds started, along with the combined herds in the case of Scandinavian-Native marriages. For instance, Donny Olson recalls how his Finnish great grandfather, Oolie Olson, came to Alaska in 1898 on the *Manitoba*: "He had a contract with Sheldon Jackson and that group to be part of the Laplander herders that came over and were teaching the local Natives to go ahead and herd reindeer that had just been brought over from Siberia 6 or 7 years ago . . . about the time there was a the gold strike here in the Nome area . . . and that's why reindeer have been such a big part of my life."[53] Olson reinforces the fact that the marriages not only cemented financial partnerships but also blended cultures.

Strict school attendance and reindeer herding were often not compatible. Dan Karmun recalls, "Back there in the days that I was growing up, they pulled out all the school kids from school. . . . This was the way to show the kids the custom and culture of the people. And they're absent from school for about upward to two months." Sometimes a hunter just happened upon the reindeer business, as in the case of Palmer Sagoonick's grandfather from Shishmaref, who started out working for the Lomen Company before forming his own herd. When Palmer's dad, Gustaf Sagoonick, was working for another Native company (the Katoonin herd) the Bureau of Indian Affairs came around and "said would you like to take over this herd? And that's how my dad got started with a small herd."[54] Iñupiat leader and historian Willie Hensley reinforced the idea that the bureau was "real good" about "suggesting" what the Native men should be doing with the herds back then.[55]

NONETHELESS, THE IÑUPIAT adapted reindeer herding into the culture, and as the Native herders drove their reindeer to find more grazing lands, they were likened to Arctic cowboys on the old cattle drives, especially with the incorporation of open herding or free ranging. The problem was these men (and a few women) were not Western buckaroos but rather marine mammal or caribou hunters who had never truly faced this type of governmental dominance or competition. "Native owners wrote notes to Congressmen, government committees, and employees in volume and lucidity" in an attempt to regain control over their homelands.[56] The Natives and their sympathetic supporters, usually agents for the Office of Indian Affairs, were united in efforts to diminish non-Native interference and clarify Native holdings, but beyond this method the Iñupiat needed someone ingrained in the government network to act as an ally and conduit. The answer was Delegate James Wickersham, who had previously worked with the Athabascan and the Tlingit on civil justice matters. Being a consummate politician, he fancied himself as the "protector of the Indians and Eskimos" when it suited his ambitions or image.[57]

Wickersham was asked to review the facts surrounding the Lomen Corporation and the infringement on Native land for deer grazing, but the case was complicated since the Lomens employed Native men in herding and butchering while the women made parkas, fur pants, mukluks, socks, and sleeping bags.[58] Was there a conflict of interest? He believed that "Alaskans [Natives] are regarded legally as Indians and are citizens of the United States," and so their property is protected. There were many instances to prove his assertion wrong, but he went on to say that the group, including the Lomens, were not given the authority to make decisions on ownership or the sale of female deer. He finalized his statements, reminding the group that no plan can "be in violation of the law—the Acts of Congress."[59]

Simultaneously, the overstretched Lomens were facing down a battle with the U.S. meat-packing industry (particularly in Kansas and Nebraska), whose representatives had organized a boycott of Alaska reindeer imports to protest unfair competition. Wickersham did not want to be drawn further into what he termed "turmoil" in the Department of the Interior, and he certainly did not want to testify about governmental favoritism toward a private company. He concluded, "The legal authority of the Secretary of the Interior to sponsor a proposal for the handling of reindeer in Alaska, such as was submitted by the representatives of the Lomen Reindeer Corporation and the Alaska Livestock and Packing Company is questionable . . . and [he] objected to the creation of a monopoly favorable to one company." Instead, he found himself on the side of the Native herdsmen. Wickersham declared that Alaska Natives were qualified for exclusive title to their deer based on their U.S. citizenship, and this included grazing rights that must be protected. The disagreements persisted, and Wickersham was invited to meet with all parties as an Alaskan representative. He agreed to do so but made it clear once again that he "did not intend to approve any plan which I think to be in violation of the law."[60] But how does one decipher the law in such uncharted circumstances?

ALTHOUGH THERE WERE key people in Washington DC pushing for reform in Alaska's reindeer industry, there was a critical lack of understanding about the situation, meaning "the Eskimo owner was for the most part without intercultural representation."[61] The Iñupiat relied on steadfast values and were no match for the Lomen machinations as they tricked the Native herders into assuming debts not their own.[62] This deception, however, could not last forever, since during the Depression the Lomens were subject to the same economic stresses as the rest of the nation, plus the Lomen Corporation, consisting of the Northwestern Livestock Corporation and five subsidiary organizations, was already heavily in debt and under investigation by the federal government.[63] It was reported that the Lomen companies consistently broke the rules by taking fawns and unmarked deer as collateral or selling the female deer that were necessary for breeding.[64] This might sound like a minor charge, but it served to slow them down and attract national attention.

For years the Native herders struggled against this criminality, but they were not without supporters in strategic places, including Clarence Andrews, who had led the reindeer project from 1923 and 1929. In his book, *The Eskimo and His Reindeer in Alaska*, he chastised the Lomens as interlopers in Alaska Natives' spiritual and economic well-being. "They [the Natives] were being demoralized both personally and in towns by strong drink and vicious associations— and in their herd management by wrong theories of stock management." Andrews backed Native independence and believed it could be achieved without destroying their ancient way of life. There would be no prophesied Eskimo downfall if they retained their independence while maintaining a position of "good shepherds."

Not everyone shared Andrew's optimism about the Native reindeer industry. Ben Mozee, field agent for the Reindeer Service, antagonized officials by revealing the incompetence of the Reindeer Councils, condemning the bodies as a political instrument for the Lomens. As proof, he cited how in 1931 the Reindeer Council had at first favored keeping the Lomens off Natives ranges, but later the council ignored previous rulings concerning deer markings, stray ownership, or mixing of herds that would have protected the Natives.[65] Mozee's arguments were compelling, and in the end the council was stripped of its regulatory powers, but Mozee was also dismissed as a trouble maker, effectively shutting down further opposition. The Native protest was instantaneous—Mozee had been one the few men in the field who understood their problems, and now they had no one to hear their issues.[66]

Simultaneous with these complaints, other related controversies were exposed through a 1930s report submitted by Roy Nash, a special agent in the Division of Investigations for the Department of the Interior. He described how the original purpose for the reindeer had been thwarted and that cross-cultural relationships were acrimonious. "The entrance of whites into the industry will tend to weaken our hold on the natives and will create a marked feeling of uncertainty among them. That native interest, which is the only thing in the reindeer industry that has interested us . . . will now have to fight its own fights and is likely to be much diminished, if not eventually wiped out." In addition, Nash spoke of how the Lomens recklessly invaded Native ranges that were legally occupied by "government wards," using the term to emphasize the sanctioned protection yet serving to reinforce the Alaska Natives' second-class status.[67]

Nash went on to make it clear that the Natives had been financially victim-ized through the Lomens' procedure of reimbursing themselves for "whatever they considered the Eskimo's share of these costs."[68] In a second report, Nash punctuated his initial accusations: "restricted Indian property had been taken by the Lomen corporation from the Eskimos during a long period of years for herding fees and for butchering," and legal action was indicated either through the courts or legislature.[69] Before this could come about, however, a dynamic new policy was passed by Congress, which would change the nature of the game.

After hearing about the Alaska Native situation in the 1930s, the prominent "Indian" advocate John Collier, commissioner for the Bureau of Indian Affairs under President Franklin Roosevelt, came to the defense. He believed the reindeer industry was part of the Alaska Native heritage, and "what [Sheldon] Jackson had promoted as a means of Eskimo assimilation almost forty years prior, Collier now saw as an important part of Eskimo culture that should be preserved" through the Indian Reorganization Act.[70] In Alaska the legislation had already strengthened Native economies and reaffirmed "tribal" sover-eignty.[71] Collier was a visionary, but he needed an implementer, which he found in Harold Ickes, the secretary of the interior, who would come to play a decisive role in Alaska Native matters. He had been a social activist since his Chicago college days and was a staunch supporter of Roosevelt's New

Deal policies. The problem with Ickes, however, was he was so enmeshed in theories and righteous crusades he sometimes lost sight of the practical day-to-day life of reindeer herders.

In the 1930s, in conjunction with New Deal legislation, Washington DC took notice of Alaska conditions, and one of the important agenda items concerned the reindeer industry. Oscar H. Lipps of the Office of Indian Affairs reported on the situation in northwest Alaska and noted the Indian Reorganization Act could be a valuable tool for the Alaska Natives, particularly the revolving loan system, if used to capitalize existing businesses. Before this scheme could be successful, Lipp concluded that the Natives must first recover from the great debts that communities had accumulated, leaving them in "semi-economic peonage to the traders" and no longer free agents.[72] Non-Natives, like the Lomens, were no small part of this crisis.

By now there was a new delegate to Congress, Anthony "Tony" Dimond, and with his background in Alaska Native issues, he felt certain the reindeer problem was a congressional matter, but he was surely not ready for what transpired next. Dimond informed Congress that conglomerates had taken over the once Native-only reindeer industry, and to rectify the situation he proposed a buyout of the reindeer from the non-Native companies, with the government fitting the bill for this endeavor. This was a radical idea on all levels. In 1937 he went before a skeptical Congress with his idea, endeavoring to uphold Alaska Native independence and civil rights: "I am not coming here to ask you to take care of the Natives today. . . . I am asking you to assist them in setting up a system which will enable them to take care of themselves. . . . We are setting up a business establishment they can operate and their children can operate after them."[73]

Not surprisingly, Dimond's proposal was reduced to a frivolous joke, reinforcing the lack of knowledge and respect for Alaska and its inhabitants. According to the *Congressional Record*, the debates moved from the issues surrounding the Alaska Native herds to a discussion of Santa Claus and his need for eight reindeer. In fact, to heighten this absurdity, one representative proposed that instead of the "Reindeer Act," the bill might instead be labeled the "Santa Claus Act."[74] Further, representatives questioned the role of the Lomen Corporation in this situation. By this time it was generally known that the Lomen Corporation had taken a hit during the Depression, and it was imagined the company had quite a bit to gain through any buyout scheme. To punctuate this reality, remarks followed such as: "Why should we bail out a white man?"[75]

After discussing the non-Native ownership of reindeer, the dialogue once again shifted back to Santa Claus, with a query from the Pennsylvania representative (Mr. Rich), who informed all that "it is a mighty fine thing to be a Santa Claus, but Santa Claus should come only on Christmas Eve. We have been a pretty good Santa Claus to the citizens of Alaska. We have been a good Santa Claus to the Eskimos." As the dialogue was reduced to a baser level, the representative from Kentucky, Edward Creal, asked "whether or not the eight reindeer that Santa Claus drives will be provided for in the bill," while William McFarlane derisively confirmed that reindeer and Santa Claus must be important to Alaska and the Eskimos.[76] The mockery might have been amusing to the legislators, but it disgusted Delegate Dimond. He grew exasperated with the inconsequential banter.[77] Steering the conversation back to the genuine matter at hand, the delegate hoped to finalize a bill, but Congress was unconvinced that U.S. taxpayer dollars should be used for "Eskimos" or failing "white men," and there were those questioning if Alaska was part of the United States. Apparently some had forgotten the geopolitical reality of its northern colony, but it did not erase the conclusion that Alaska was remote and not a priority—there were more pressing needs, such as getting enough mules to Kentucky farmers, who had lost animas due to flooding.[78] The argument was also put forward that a large distribution of money to a small Alaskan population was outrageous, and J. Parnell Thomas of New Jersey, an opponent of Roosevelt's New Deal policies, remarked to the pleasure of his fellow representatives that the proposed Reindeer Bill was "a case of bringing Santa Claus to the reindeer instead of bringing reindeer to Santa Claus." In an eleventh-hour plea, there was a question of why the reindeer industry should be subsidized for Alaska Natives who have supported themselves for thousands of years.[79]

Despite congressional attitudes, debates, and inane banter, the Reindeer Act was passed in 1937, granting Alaska Natives sole ownership of the deer—at least on paper. The act was intended to protect Alaskan Natives in their pursuit of self-sustaining industry, and the reindeer herds were to be managed through Native values, which meant, according to Representative Theodore Green, that the herds would stay on Native land, although that was difficult to define.[80] This legislation was without precedent and came as a shock to both the industrial reindeer companies and the Sámi, who were suddenly required to turn their herds and equipment over to their Native neighbors at a loss. The Scandinavian herders who were married to Natives were safe, but other Europeans were outraged at what they considered an injustice. When interviewed in 1982, early Sámi pioneers, Marit Baer and Anders Bongo, remarked, "We had worked hard, we had a decent herd of reindeer and then we had to give them away. . . . It did not seem just at all. But our people said, We should not make any quarrel."[81]

The 1937 Reindeer Act sent a jolt through a capitalistic society recovering from the Great Depression. Privately owned businesses were forced to sell their herds to the government "on behalf of the Eskimos and other natives of Alaska, including reindeer-range equipment, cold-storage plants, warehouses and other property, real or personal."[82] Of course there was no mistaking the use of the phrase "on behalf"—the Natives were still under the oversight of the Department of the Interior. Over the years autonomy had been regained in increments, but it was not complete.

In essence the New Deal philosophy, with its socialist overtones, had struck a blow to the still evolving legacy of the Guggenheims, Carnegies, and Rockefellers, personified by the Lomens in Alaska, who asked Congress to reconsider this legislation.[83] In their defense they declared they had employed many "Eskimos," and they were actually part of the solution and not the problem. Carl Lomen added, "The Lomen Corporation had fully demonstrated its constructive aims. . . . It had purchased hundreds of surplus male deer from Eskimo deer men. It had developed improved methods for handling deer. . . . In one winter season alone we shipped out of the port of Seattle fifty-one carloads of reindeer meat, each of approximately 30,000 pounds." When these desperate arguments went unrecognized, Carl Lomen resigned himself to his fate: "So ended our reindeer adventure. Without withdrawal from the industry, we could think only that it would be interesting, and doubtless not a little heart-rending, to sit back and watch how the Government would deal with the problem. . . . When we were forced to quit, most of the Eskimo followed suit, although they were now the only ones permitted to own reindeer. Wolves entered the grazing lands and killed thousands of reindeer."[84]

Indeed, there were ecological threats. The carrying capacity was burdened, and the deer fell prey to diseases, while several herds wandered off to become feral and mixed in with wild migratory caribou herds. In turn, because of habitat insufficiencies, caribou moved out of the sight of traditional hunters. Beyond problems with the reindeer herds, the wider environment had been badly damaged by overgrazing on lichens (deer grass). Tundra land may appear barren to the untrained eye, but in reality it is a rich ecosystem that provides for animals and other biota, including humans. As the reindeer and caribou populations grew, there was more competition for scarce resources, leading to further land degradation, often called desertification. The villagers, with their proximity to the resources, were the first to report the diminishing vegetation and bird scarcity. On the whole the intermixing of domesticated reindeer with wild stock resulted in genetically weaker animals, subject to disease and predators, such as wolves and bears.

AFTER THE PASSAGE of the legislation, there were two chaotic years without precise enumeration or ownership title of the reindeer stocks. Not only was there a question about how many reindeer the Lomens or other non-Natives and Europeans owned—some figured in the thousands—there were no efficient methods for counting. The owners and families were reimbursed for their losses but contested the fairness of these transactions. For instance, in Unalakleet, along the northern coast, once a site of large reindeer operations, the Sámi were paid only three dollars for each deer, far below market value. Now reduced to poverty, many left Alaska or returned to their homeland. Others, like Marit Baer and Anders Bongo, descendants of some of the original Scandinavians, made their resentments clear about the government's actions: "We did not want to give away the animals. My father did not want to fight it. . . . The pay they got was too small. To me [Baer] it did not seem just at all."[85]

THE IÑUPIAT CULTURE had been altered forever by the introduction of capitalism, Western goods, and wages. Native herders seldom grew accustomed to the required nomadic way of life that herding demanded, and even today the few remaining reindeer farms are close to home. Ironically, by the time of the 1937 Reindeer Act, herding as an occupation had largely waned, brought on by herd starvation and wolf predation. The original rationale of bringing Western education to the Natives through reindeer herding had not been accomplished, and the so-called cooperatives were nothing more than reindeer herds managed by extended families, but under government control. The fiduciary guarantees had been weak and ineffective. To stand up for themselves and their enterprise, the Iñupiat built up their political stance, and some historians believe that "by the late 1930s the Eskimos of Alaska had taken both legal and cultural control of what was originally designed to be a project of assimilation. . . . Native involvement and economic development was often part of a larger strategy of adaptation and cultural endurance."[86] One overall conclusion was clear: political fundamentals would be necessary to cope with the increased number of interlopers in the Arctic, particularly when oil was discovered in the next decades.

For example, in the Barrow area (now called Utqiagvik), the National Petroleum Reserve opened in the 1950s, and according to culture bearer Sadie Brower Neakok, after the commotion associated with the oil operations started to take place, "the reindeer wandered off and they never came back." She tells the story about hunters spotting strange animals among the caribou herds and then realizing they were actually reindeer turned feral. She blamed the oil reserve, all the traffic, and the noise for the disappearance of the original reindeer herds. Simultaneously, would-be herders turned to the wage jobs that oil provided, and there were no longer many people to keep track of the few remaining herds.[87]

THERE ARE STILL a few active ranches and grazing areas today. One of the largest populations is on Nunivak Island, off the coast of southwest Alaska, where the residents depend on reindeer herding for their sole livelihood outside of subsistence hunting and fishing.[88] The herders from the past would have never dreamed their descendants would someday become corporate shareholders or, paradoxically, executives themselves through the Alaska Native Claims Settlement Act, the legislation that oil built. One of the twelve initial corporations created by the settlement was the Northwest Arctic Native Association, located in the same territory as the first Iñupiat reindeer herders, and when pressed to find moneymaking enterprises to keep the corporation afloat, it turned to a surprising commercial idea. John Schaeffer, one of the early leaders during the corporation start up, suggested a return to reindeer herding as a moneymaking scheme, but no one was quite sure how to get started. Iñupiat leader Willie Hensley writes in his book *Fifty Miles from Tomorrow* that, when they decided to go into the reindeer business, there was much to learn: "Neophytes that we were, our deer-raising techniques were at first chaotic and crazed."[89] One critical problem concerned boundaries and the unintentional mixing of deer into the wrong herds, until once again the question had to be asked: Who owns these reindeer?

5   Baleen to Bombs, Project Chariot

The woman in the crowded meeting room called out from the back, "What happens to my children if I die from a heart attack?" She was referring to the deep scare that could be caused when bombs were detonated near her home. Her neighbors were not surprised by her question. They knew she had a weak heart. The purported professionals at this meeting disguised their uneasiness in this foreign environment. This Point Hope woman's first language was Iñupiaq, the ancient regional language, and although she may have spoken haltingly, mixing in English at the same time, she carried the convictions of her ancestors and felt sure she would have the support of her community. In early times the people had formed robust councils for Arctic conflict resolution, necessary in an unforgiving environment where harmony was essential for life. This latest development certainly fit into the life or death category.

AS SEEN IN archaeological findings, the Iñupiat have occupied northwest Alaska for more than ten thousand years, making it their home through all seasons. A nomadic way of life was temporary, and permanent settlements occurred quite early in history. The flora and fauna provided for their needs as long as they practiced reverence, using caution not to damage the fragile ecosystem, the marine mammals of the Bering Sea, and the tundra animals. Shelters were constructed from sod, mirroring the landscape, and were thermodynamic wonders. For many generations the people of this northern clime were not intruded on, and their way of life continued from generation to generation in this village called Tikigaq, translated from the Iñupiaq as "index finger," so named for the spit of land that juts out into the Chukchi Sea. Later, in 1826, the area was named Point Hope by Capt. Frederick W. Beechey to honor Sir William Johnstone Hope, but that name meant little to the first inhabitants. And years later, after the arrival of the missionaries, the government agents, and the teachers, the whaling village remained a vibrant traditional site.

The old prophet Maniilaq foretold of a time when newcomers would endanger their way of living.[1] By the turn of the century, those words were a reality, as Western-defined progress and modernity were introduced to the first people of the North. Besides an alteration in clothing styles, often unsuited for the environment, the conventional sod houses were replaced by wood dwellings, and government buildings were erected, establishing a new Arctic presence. As anthropologist Norman Chance described, there were "two or three room homes constructed of scrap lumber taken from machinery-packing crates" and other usable items.[2] Perhaps the most alien conversion was the switch from Native stewardship of the environment to the rise of governmental oversight agencies charged with monitoring wildlife and making rules, boldly preempting age-old Indigenous knowledge. The culture shock required adaptation. Increasingly, the people of the Northwest adopted the cash and wage economy and acquired Western goods while retaining a subsistence lifestyle, critical for survival and cultural well-being.

In the 1940s Alaska's northern region was isolated, but it did not stop the residents from learning the details concerning the global war. Through the few newspapers and radio reports that made their way north, they learned about the horrors of the conflict and fully realized their geopolitical placement in proximity to the Soviet Union. Though the war ended in 1945, the enduring hostilities constructed a barrier between nations, and in the Arctic region this was referred to as the Ice Curtain.[3] Past trading with Siberian neighbors across the Bering Sea became a distant memory, while an international arms race sparked from the embers of previous combat on foreign soil.

Although Native veterans told fantastic tales from the war, the northern villages remained relatively isolated until federal agencies entered the scene and shaped the region into a U.S. outpost. In the 1950s Episcopal minister Keith Lawton remarked that the village still had many sod houses among the modern buildings, yet it was the National Guard station that stood out as a reminder of the Alaska Native contributions to the war. Lawton described how the "mission buildings, schools, and the village store . . . and the post office" did little to change the village landscape, never realizing they were on the cusp of great change.[4] Shortly, Lawton, would advocate for the Point Hope residents against further governmental intrusion.

BECAUSE OF INTERNATIONAL tensions and an unwavering defensive posture between the United States and the Soviet Union, the Cold War grew to dangerous proportions during the 1950s, culminating in a contest for superiority. In this hostile atmosphere, nuclear capabilities were a priority. Politicians supported further testing and campaigned on a show of this dominance against the Soviet Union. The subsequent nuclear experiments were coupled with anticommunist hatred and an all-encompassing xenophobic wave that crashed over the United States. Sensational newspaper headlines warned that if extreme heed was not taken, dangerous foreigners would take over the country. In this jingoistic turmoil, the prestige of the scientific community was elevated in the nation's eyes, along with the H-bomb, which many believed had singly ended World War II. In the midst of this patriotic fever, it was suggested the nuclear bomb could be used for beneficial purposes, and when that idea took hold, there was no stopping the march of progress, regardless of definition.

In the 1954 Atomic Energy Act, Congress declared that atomic energy could promote diplomatic world relations, improve the nation's general welfare, and increase the standard of living by strengthening free enterprise—tall promises for the postwar era. By 1957 the Atomic Energy Commission (AEC) approved a program code, named Project Plowshare, with the purpose of exploring "peaceful" uses of nuclear power and to further domestic capabilities through the hoped-for scientific breakthroughs. In less than a year, the AEC turned their attention to a possible testing site about thirty miles from the northern Alaska village of Point Hope. The government thought of it as an icy wilderness, without acknowledging this site had been occupied for over ten thousand years. Once again Indigenous land and waters were considered worthless if they were not producing something for the nation.

The initial work in the area had already begun before Point Hope dwellers were aware of the activity. Obviously, the residents were never consulted about any plans, but when the plot was uncovered, the village residents were shocked. Since it appeared to be a clandestine operation, they feared it was dangerous. The first local sighting of the project was discovered incidentally by Daniel Lisbourne, the president of the Point Hope Village Council at the time. One day he returned home after scouting for hunting opportunities and told his wife he had seen caribou in the distance, but something else puzzled him. Lisbourne told his wife he had seen strangers and tents out by Ogotoruk (a freshwater stream).[5] He was curious about his observations but had no idea at the time that he had stumbled on the Atomic Energy Commission's new pet scheme, already identified as Project Chariot.

In a radical proposal, the AEC sought to "bomb" the area to create a deep-water harbor to not only advance scientific uses of nuclear power but also provide a central point in the Arctic for trade routes between Asia and Alaska—how was this a reality in the frozen north during the Cold War? The proposed harbor would be built using a 2.4 megaton thermonuclear device. This tremendous undertaking had not undergone thorough planning, had little oversight, and was before significant environmental standards were in place, but the frenzy could not be halted. Eventually, after the master proposal was exposed, it was determined the actual testing site would be near Cape Thompson, about 125 miles from Kotzebue and 30 miles southeast of the village of Point Hope. Although hidden for a while, scientific speculation indicated the potential damage could be widespread, affecting the whaling villages of Kotzebue, Kivalina, and Noatak due to the nuclear fallout that would be carried across the tundra by the prevalent winds or waters.[6]

This project was headed by physicist Edward Teller, best known as the father of the hydrogen bomb, a dubious title and not his only distinction. In his enthusiasm Teller was relentless promoter of nuclear energy and all the miracles it might allegedly produce; that was his reckless pitch. He based his findings on the previous detonation of five thermonuclear devices and argued the resultant radioactive threat was minimal and "would add even less radiation than the background amount in which all persons are constantly exposed due to cosmic rays."[7] Scientific sources, however, concluded that in reality "the detonation would send debris 30,000 feet into the air and create a crater that could be filled by the overlapping Chukchi Sea."[8] Picturing this huge displacement of the natural landscape and oceans was horrendous but did not faze the planners, who boasted the project was another example of U.S. ingenuity, while in truth the project had no viable path toward success, and the promised vast trade route was a preposterous claim. Teller, lost in his own world, ignored sociopolitical problems, good sense, and the immediate pleas from local residents. In essence he took his scheme to extremes.

Because of the potential devastation, the project should have been shut down from the beginning, but the AEC carried weight in governmental circles, and the proposed experiment gained momentum from Washington DC to Juneau. It appeared the Point Hope residents were outflanked, but help was on the way. The environmental movement was gaining strength, and its leaders were prepared to fight against the known dangers of nuclear radiation in the ice, snow, and air, accompanied by the knowledge that both humans and animals depended on the land and waters for their survival. In the long run, however, it would take more than environmentalists and freethinking politicians to stop this project—the genuine potency came from the Iñupiat themselves.

The people of Point Hope were more savvy than scientists gave them credit for, and their local council stood up to take decisive action, noting that the potential "poison," as the people called it, was targeted toward their ancient village of Tikigag. This was an offense to the ancestors, who had walked on this soil and hunted whales in the sea for thousands of years. In response the Point Hope Council protested through any means possible, particularly by sending letters to Washington DC in the hopes of reaching the ear of an effective and sympathetic politician. The one answer they received was from Alaska senator Bob Bartlett, who was already angry that he had been duped by the AEC and Teller with false information. After hearing from the Native dissenters, he withdrew his tenuous support for Project Chariot, stating that he was discouraged about the "whole situation" and that his initial interest for the AEC project had "evaporated."[9] After securing this support, the Point Hope residents breathed a sigh of relief, but the council also recognized they were no match against the federal government and the powerful scientific community. They needed to do what they did best—galvanize their efforts at the local level and acquire trusted and powerful allies who would take up the dual cause of civil and environmental rights, bolstered by an understanding of the Iñupiat relationship to the land, air, and waters. This was no place for nuclear destruction.

IN THE BEGINNING of this dispute there was little discussion of land ownership. The presumption was the federal government could take what it wanted without question. For the Alaska Natives the concept of ownership is foreign; the land provides for those who show respect and act as stewards—an ideal that the scientists and politicians had trouble grasping. The federal government, fueled with thoughts of pervasive domain, believed that other than the few specific sites of obvious individual ownership, everything was under their dominion, which was not so far from the truth in Alaska. In the 1950s, before statehood, the federal government "owned" the majority of fisheries, forests, tundra lands, and other reserves, while the Iñupiat merely "occupied" certain lands, an active concept that had not been updated since the days of Justice John Marshall's Supreme Court in the 1820s. In terms of land and tenure, however, there are pervasive differences between the Alaska Natives and those of the lower states. Alaska Natives have never signed a treaty with the federal government nor been assigned to reservations. Although these factors limited the available repertoire of beneficial legal precedents, it opened the door for innovative outcomes free of a malevolent yoke. At times Point Hope residents believed they must appeal to the wider court of public opinion, but that was difficult given the geographic barriers and the pervading nationalism reinforced by Cold War policies and the competitive race for U.S. dominance.

LOCALLY, ALASKAN ENERGIES were directed toward the quest for statehood, perpetuating earnest efforts to prove the territory was rich in resources, as Alaska's bounty was showcased through its fisheries, timber products, and precious metals to demonstrate its worthiness. Being on the edge of technology was a bonus. What difference did it matter that this project had been compared to a Hiroshima in the Arctic? But for the northern dwellers, it was of grave concern, since this was their home, prompting the necessity to raise public awareness beyond the fleeting magic of science. Moreover, comparisons to Hiroshima revived memories of the atrocities that had been committed to innocent civilians, and this was not good press.

Edward Teller himself was also a formidable obstacle. With an eccentric charm, he had a way of twisting facts and turning doubts into fantastic promises for the future. In a 1959 speech at the University of Alaska at Fairbanks commencement exercise, he boasted that "all Eskimos could be coal miners" and that the Japanese could be the first recipients of Alaska's oil and coal products as a function of nuclear excavation. In his portrayal the Japanese, still recovering from World War II, would benefit from Alaska's natural resources, after suffering the devastation of the atomic bomb firsthand.[10] The cultural insensitivity on both counts was beyond the pale and an indication he was operating in dystopian world while his loyal followers were equally smitten by delusion, but they had misjudged the American public.

Contrary to Teller's rhetoric and despite measures to cover up World War II atrocities, word leaked out concerning nuclear radiation and other harmful effects that had devastated the civilian Japanese. The AEC attempted damage control but skirted safety issues. Instead, they promised that the benefits of nuclear-power exploration would provide year-round employment, ostensibly lifting Alaska Natives out of the poverty they never realized they were in. This charade was kept up until finally the AEC had to admit there were potential hazards associated with nuclear blasting, including cancers and leukemia. Teller's response was that northern Alaska was remote, and science ranked higher than any significant danger to a handful of Eskimos.[11] Filled with hubris, Teller and his cronies continued their mission and ignored those who voiced alarm. After all, risks would be minimal since so much of the radioactive material would be buried underground. Their statement was based on either blind ambition or outright deception.[12]

Many inside and outside of Alaska believed Teller and his staff because they were "scientists" and therefore must be right. This was reinforced through public speeches and patriotic anthems of national growth and modernity, but in village meetings the people saw things differently and believed the underground vats of nuclear waste were murder weapons. The dissidents increased their opposition and attempted to convince others that the real facts were being suppressed. In turn the AEC bolstered their crusade by setting up more rallies and meetings to increase positive public relations, understanding this was the only way to ward off nuisance protests so they could get to work, starting at the mouth of Ogotoruk Creek on Cape Thompson. They did not want anything leaking out to the newspapers that would alter the public's good opinion, while the residents of Point Hope did not want anything leaking out that would kill them.

In the face of increasing threats, the Point Hope Council increased their offensive measures and rallied more concerned Alaska citizens to complain about the project, which surprised the AEC because originally they had been under the impression this operation would be a simple matter. Beyond ignoring the concerns, the AEC also suffered from poor communication methods, exacerbated by the cross-cultural setting—the government was a fish out of water. As strangers to each other, the Point Hope residents and the AEC representatives were working at cross-purposes, and communication was stilted. When the transcripts were finally released to the public years later, the narrative clearly indicates that the officials answered questions either in highly scientific terms or in a condescending manner.[13]

In one of the original public relations visits, the AEC went to Point Hope to show the community an eleven-minute film. If this documentary was meant to allay doubts, the government sorely missed their mark. The film was described in this way: "The first thing the Eskimos saw after the title faded was a white flash followed by a churning, red fireball lifting off the earth." These Arctic dwellers were no stranger to danger, but this was something out of their worst nightmares, as they imagined these catastrophic explosions on their soil. The Point Hope Council, under the direction of David Frankson, sent a protest letter to the AEC, stating they did not want to see the blast, and Frankson added, "when we say it, we mean it." At one of the meetings, Kitty Kineeveauk, from Kotzebue and the wife of a whaling captain, spoke directly to the men from Washington DC: "We really don't want to see the Cape Thompson blasted because it is our homeland. I'm pretty sure you don't like to see your home blasted by some other people who didn't live in your place."[14] Kitty knew she was speaking for all the people, and it was tough to beat her logic. She was not alone. The village might not have been able to summon up fancy technical jargon, but they made their point clear. Unfortunately, the communication chasm deepened because of mutual distrust. Local anger was ignored in favor of the AEC and their drive to complete this project at any cost. The Point Hope Council was strong, but they needed to bring outside activists into their circle—those possessing political acumen or the voice of money. In the end they found both.

By mid-1959 the clash between the north coast residents versus Teller had reached a deadlock. While the Iñupiat were looking for allies, including the University of Alaska at Fairbanks professors, the AEC challenged the opposition and adjusted their tactics from a purely technical premise to appear more benign. In a show of good faith, the project coordinators excavated a small plot for experimentation to prove there would be no long-term consequences. The plan was to bury nuclear waste from a former testing site in Nevada to show nothing adverse would occur, but before this smaller project commenced, archaeologists demanded a study to evaluate artifacts and the historical value of the site.[15]

Archaeology in the Arctic is fraught with the difficulties involved with access, transporting equipment, permafrost conditions, and expense, but nevertheless work was ordered to determine if any artifacts or other ethnological or historical remains might be destroyed in this "experiment." The pursuit was funded by the AEC, and several artifacts were uncovered and cataloged, and the accompanying report concluded that the outlying region had been in continual use for residency and subsistence purposes for thousands of years, and the archaeologists believed these findings must be part of the public record. Based on these findings, the archaeologists, along with human geographer Don Foote, proceeded to dig up the past. Human geography is the study of how people and their cultures are shaped by the terrain, fauna, and flora. At the time it was a new scientific branch, but effective for documenting the damage that would likely occur should Project Chariot come to fruition.

Foote was an interesting character in this mix. He was a trained scientist yet understood how lands and waters are central to cultures. He was hired by the AEC as part of a public relations campaign and began the work as a self-professed novice on nuclear devices and politics. As he uncovered more and more, however, he developed an animosity toward his employer because of the duplicitous nature of this venture. In his words, it was necessary to expose a scientific experiment that was "rotten to its very bottom." Later he explained to John Wolfe, the chief of the Planning Committee on Environmental Studies, an appendage of the AEC, that he had been naive in every way and "politically immature," but it was that fresh, untainted mind that understood the interaction between power and science, with their potential dangers.[16] Even though Wolfe was connected with the AEC, he was in touch with Arctic life and claimed that the area was not barren but rather displayed the "showiest natural floral display of any vegetation in the world." He also believed there should be a new philosophy of development that embraced bioenvironmental knowledge.[17]

Several government agencies employed Iñupiat workers on archaeological digs and in the implementation preliminaries, but obvious language barriers and the high degree of secrecy meant these employees had no idea what was going on, including Alaska Native leader Willie Hensley, who recalled that he did not realize he was in the midst of a confidential government test site. In his autobiographical book, he recalls working for the Cold Regions Research and Engineering Laboratory. His job was to dig posts for storing atomic bombs to be detonated at a prescribed time. "I had no idea I had been hired to work on the controversial 'Project Chariot,' as it was called, the brainchild of Dr. Edward Teller. . . . It could have come right out of the script for *Dr. Strangelove.*" When I talked to him many years later, he expressed the view that they were tricked into working on this job.[18] This was but one of the examples indicating how subterfuge was necessary to disguise the government's goals and Teller's madness.

Those involved at the higher levels were aware of the effects of nuclear waste and other problems associated with the bomb, but available reports sublimated the dangers while assuring safety. In determining the suitability at the proposed site at Ogotoruk Creek, a site where the villagers obtained their fresh water, negative physical findings were put aside and deemed unimportant, despite the reality of people living, working, and hunting on these lands. An example of the myopic assumptions included the statement that the "Eskimo culture maintained an autochthonous character" even after churches were established or trading companies made their way up the Arctic coast.[19] There was no acknowledgement of the tremendous culture change that occurred after Western encroachment and certainly no responsibility was taken for what might happen to these villages if hydrogen bombs were exploded in their waters and nuclear waste buried in their land.

Yet Teller and his supporters remained cavalier. When told that the people depended on whales and caribou, he replied, "Well they're going to have to change their way of life."[20] There was no consideration of ecosystem destruction, food-chain disruption, or the contamination of the tundra and waters. In ignorance Teller even mentioned that the testing would go on during the winter when there was less wind and no hunting.[21] His erroneous evaluation was accepted as truth by the authorities in charge, and adverse outcomes were categorized as collateral damage for the good of scientific exploration. In essence it was a modern-day throwback to the age of discovery. Claims on Indigenous land were justified based on the American idea of best use in the old game of pitting Western expansion against the well-being of the original dwellers.

When pressured, the AEC continued its pacification exercises by slightly changing their stance of no risks to the old standby that if any harm should come from nuclear testing or fallout, the Iñupiat residents could be relocated, but the people of Point Hope and Kivalina would not accept this solution. There was even talk of removing the people from Noatak to Kotzebue and even Nome. The AEC appeared to have no respect for the longevity and traditions on the Arctic coast or the importance of the land and sea to the northern people. This "removal" proposition shocked the activists and confirmed their worst suspicions—the AEC had been lying to them from the start. Was the government willing to go to such great lengths and expense to relocate entire villages into so-called model communities just to build a port facility? There had to be something more.[22] The irrational move did not fool the villagers, and even guarantees of future employment, such as it was, did little to sway those who would ultimately be affected. The AEC, Teller, and proponents were seen as empty hyperbole vats, and the Iñupiat grew more skeptical of every word, meeting, and action. They would not yield in their demand for truthful answers from the scientists and politicians, while their voices were tinged with fear of the future for themselves and their children. What would be the terrifying results of the bombs from those men, whom author Dan O'Neill labeled "The Firecracker Boys"?

The Iñupiat were not naive or uninformed about global events, and a few Native leaders knew about the Bikini Island testing site and passed on the information to others.[23] Fundamentally, the AEC and other government agencies had "underestimated the acuity of the Tigaraqmiut."[24] Kitty Kineeveauk was one who had heard about the failures and hazards of other nuclear experiments, reinforcing her distrust of AEC agents. In a crowded Point Hope meeting, she interrupted the government speaker by referring to an article she had read, where "Indian" homes had been blasted and destroyed. The officials countered by saying, "It wasn't us," adding they had tested only in Nevada (Sedan Project) and way out in the Pacific (Bikini Island).[25] It was too late for the AEC. Kineeveauk and others had already shored up their ranks, forcing the government into a defensive posture.

The AEC was determined that a few disgruntled "Eskimos" would not stop the project, but they continued to lose steam when outside organizations, backed by money and influence, got into the act, starting with biologists Leslie Viereck and William Pruitt, who were both connected to the University of Alaska at Fairbanks and hired to work on Project Chariot under an AEC grant. Pruitt and Viereck innocently believed they could be impartial, but as scientists they could not ignore the obvious probability of regional damage should the project continue, and in good conscience their only recourse was to support the Native cause.

William Pruitt had come to Alaska in 1953 and worked as a field biologist, living a rustic lifestyle and traveling throughout the Alaska landscape. Leslie Viereck was from the old whaling port of New Bedford along the coast of Massachusetts. As a graduate of Dartmouth, he was educated in the sciences but also saw himself as a naturalist with a particular interest in the relationship between ecology and biology in conservation strategies. Soon after arriving in Fairbanks, he went to Ogotoruk Creek to engage in botanical studies for the AEC. What he found concerned him, but he kept his suspicions under wraps until he could find out more.[26]

When Pruitt and Viereck found themselves knee-deep in the quagmire of controversy and "suspect science," their keener knowledge of the circumstances resulted in an ethical choice to become whistleblowers. Their first step was to sound the alarm concerning the potential of radiation in the caribou herds, but that was only the beginning. The biologists publicized their findings in hopes of encouraging officials to shut down Project Chariot, but their efforts met with limited success. No good deed goes unpunished, and in the end they lost their jobs, and the newspapers destroyed their reputation and further career possibilities. Yet they had sown the seeds for discord, and in the early 1960s the Alaska Conservation Society sprouted to fight against Project Chariot, with Don Foote as one of the charter members.[27]

Don Foote, the human geographer, had previously mapped the area and documented Iñupiat land-use patterns while gaining a voice as an opponent of the project.[28] Although the AEC wanted to keep Project Chariot out of the press, Foote made sure the word got out, and his position was respected in the village since he had shown himself to be more than a mere drop-in scientist. Instead, he had worked and lived in Point Hope during his research, keeping himself close to the heartbeat of what was going on. In his position he was able to work with leaders, such as David Frankson and Dan Lisbourne, who had already rallied the villages. Ultimately, it was these leaders and their supporters who stopped further site testing before the most detrimental aspects of radioactive materials could be realized. Author Dan O'Neill describes Frankson as "an important *umalik* (whaling captain) who was also the village postmaster and had just succeeded Dan Lisbourne as president of the village council. . . . [He was a] shrewd, tough man . . . one of Point Hope's strongest leaders in modern times."[29] Frankson and Lisbourne acted as trusted cultural brokers with coordinated efforts, but even they could not slay this dragon with outside help.[30] Filled with moral vigor, the Point Hope Council believed that if they had the means to travel to Washington DC, they could generate more exposure and connect with the right people.

In the meantime the village council solicited help from the Association on American Indian Affairs, an advocacy organization founded in 1922. The outcome of this move brought together a pair who were as out of place in the Arctic as a sod house on a California beach, but for all their societal privilege, they were adaptable and without pretense and genuinely committed to this crusade.[31] To make headway La Verne Madigan, secretary of the association, had to change the organization's stance on Alaska. Many believed it was out of their scope, until Madigan convinced the doubters with her carefully tuned Arctic strategy. The other activist was Dr. Henry Stone Forbes, grandson of wealthy New England banker John Murray Forbes. Initially, the two were eyed with skepticism, but once Madigan held the first meeting, the audience noticed she listened to their concerns and her approach was practical. To form an effective plan, Madigan drilled down to the nucleus of the issue and asked, Whose land is this the AEC is considering for testing? For centuries, according to the Native way, the land had been owned collectively, and everyone took care of the resources. That is why it came as a surprise to many to find out that the actual site was "owned" by the Rock family and a few other villagers. Moreover, an official claim had been filed in the 1950s.[32] Now there was something to work with, and this drew Howard Rock, editor of the *Tundra Times*, deeper into the picture.

Howard Rock was an artist, an activist, and at times a deeply troubled man, but when he discovered his father had claimed the land where the testing was taking place and after hearing the pleas from the elders in his village, he was committed to do whatever he could to halt this project. He needed cash and guidance, however, and a media outlet to disseminate the issues over a wider range. A reliable connection for these goals was found in Tom Snapp, a former reporter for the *Fairbanks Daily News-Miner*, who had already rejected that newspaper's stance on Project Chariot. The newspaper had once (and often repeated by other newspapers) editorialized, "We think the holding of a huge nuclear blast in Alaska would be a fitting overture to the new era which is opening for our state."[33]

To rebut this declaration, Rock relied on Forbes's experience and financial backing to produce the *Tundra Times*, providing a crucial conduit connecting people throughout villages in Alaska so they might understand what was occurring and ultimately open a wider platform. Ultimately, the newspaper brought Alaska Natives together to push for land claims, but the first 1962 issue focused on Arctic problems, particularly Project Chariot and the Herculean effort to stop the AEC from continuing their dangerous experiments. There was no underestimating the influence of the *Tundra Times*, but there was also a need for more power brokers to enter the arena.

This essential energy was found through passionate environmental groups that were taking hold in Alaska and naturally viewed Project Chariot as the embodiment of everything they were against. With the ecology movement publicizing the damage to the fragile Arctic ecosystem, the Alaska Conservation Society called for an independent study to assess the potential outcomes and merits (and demerits) of the project. Charter members Viereck and Pruitt acted as environmental watchdogs and fed information to the society and other groups to construct a stronger case. Simultaneously, the coordinated outreach drew Alaska Native villages solidly into the fight to protect the Arctic and an ancient way of life against the neoscientific revolution brought on by the nuclear age.[34]

The Iñupiat were up against tough foes all the way to the White House. In March 1961 the Point Hope Council sent an additional protest missive to President John Kennedy, complaining that these potential explosions and the expected fallout were too close to their homes but received no reply.[35] The Point Hope Village Health Council sent an additional letter to the president, stressing the need to preserve the pristine nature of their area to continue the subsistence lifestyle. They emphasized the importance of fresh water and added, "We are concerned about the health of our children and the mothers-to-be after the explosion."[36] As these issues continued to fall on deaf ears, it was obvious that a letter from a small, unheard-of whaling village was not going to make a difference. They needed a breakthrough event. The tide turned after an article was published in the well-read *Harper's* magazine, outlining the dangers of Project Chariot to the nation. The authors were Paul Brooks of the Sierra Club and Joseph Foote, brother of Don Foote, who had already done so much to stop the AEC through his own scientific reports.

These efforts were bolstered by the homegrown Inupiat Paitot, founded during a 1961 meeting organized by Madigan and Forbes to discuss Native rights. By banding Native communities together, they believed they could effectively fight the AEC. After appointing regional delegates, they met in Barrow (now called Utqiagvik) to form a strategy, augmented by a common goal to regain their heritage and not take orders from the federal government. "That [we do not own the land] was a lie told to us Inupiat to take away our aboriginal land and mineral rights. Talking at this meeting about what we were told about aboriginal rights and reservations, we found that each one of our villages were told the same lie. But we never knew that, because we never had a chance to talk to each other."[37]

This statement summed up their campaign. Once armed with knowledge, means, and political esteem, they were unstoppable. This energy was coupled with growing negative public pressure and feckless government studies failing to prove economic feasibility. Faced with this backlash, the AEC reluctantly gave up the project in 1963. Although excuses were made, mostly as a face-saving measure, the official governmental word was that Project Chariot was no longer necessary for the purposes of testing nuclear energy because the scientists had learned all they needed to through Project Sedan. Allegedly, the Nevada Sedan project had proven how effective and safe nuclear land excavation might be, and the arguments for continuing on with the Point Hope site became superfluous. No one mentioned the less than brilliant proposal for an Arctic trading port—that ship had sailed long ago.

If Project Chariot had proceeded it would have been larger than Sedan, and in the Arctic the damage would have been greater. It was a bitter irony the nuclear waste from Sedan had been buried near Port Thompson. Naturally this meant that the environmental damage had already begun and indeed persists to this day in a textbook example of environmental injustice. Unveiled documents revealed that radioactive soil from Project Sedan had been buried near the Ogotoruk Creek area, the only location for fresh water. The contaminated soil had also been buried in a mound in the vicinity of Snowbank Creek, where it was allowed to seep into the ground water and permafrost and to escape in the air.[38]

For years these events were unknown outside of Alaska. While the otherwise ignored territory was busy proving itself as a new and worthy state, no one paid much attention to a secluded "Eskimo" location. There is a disproportional rate of cancer among the people, and animals and hunters continue to find dead animals with malignant lesions on their body.[39] These northern people depend on the bowhead whale, and testing has indicated radioactive particles and other signs of damage in the animal.[40] Without a doubt, the Point Hope community, the *Tundra Times*, and Inupiat Paitot stopped the project but not without permanent devastation.

Another stated reason for halting the project centered on international political pressure during the Cold War era. In 1958, to ease tensions, a moratorium on nuclear military testing had been agreed to by President Dwight D. Eisenhower, and when the Soviet Union heard about the AEC project, they accused the U.S. government of secretly breaking the pact through a "legal camouflage for the continuation of nuclear tests," and they were not going to be fooled.[41] Even though this was a diplomatic controversy, it was one of the factors, along with the cost-benefit ratio and public sentiment, that led to the downfall of the AEC's pet project.

IN THAT EARLY meeting between the Point Hope Council and the AEC, a woman questioned the officials about what would happen to her children if she suffered a heart attack if bombs were detonated near her home. The reply she received encapsulated the entire project. Russell Ball, assistant to the technical manager for the AEC, responded, "Damned if I know." Years later critics are repulsed by how disrespectful Teller and the AEC were to the Iñupiat—how they had even boasted they could carve out the likeness of a polar bear through the calculated placement of bombs. Above all, the residents knew "Teller and his associates were not honest. . . . Practically everything Teller told the Alaskan people . . . was misleading or untruthful. We should be glad he never got the chance to complete his original desire to make a harbor using a 2.4-megaton nuclear detonation in Northwest Alaska."[42]

Barry Commoner, the founder of the Committee for Nuclear Information and an early watchdog on AEC undertakings, attributes the dissenting documentation concerning Project Chariot to the advancement of the environmental movement.[43] Commoner condemned the notion that scientists held some godlike power and instead advocated that the real authority resided within the electorate, and those elected must serve the needs of the people. The events surrounding Point Hope spotlighted the need for an informed nation that could not be hoodwinked by profit-seeking and all-knowing experts, and it also pointed to the necessity for holding the government accountable for the consequences caused by bad actors or ill-planned projects. They should no longer have the luxury of hiding behind agencies or special-interest groups. The lessons learned from Project Chariot reinforced the ideal of a genuine democracy, where every citizen is equal under the law, regardless of economic status, residence, or ethnic background. Alaska Native villages were not laboratories for scientific experiments, and the downfall of the AEC gave other Alaska Native villages a tutorial for future environmental challenges. Through village unity and grassroots organizations, Alaska Natives increased political clout in the 1950s, growing even stronger in the 1960s.

Unfortunately, problems still exist in the northwest region, including health issues. The residents have never received justice or compensation, but instead the episode has been rather mired in denial.[44] We should be thankful for the efforts of author and investigator Dan O'Neill, who unlocked the historical vault and exposed the atrocities. To bring the story up to date, in July 2021 Iñupiat leader Delbert Rexford testified before the U.S. Senate Environmental Justice Committee, informing the senators that contamination still exists in Ogotoruk Creek, the main freshwater source for Point Hope. This creek has been tested on numerous occasions for radioactive particles, and Rexford testified that he personally knew five members of a single family who regularly used the creek before developing cancer and dying. Though this may seem to be anecdotal evidence, Rexford believes it was no coincidence. He called it a manmade tragedy that did not need to happen.[45]

6 Boreal Forest to Floodplain, Rampart Dam

When the Cold War set its icy stakes into U.S. culture, politicians became obsessed with the notion of beating the Soviet Union in every way possible, including technology. Leaders were invested in the country's jingoistic exceptionalism. By the end of the Eisenhower years, there was a rising star in the Democratic party, John F. Kennedy, a war hero from a prominent Massachusetts family. As he became more involved in political life, he voiced his "New Frontier" philosophy, aimed at reinforcing U.S. hegemony, which put other nations on notice, particularly the Soviet Union. His pet projects involved space and Alaska. Consequently, when the Rampart Dam Project, the brainchild of the Army Corps of Engineers, was announced, Kennedy was fully behind the scheme. On his campaign trip to Alaska, an anomaly in itself, he spoke to a group of farmers at the Alaska State Fair, declaring the importance of the potential dam, and then carried the same message to gatherings at an Anchorage hotel and to Juneau, the capital of Alaska. He promised, without evidence, that such new projects would lift Alaska out of its colonial status to that of a sovereign entity, fitting of its nascent role as the forty-ninth state. From here a major battle was initiated between prodevelopers and Alaska Natives protecting their homes with the help of emerging environmental groups.

In essence John F. Kennedy was leaning on Frederick Turner's nostalgic thesis concerning the character of the U.S. nation as one of building moral and democratic fiber through the expansion to the West. Kennedy vowed they "would overcome hazards and hardships, to conquer the enemies that threatened from within and without." Western historian Patricia Limerick reviewed these expansion myths and concluded that Kennedy believed the enemies were "a combination of natural forces, natives, and cautious naysayers who dragged their feet against the currents of Manifest Destiny."[1] Kennedy and other "progressive" politicians were not counting on the rise of Indigenous activism and influential supporters. In unison these passionate environmentalists were convinced that Interior Alaska was not an experimental stage for flawed ventures, leading to the detriment of Alaska's interior ecosystem.

For the opponents of the dam, it was an uphill battle to squelch the revived excitement for taming unknown lands and creating monuments to the conquest of landscapes. The prodevelopment faction reasoned this could be accomplished by providing hydroelectric power, irrigation, and, incongruously, flood control at a site located on the Yukon River, at the end of a hundred-mile gorge and the Rampart Canyon. The dam site would lie downstream from the Yukon Flats area, regarded by the planners as vacant, although the Athabascan have lived and hunted in the area for hundreds of years. Proponents touted the glories of the project but were oblivious to the consequential aftermath, including increased flooding, erosion, and loss of wildlife habitat. As for the Athabascan—they were a politically invisible people.

In the early period of evaluation, the U.S. Fish and Wildlife Service offered an estimate that the region in question was the "summer habitat of 1.5 million migratory waterfowl" and a number of fish species, including salmon. A project of this magnitude would upset the ecosystem, but potential harm was disregarded and so were the realities. To fill the Yukon Flats area, a site larger than Erie Lake, would take between eighteen to twenty years, but the time factor did not bother the promoters, nor did they flinch at the construction price tag or the lack of consumer base.[2] The prodevelopers, often politicians, believed this was an opportunity that could not be missed. After all, before this time the region's only apparent fame had been as the site of Rex Beach's cabin, where he penned several of his novels.

The project news traveled as far as New York newspapers. Editorials contrasted the conflict between those who wanted to save a natural wilderness and those who aimed to conquer it. Meanwhile, Athabascan villagers realized they must confront the dam dreamers who had prejudicially decided their homes were on wasted land, but before they became a unified force, the project proceeded, despite confirmed scientific analysis that the dam would regularly flood seven to nine Athabascan villages, and subsistence lands would be irreversibly harmed. In defense, as the Unangan and Iñupiat had done before this time, the Athabascan formed their own grassroots organizations and rallied nearby communities to support their cause.

In the past the Athabascan had experienced culture contact with the Russians, followed by the English, but in relative terms these remote villages had been largely ignored until the 1950s, when the indomitable pursuit of technological superiority mushroomed. For protection the Athabascan constructed political fortresses to guard against intrusions. Fort Yukon (Gwichyaa Zhee) is located near the Canadian border and had once been a trading post for England's Hudson's Bay Company. With this history and its central position, this village formed a natural hub for Native meetings, along with the more northerly Minto Flats area (Tanana Athabascan). Dealing with newcomers was not an unfamiliar obstacle, but the Athabascan were not intimidated and stood their ground, as illustrated in the following historical episode.

The Minto village, located 126 miles from Fairbanks, was the site of a dispute over building a park and road on traditional Athabascan land. In the early 1960s, Richard Frank, renowned as a protector of subsistence and land rights, was an outspoken critic of the Bureau of Land Management and their plans to usurp land for development purposes. Frank explained these were their hunting grounds and should be protected as such. Any changes to the terrain would interfere with subsistence, leading to an unfavorable outcome. Frank emphasized that the people were trying to follow U.S. ways, even supporting charity drives, but when hunting lands were threatened, that created a red line. Conversely, the Bureau of Land Management claimed they had the right to move forward since no Natives were physically occupying the site in question. That is when the Bureau of Indian Affairs got into the act and persuaded Frank and his supporters to claim as much as they thought necessary. This solution suited Frank. He understood his village could not compete with the government or Western business interests. Consequently, it was important to hold onto the land, emphasizing he could not bear to see hungry children, and that is what would happen if the proposed development took place.[3]

The Athabascan were not strangers to the government's attempts to quantify their traditional land base. Back in 1937 the Minto Flats villages had rejected the idea of a reservation for the second time. The first time occurred in 1915, when a railroad had threatened the Nenana region and the Tanana Chiefs Conference was formed to fight against this incursion. The conference was supported by judge and Alaska delegate James Wickersham, who proved to be an effectual voice against those who wanted to seize Indigenous land or water resources for their own private enterprises. The railroad builders promised that the Athabascan could be moved to a "better" place, but of course that smacked of reservation status. The time had long passed, realistically, philosophically, and legally, for any new federal reservations, particularly since it had proved disastrous for Native Americans in the contiguous states.[4] With the knowledge of this earlier dispute, Frank continued to stand up for their rights, dismissing Western definitions of best land use and tenure.

Frank had the respect and experience necessary to build a strong coalition. He looked back at previous cases when, against Native objections, the Bureau of Land Management had forged ahead with government-sponsored plans for the region without a care for the occupants. Yet it was difficult for the officials to ignore the resistance. As evidence for his claims, Frank shared a map his father had created (he had been considered chief at the time) in the hopes it would confirm ownership.[5] The map outlined the usual sites for hunting and fishing—the same areas the authorities were thinking of building the recreational area. With this evidence Frank filed a claim with the Fairbanks bureau office, protesting any road that crossed Athabascan lands. His sentiments were emphatic: "Now I don't want to sound like I really hate you people, no," but to him this was like someone taking another's home without compensation or benefits, and he needed to protect the people of Minto.[6] When the issue of land development became paramount, and it looked like the bulldozers would be arriving any day, Frank declared, "As long as I'm chief, we won't give up our land. We have the same idea the state has. That state wants to develop our land, and that's our aim too."[7]

Frank did not explain further but instead hired a young lawyer to fight the battle in the court system. His name was Ted Stevens, and he went to work to uncover the veracity of these claims and also to understand the varying definitions of the land and resources between oversight agencies and the Athabascan. Stevens came with experience. He had worked as a solicitor for the Department of the Interior during the Eisenhower administration, including pro bono work for other Alaska Native legal issues.[8] Together they won their case, due to the artful skill of Stevens's and Frank's steely resistance.

In 1968 Stevens was elected to the U.S. Senate, increasing his influence and ability to control future projects from the federal level. Stevens joined forces with Don Young, a non-Native schoolteacher living in Fort Yukon with his Athabascan wife, and they were both drawn into the political maelstrom. Based on his opposition to the dam, Young campaigned for the U.S. House seat in 1966 and won. He was immediately up against prodevelopers, like former Alaska governor Ernest Gruening, who was his fellow inaugural U.S. senator. Gruening claimed that stopping the dam project would set Alaska backward and argued against any scientific or political objections, and he opposed Young's opposition, calling him a fanatic.[9] This volatile climate and polar factional debates fueled the battle, kept burning by the anticipation of economic gains. One side was determined to set a financial boon in motion, deeming the project crucial for the fledging state, while others argued that the proposed project spelled certain disaster. In all this uproar, the Native voice was loud, but money and reputation spoke louder.

Although Ted Stevens and Don Young were sympathetic to the Native cause, while simultaneously shocked by the project's price tag, they also represented other constituents who had to be considered in any decision or stance. Many Alaskans, tired of being treated like a colony for the rest of the United States, were enthused about the greatness of the project and how it might generate more respect for the Last Frontier. In local newspapers they read Senator Kennedy's words when he opined, "I see a giant electric grid stretching from Juneau to Anchorage and beyond. I see the greatest dam in the free world at Rampart Canyon, producing twice the power of TVA to light homes and mills and cities and farms all over Alaska."[10]

THE PERIOD FROM 1958 to 1962 ushered in a tremendous social and political transformation for the nation and Alaska. When Alaska became a state, it was believed the long battle for self-determination against federal paternalism had ended, but Alaska Natives were leery, wondering what it might mean for their lives. In effect the chasm between governmental ownership and Native stewardship increased, but nothing compared to when the state started land selections following the passage of the Alaska Statehood Act, which allowed the rule-makers to sort out state and federal government domains. Alaska selected about 105 million acres of unappropriated lands, but the question arose over definition. These supposed vacant lands were used for Native hunting year-round, hardly unappropriated. The state was placed in a bind to either honor Native rights or make money to survive. The overriding presumption of the state was that these vast untouched expanses could not remain a wasted opportunity.

While land ownership was debated, the contest between resource extractors and the Athabascan villages reached crisis levels in the early 1960s, when the dam project, first proposed in 1954 by the U.S. Army Corps of Engineers, started its final planning phase to create this mammoth reservoir within the Yukon River, located about 31 miles from the Athabascan village of Rampart and 105 miles from Fairbanks. Immediately it was recognized that this extraction and water diversion would produce an ecological disaster by overflowing the natural water bodies and disrupting the ecosystem, already prone to seasonal flooding. Environmental groups, particularly the Wilderness Society and Sierra Club, were gaining prominence throughout the United States, and the activists confronted the prodevelopers, explaining that there would be disastrous effects to the wetlands and its inhabitants, including waterfowl and moose populations. But the environmentalists were met with indifference, while dam enthusiasts answered the complaint by assuming the wildlife were either expendable or that the animals would just instinctually move out of harm's way.

Ernest Gruening was not about to give an inch, although his allegiance was split. On one hand he advocated for Native rights and encouraged Native men to run for public office to better represent their people. Yet he relentlessly promoted natural resource development so that Alaska, according to his viewpoint, could occupy its proper place among the other states and territories—regardless of how these actions would throw Native villages into a crisis mode. In his words the project would result in "a concrete gravity dam with an installed capacity of five million kilowatts. . . . It would be the largest hydroelectric dam in the western world, generating two and half times as much power as Grand Coulee."[11] With solid connections in Washington DC, people like Gruening could make things happen, including securing large funds. The minority, expressing concerns about the financial and ecological cost, could not stand up against those who wanted to develop the "howling wilderness."

Politicians saw the Rampart Dam Project as a means of boosting Alaska's economy and a way to beautify a site deemed a "vast swamp and uninhabited except for seven small Indian villages," so construction would "destroy no property values." Any difficulties would be offset by new employment, the ever-present dangling carrot offered to Indigenous habitants so they would leave their homes in a modern-day episode of Indian removal.[12] Gruening and others in government did not realize that the Athabascan already had jobs. Their lifestyle might not be analogous to mainstream America, but it remained vital, and what the dam builders called ugly was a beautiful forestland that provided for the people. Famed anthropologist and naturalist Richard Nelson describes the discrepancy: "Westerners identify this remote country as wilderness, reflecting their inability to conceive of occupying and utilizing an environment without fundamentally altering its natural state," while the Athabascan have "made a highly effective adjustment to living as members of an ecosystem . . . that fosters the successful coexistence of humanity and nature within a single community."[13]

NONETHELESS, THOSE WHO wanted to dig a mammoth hole in the interior reduced the region to a withering swampland, not unlike the land speculators in the early years of the nation. Politicians downplayed the flooding possibilities while generating false or misleading information concerning the greatness of the project and how it would bring economic miracles to the Natives. These dam dreamers were further bolstered by the Yukon Power for

America organization, which sent out propaganda pamphlets to the public. As Alaska historians Claus-M. Naske and Herman Slotnick determined, this organization was the leading proponent for the Rampart Dam: "Businessmen, newspaper publishers, chambers of commerce, and mayors of Alaska's principal cites belonged to the group. The organization published a colorful brochure titled 'The Rampart Story,' which extolled the benefits of cheap electrical power, specifically three mills per kilowatt hour. This power would in turn attract industry, it was said, notably the aluminum industry."[14] During these Cold War years, especially after the sacrifices made during World War II, the public was ready to jump on the consumer wagon, but nobody foresaw the growing power of environmental groups. They demanded an audience with governmental agencies and were supported by the changing public opinion about Native Americans and the environment.

Ira Gabrielson, the director of the Wildlife Management Institute, listened to the Athabascan's complaints and offered his analysis: "The 500 foot dam would block sizable upstream migration of salmon on the Yukon. . . . The impoundment would cover the Yukon Flats that produce on the average of 1–1.2 million ducks and geese a year. . . . Moose and fur bearers would suffer. . . . Rampart Dam is synonymous with resource destruction." Gabrielson gathered those of like mind to fight against this project and stressed that the harm to wildlife, water bodies and villages far outweighed any imagined gains. Instead of making his point, his motives were questioned, and he was accused of being influenced by "gunmakers and ammunition manufacturers." Further, he was questioned on whether his efforts to save Alaskan ducks was only a pretense so that they may later be "blasted from the skies in the States."[15] Paradoxically, it was the real danger of destroying duck habitats that posed the greater threat to "visiting duck hunters," and when wildlife guides and other business owners uncovered these pesky facts, they aligned with Gabrielson's efforts to stop the dam. The moose question was a different matter. In a twisted bit of fate, it turned out that the out-of-state duck hunters were favored over local moose hunters.

With the nature of this controversy, it was a foregone conclusion that Wally Hickel, Alaska's quintessential entrepreneur and later Richard Nixon's secretary of the interior from 1969 to 1970, joined the dispute.[16] He was imbued with a prodevelopment philosophy and the idea that Alaska's resources belonged to Alaskans only, but not necessarily the original Alaskans. To this end he created the user-state philosophy, which encourages government intervention if it results in more infrastructure and expansion.[17] At the time of the proposed project, Hickel was making a name for himself as a financial prophet and in real estate and resource development, and he could not understand what all the ruckus was about when there was money to be made. He scoffed at impediments, including the Athabascan. These longtime interior residents, according to Hickel, did not possess any jurisdiction because genuine ownership came only through conquest or purchase.[18] In his usual condescending and incendiary manner, he remarked, "Just because your granddaddy chased a moose around doesn't mean you own the land."[19]

To Hickel and his ilk, the quixotic Alaska Native past could be replaced by a modern vision, and his ideas were shared by Alaska's new governor William Egan, who imagined "busy factories, modern cities, crowded ports. We see the vast potential wealth of Alaska being utilized to improve the material well-being of the people. . . . It is a long standing [dream] shared by all who know Alaska's enormous potential for economic and social growth."[20] During the height of the debates, Egan and a congressional delegation addressed the Pacific Trade Association Conference in British Columbia and were adamant the dam would be built, and any detracting fish and wildlife reports could easily be exposed as weak.[21] Similar to Gruening, Egan found himself in a personal and political dilemma, since he had previously been sympathetic to the Native cause but also felt the burden of running a new state.

Meanwhile, Fairbanks labor unions were all fired up to get working on what appeared to be a beneficial undertaking for their wallets. The Athabascan protest was shrugged off without recognizing the rapid growth of Native strength and anger, as their leaders forged the path necessary to traverse the thorny diplomatic landscape consisting of federal and state government bureaucracy and fervent environmental groups. At a glance it would seem as if big business had the upper hand, but its viewpoint was influenced by dollars without sense. Those opposed to the dam targeted the cost, believing this would discourage the federal government, while others continued to mount a scientific defense, finally taking their complaints to the Department of the

Interior and the Fish and Wildlife Service. When they presented their case, they explained the absurdity of any project that proposed to provide Yukon power to an unnamed population. But the politicians had to have the last word. Ernest Gruening, with a voice in Washington DC, exposed his jaundiced view of the Yukon Flats and Minto Flats: "In a land of infinite beauty with towering peaks rising from the ocean, tidal glaciers, high waterfalls and many other sights to lift the spirit of man, the Yukon Flats are, in my opinion, anything but beautiful." Further, Gruening claimed environmentalists were "interested in preserving the habitat of a variety of feathered, furred, and scaled creatures" at the sacrifice of a robust economy.[22]

The Athabascan were in an uphill fight, as delineated by historian Dan O'Neill, who documented the Project Chariot crisis and was a major critic of this potential environmental nightmare. He noted, "When Rampart Dam proponents paid any attention at all to the 1,200 people whose homeland and livelihood would disappear, they sometimes did so with a degree of ethnocentrism not readily distinguishable from insult." Similar sentiments were countered by Gruening's continual barrage of invectives, stating that the Athabascan lived in "an area as worthless from the standpoint of human habitation as any that can be found on earth."[23] The incendiary language drew the attention of secretary of the interior, Stewart Udall. He reviewed the environmental reports and complaints in conjunction with documenting other Alaska Native problems during this period.[24] After careful study, Udall concluded there was a potential for environmental catastrophe. Gruening, in full asperity, groused that Udall must have been taken captive by conservationists, but it was enough to turn the tide.[25]

Between 1963 and 1968, the political jockeying continued until it was shown without doubt that the project was too expensive and there were no benefits. Alaska was still a relatively unknown region, and Congress did not want to take a risk on such a large investment. When the dam idea was finally shut down, it was assumed to be a victory for environmental groups, but they did not do it alone. The winning strategy had its origins in village unity, Native leadership, and grassroots groups who sprung up to meet the exigency.

Gwitchya Gwitchin Ginkhye (Yukon Flats People Speak) was formed to address the Rampart Dam Project. Their mission statement read, in part,

"This land is dear to us. . . . It has provided life for our fathers. It provided the means of life to us and would provide for our children."[26] The members were opposed to any forced move that would dangerously disrupt their lives, such as the suggestion of relocating nine villages to Minto Flats. If this had occurred, not only would there be resentment, but suddenly that village would have two thousand new residents and no infrastructure in place to accommodate these people. The Fort Yukon group raised their fists in protest against the Civilian Corp of Engineers and won.

Jonathon Solomon served as traditional chief of Gwitchya Gwitchin Ginkhye and was joined by other political warriors from as far south as the Copper River Valley, more than four hundred miles away. Noted Ahtna elder Fred John Jr. told me how several Mentasta people, including his father, Fred John Sr., participated in meetings dedicated to halting the project and protecting their way of life.[27] Above all, there was a need for substantial documentation to support their claims. By the fall of 1963, four Yukon Flats villages had created maps to show traditional trading and hunting trails, fish camps, and sacred sites from as far back as their memories and oral narrative could reach, believing this demonstrated the Organic Act occupancy requirements. In addition, false statements in newspapers were rebuffed, particularly when "fake Indians" were quoted as saying, "Who cares about little piece flooded? I for Rampart." They countered with their own statement: "I am against it because a way of life would be changed. I do not want to relocate."[28] The added, "We do not think the mighty Yukon, which in our Athabascan language means broad and wide river, should be tampered with. The dam would ruin the river."[29]

Gwitchya Gwitchin Ginkhye persevered by advocating they were the rightful owners of the land, and the legacy belonged to their children. The word spread through *Tundra Times* editorials, condemning the project, but these communications were offset by other reports that negatively portrayed the Athabascan as living in poverty and forecasting that the true cost of halting development would result in running a welfare state in Native villages, a charge that had found fertile soil in past arguments, regardless of veracity.[30] As unsound as this latter argument was, it had run headlong into the evolving national social policy. President Lyndon Johnson's new domestic program, "the Great Society"—with its promise to lift everyone, including the "Indians," out of poverty—was in the forefront, though challenged as reckless spending. President Johnson's War on Poverty was antithetical to a nascent state attempting to make its mark, and Alaskan statespeople and entrepreneurs surely did not want Alaska to appear as a welfare state, while the Natives did not want to be the wards of any government.

To strengthen the troops, Gwitchya Gwitchin Ginkhye teamed up with other Native organizations, such as the Alaska Native Brotherhood (urged on by William Paul Sr.), Arctic Native Brotherhood, Dena Nena Henash (Our Land Speaks), and Inupiat Paitot (from Project Chariot), to form the Conference of Native Organizations, with the chief purpose of combating false information whether it was coming from Washington DC or Juneau or Fairbanks.[31] Dena Nena Henash had previously spoken out on land issues and what it meant to the people: "The state is invading and selling our land. There are no jobs in the villages, and our hunting grounds are being taken away. We no longer have any way to feed our children."[32] These were almost the exact words of Richard Frank in speaking of their subsistence way of life.

In this protracted crusade the Alaska Natives were helped by the changing U.S. culture, as the nation woke up from the sleepy 1950s into a setting that witnessed growing social unrest. The pan-Indian movement called for a reckoning on Indigenous lands and demanded their cause be heard. Yet, despite the growing turbulence and protests, John F. Kennedy's past words persisted in gaining a foothold on the political landscape with taunts like "If Alaska still belonged to the Russians, Rampart Canyon would be underway today." Yet times had changed, and the dam proponents saw their vision fade. There would no longer be the hope of a "giant grid stretching from Juneau to Anchorage and beyond." Kennedy's dream of "the greatest dam in the free world at Rampart Canyon, producing twice the power of TVA to light homes and mills and cities and farms all over Alaska" had come to an end.[33]

For a while the dam project had thrived on an ignorance of terrain, necessary infrastructure, and transportation realities. The Army Corps of Engineers had no idea how to safeguard waterfowl and fish. Finally, the Athabascan were heard, and Alaska residents were made aware of the dangers of continual flooding. Moreover, there were international concerns. The Canadian government opposed the Rampart Dam project on the basis of the 1871 Treaty of Washington, which guaranteed Canada free access to the Yukon River, stemming from a longtime agreement between the English and Americans along the Canadian border. There were fears that construction of such a dam would violate the treaty by taking away the navigation rights in the shared territories along the Yukon and Porcupine Rivers. Athabascan on both sides of the border would be adversely affected by conflicting legislation and natural resource regulations by either the Canadian government, the U.S. federal government, or Alaska's Fish and Game Department.

Alaska and the nation dodged a situation that could have turned into "the world's biggest sinkhole for public funds."[34] The Spurr Report, which influenced the Department of the Interior's decision to shut down the project, outlined the negative effects on wildlife, fish, and habitat and determined any dam would be "the most expensive gamble ever suggested in hydroelectric development" with a "detrimental impact on the Native population." In conclusion the project could not be profitable and would in fact end up costing both the federal and state government.[35] By June 1967 Secretary Stewart Udall announced there were "less costly alternatives" and reemphasized "the fish and wildlife losses" that would occur if it was allowed to go forward.[36] Even at that point, Governor William Egan pleaded with the Army Corps of Engineers to reopen the project. The matter was turned over to the U.S. Senate, which closed the case in 1978. To eliminate any further attempts to resurrect the proposal, President Jimmy Carter designated the area as a federal reserve, the Yukon Flats National Wildlife Monument, and by 1985 the Bureau of Land Management had released all former lands that had once been considered or reserved for the dam.[37]

THIS ULTIMATE SUCCESS brought together Native communities from across the state in a common cause, reinvigorating the fight to redeem land and resource rights and consequently exposing Alaska's provincial politics, peculiar priorities, and the common struggle against the forces of Western expansion and colonization. Primarily, as has been noted in the previous conflicts, this had been a tug-of-war between human advancement as determined by a Western yardstick pitted against Indigenous survival. The Athabascan were lucky to have escaped the fate of other regions where dams had been built and experienced "impacts ranging from population displacement to environmental disruption," including to the subsistence cycle. Specific problems included temperature differentials and "changes in nutrient and toxin concentrations in rivers, and increasing erosion and sediment deposition" alterations that harm fisheries. Pacific Northwest and Alaska Native residents depend on salmon, and dams have been known to cause a "sudden loss of salmon-based economies and spiritual traditions," sending "a seismic shock to the cultures and psyches of the people."[38]

The Athabascan blazed a trail for environmental justice and had the scars to prove it. The *Tundra Times* documented the blatant racist language in newspapers, governmental reports, and other media that proclaimed Natives were standing in the way of a healthy economy. The *Fairbanks Daily News-Miner* from February 22, 1964, stated, "You don't buy electrical power and gasoline with moose meat and duck feathers." Rural or village Alaska was likened to a poverty-stricken country, and editorials lamented the loss of jobs that the Rampart Dam would have supposedly provided so the poor people would not be "forced" to live off the land. The incendiary language was a gross failure to understand the concept of place in traditional and contemporary identity, as well as the validity of Native land rights.[39]

Similar to the perception in the Pacific Northwest, the salmon were "not looked upon as important . . . compared to development or progress. Progress means conquest of nature, industry, highways, suburbs, bulldozing, dams." Roberta Ulrich, in her book *Empty Nets: Indians, Dams, and the Columbia River*, explains that in "the world where Indian lives were regulated by the seasons and by customs that extend beyond memory came Bonneville Dam. It disrupted life on the lower river as Grand Coulee Dam did for other tribes. . . . The dam would change the Columbia into a mile-wide stream flowing sluggishly . . . where Indian fisherman had caught their family's food since time immemorial."[40]

Through the work of Native villages and tribes and the growth of environmentalism, there was a demand for government accountability. Sports hunters became aware that their expeditions might be in jeopardy, and the public demanded proper resource management and the sustainable use of fauna and biota. Yet, even after the downfall of Project Chariot and the Rampart

Dam proposal, the struggle for justice did not stop. Ecological skirmishes were being fought simultaneously with the Native land–rights pursuit that escalated when oil was found in northern Alaska at a place called Prudhoe Bay. Alaska's socioeconomic landscape was altered forever when the Atlantic Richfield Company made this discovery in 1968.

1. Harvesting a walrus that washed up to shore. This was a common practice. Nothing would go to waste. Courtesy of the Michael Nore Collection.

2. Whale hunting and harvesting at Akutan on the Aleutian Chain. Courtesy of the Michael Nore Collection.

3. Northwest Alaska men living in tents in seasonal camps. Courtesy of the Michael Nore Collection.

4. The blanket toss was part of an annual celebration to celebrate the earth's bounty. Honored individuals took part in this ritual, and jumpers were known for their skill. Courtesy of the Michael Nore Collection.

5. Young Iñupiat girl. Courtesy of the Michael Nore Collection.

6. Counting seal skins for the government. This labor was coerced, and there were no privileges. This photo shows the depth of the operation. Courtesy of the Michael Nore Collection.

7. Seal harvesting activity to get ready for shipment, Saint Paul, Pribilof Islands, 1905. Courtesy of the Michael Nore Collection.

8. Sorting through fur seal skins, Saint George, Pribilof Islands, 1905. Courtesy of the Michael Nore Collection.

9. This marine vessel was called a *qayak* in the traditional Unangan (Aleutian Chain) language, but the word was changed to the Russian *baidarka,* or *bidarka,* when the Russians arrived. These men and their families were subjugated to work in the sea otter trade or to harvest fur seals. Courtesy of the Michael Nore Collection.

10. Unloading coal sent by the U.S. government to the Pribilof Islands. Courtesy of the Michael Nore Collection.

11. Coal delivery to Saint Paul, Pribilof Islands. Courtesy of the Michael Nore Collection.

7   Etok versus Big Oil

Charlie Edwardsen Jr., or "Etok," was a fighter—no obstacle was unconquerable, including conglomerate oil companies. While the profiteers recognized the money to be made from fossil fuels, remnants from a prehistoric era, Edwardsen feared his heritage was in jeopardy and took action. Along with other emerging leaders and resistance groups, he tried to stop the Texas oil barons and exploratory drillers from becoming a reality in the Arctic. Often it was often a solitary struggle against a behemoth, and he made more enemies than partners, but decades later his rebellion is legendary and an example for those who came after him.

From his early years, Charlie Edwardsen had the makings of a political activist. He was from the northernmost village of Barrow (now called Utqiagvik) with an ancient history, including sod houses still standing as relics of the past. His father had told him stories of their people to instill a degree of patience and pride in the young, restless boy, who sought deep answers to life's problems. His persistent inquisitiveness led to an arsenal of knowledge. During his teenage years, he consumed the details surrounding the U.S. Constitution, the Bill of Rights, and the 1884 Alaska Organic Act, and for a time he was naive enough to believe the promises in these documents in his evolving quest to achieve Indigenous rights.

In 1962 he graduated from Mount Edgecumbe, a Native boarding school in southeast Alaska, and briefly attended the University of Alaska but dropped out, giving in to a perpetual agitated state. He later enrolled in a New Jersey program RCA operated to train electronic technicians but became disillusioned with that pursuit. As he became more involved in national politics, he hitch-hiked to the Democratic National Convention in Atlantic City, which took place less than a year after the Kennedy assassination. Finding no answers there, he returned to Barrow, discouraged but still trying to find his niche in life.[1] More than anything he wanted to bring his developing knowledge to the cause of Alaska Natives and their land rights.

Edwardsen had a stutter that made it difficult to express himself at times. The speech impediment was worse when he was agitated, yet he would not be deterred, nor could he be overlooked. His zealous demeanor made some standoffish or skeptical with his get-in-your-face tactics, but despite those drawbacks he developed a personal power. In cultural terms, however, his rhetoric was considered an affront to the Iñupiat code that stressed accommodation rather than confrontation, hindering his ability to form significant Native alliances. Edwardsen's biographer summed it up as "he knew his family and relations in Barrow and the people of the Arctic Slope would find it hard to understand or approve of what he intended to do. They are a quiet society, the Eskimos, whose anger and opposition are repressed in an uneasy silence; a people loyal to the United States, trusting the white man and his laws."[2] Because of his relentless nature, though, he was determined to break out of the status quo to redeem the overdue respect for the Iñupiat people.

Eventually, Edwardsen found himself in an unlikely position: that of a negotiator between the Alaska Natives and the federal government. After returning to Barrow, he had sharpened his tool set by focusing on state and federal legislature and Supreme Court rulings. Not only did he learn all he could about each law or legal decision, but he also analyzed the circumstances that led to the final wording. Still he was conflicted over the correct approach toward issues—to engage in battle or negotiate. He recalled how his father stressed peaceful resolutions, and he had also heard other Iñupiat leaders, like Willie Hensley, speak about ironing out differences through provincial channels. He was not sure he could be so patient.

Edwardsen may have been confused over philosophies, but he envisioned speaking for the people concerning the management of Arctic natural resources.[3] He was well aware of the stake corporations had in the region, and this forced him to examine the Western interpretation of a finite land base governed by titles and deeds as opposed to the Native custom of living with the land. To reconcile these differences, he sought assistance from elders to draw a map, delineating the ancient territory. At Anny and Harry Brower's house, he unfolded a map of Alaska on the table and sketched a line "from the Chukchi Sea on the west, along the sixty-eighth north latitude to the one hundred forty-eighth west longitude and then north" and east to the Canadian border. In all it was fifty-six million acres, and even though the Indigenous population had been reduced, largely due to disease, Edwardsen claimed that land, containing jade mountains from "the far tip of Point Hope, exposed and eroding from winds and tides, north of the Bering Strait, all the way across," where the people had built hunting trails, seasonal camps, where they knew the flora and fauna—"all these were lands of the Iñupiat."[4]

Far removed from the 1960s protests and rebellion in the lower states, Edwardsen was carving a path for justice, which meant this firebrand needed like-minded movers and shakers to form a formidable force. Faithful supporters were difficult to find, and he was troubled by the enormity of the task, so he turned to his old mentor, a man now in his eighties. Tlingit attorney William Paul Sr., a born warrior, had become his cultural hero. Paul, also known for a combative style, had first met Charlie at Mount Edgecumbe, a Native boarding school in southeast Alaska, and the teenager had been mesmerized by the words of this man who was not afraid to use unconventional weapons on the political battlefield.

When Paul Sr. spoke of the Supreme Court case he had defended in 1955, Edwardsen found significance for his own people. Paul had claimed that his Stikine Tlingit (Wrangell, southeast Alaska) clan still owned their piece of the Tongass Forest because the aboriginal title had never been extinguished when President Theodore Roosevelt had locked it away in a reserve in the early 1900s. This case, *Tee-Hit-Ton Indians v. United States*, did not receive compensation for the timber harvested on Stikine Tlingit lands, but it did set a precedent for considering the legal concept of aboriginal title, or the common law doctrine that original tenure continues to exist even after "settler colonialism" assumes control over land and resources. Although William Paul Sr. lost his case, the conclusions, both favorable and unfavorable, remain in Federal Indian Law, including the clause about outsider trespassing on Indigenous land.

Edwardsen could have no idea at his young age, but he would use *Tee-Hit-Ton* in his case against big oil in defending the Arctic and its first people. From the start he was convinced that the Supreme Court decision had been tainted by the overarching desire to open the West for settlers and development, and he focused on to the due process clause, believing it applied to Native lands.[5] Specifically, he concentrated on the section where Chief Justice Marshall was quoted as saying the "tribes" were dependent sovereign nations, and outsiders were defined as trespassers. Paul Sr. had told him that the Russians never owned Alaska, so it followed that the United States did not have a genuine claim to his homeland.[6]

Edwardsen compared the *Tee-Hit-Ton* case to his own Arctic situation and was convinced that Iñupiat land had never been legally extinguished, and the "conquest theory," also advocated by Chief Justice Marshall, could not apply since there had never been Indian wars in Alaska. He felt solid in his legal arguments but also understood the power of numbers and the necessity of building a Native coalition to represent northern Alaskan interests in any land claims movement. Other village political groups had formed by this time, but Edwardsen did not think they could understand the exact nature of the Arctic problem, except for one recent lawsuit. In 1959 the Tlingit and Haida land claims suit concerning aboriginal rights in the Tongass Forest—a larger extension of the same fight that William Paul Sr. had fought for Wrangell—had been won. This judgment paved the way for other lawsuits, including the eventual pan-Alaska land claims movement also motivated by oil exploration. Edwardsen used this victory as a template.

His disdain for large organizations and the specific nature of his target led to the formation of the Arctic Slope Native Association (ASNA), built largely on the principles expressed in a January 1966 letter from Charlie to William Paul Sr., stating the organization's mission was to secure "aboriginal rights and title to said land" along the lines he had already drawn out on the map. There was a sense of urgency because oil exploration had already started at a few sites, and Edwardsen felt the pressure. Through the ASNA he started an injunction motion for the purposes of proving that "our people have not adequately been compensated," and oil drilling must be stopped.[7]

The ASNA claimed that ninety-six million acres were theirs by right of occupancy and that there was significant documentation to back the claim, legally and historically, adding that Hubert Bancroft's famous Alaska history tome contained documentation that the 1867 Treaty of Cession between Russia and the United States confirmed this land tenure. Edwardsen's reasoning followed the same premise that William "Bill" Paul Jr. had used in his 1939 law school thesis.[8] Paul Jr. had determined that this treaty, coupled with the 1884 Organic Act, guaranteed title to the lands used, occupied, or otherwise claimed by Natives, and all others were trespassers. If this argument failed, Edwardsen was ready to use "law and lawyers and politics and unite in action," which turned out to be his next step.[9] All the while oil companies were chomping at the bit to get started, and the Alaska Native political bodies were being squeezed in every direction.

Based on his readings, Edwardsen was certain that no valid exchange had occurred to separate Alaska Natives from their land and waters. The purchase of a "trading company in 1867, the Russian American Trading Company" could not "displace our original sovereignty."[10] But there was more on the horizon to consider. In 1971 the Alaska Native Claims Settlement Act (ANCSA) had been decided, and the legislation turned into the most important document for extant and future land claims. When oil companies could no longer proceed with exploration, the matter of land claims had to be decided without delay. The final settlement act was complex and a revolution in Alaska Native economies. Twelve for-profit regional corporations were set up and about two hundred auxiliary village corporations, all based on natural resource extraction by corporations. In one fell swoop, capitalism was brought to rural Alaska. In exchange the Alaska Native leaders and corporation directors agreed to quit all claims to the rest of Alaska. It would seem this legislation finalized the problems, but interpretation and misunderstandings follow ANCSA to this day. In Edwardsen's story, it is instrumental to look closer at what this legislation entailed and how it applied to northern oil exploration.

In the early stages of land claims discussions, Edwardsen fought against any legislation that would allow oil companies to have free reign on the Arctic Slope, and he often felt alone in his resistance. In 1967 the Alaska Federation of Natives (AFN) was created to negotiate the inevitable land claims, but Edwardsen had no faith in the organization. In his eyes they were not strong enough to stand up to big oil or the federal government. Further, he did not believe any congressional mandate had the power to remove Indigenous hunters from their traditional lands and replace them with oil drills.[11] The ASNA was now headed by Edwardsen, and he was ready to take on those who would usurp his home. But he had more than enemies in his path. The do-gooders were strewing boulders along the way that were hard to remove.

Alaska, as usual, was suffering from myths and legends that had nothing to do with reality, and the inherent confusion blocked Alaska Native progress in regaining their rights. Some of the misunderstandings emanated from the White House. President Lyndon Johnson had set up various poverty programs to assist in the building of his Great Society project. There were those who praised Johnson's program, while others considered it a distraction from the escalating war in Vietnam. Edwardsen had an entirely different interpretation and feared that his people might once again be looked on as dependents. When he heard that these proposed "safety net" programs might apply to the northern country, he shunned any mention of "hand outs" that would make Alaska Natives more reliant on the government, a yoke to be permanently severed. He was vehement that Great Society welfare programs for the "Indians," or what President Johnson called the "Forgotten Americans," were not only unnecessary but a newly fashioned arrow aimed at a people who have pride in their past and confidence in their future.

Later on he tempered his message somewhat while speaking before Congress to offer an honest assessment of the circumstances. While reserving his convictions, he thought it was beneficial for Alaska Native communities to receive benefits from the federal government like any other citizen on an equal plane. In his region, he explained, there were obstacles to village infrastructure from a lack of funds for skilled labor and transportation, although "the Natives have the incentive and desire to provide better homes for themselves. When you have no financial means, this is not possible."[12] Yet Edwardsen condemned any motion that attached labels presuming poverty or victim status. By now, Edwardsen had reckoned, the oil companies could not be stopped, even after picketing against oil leases, going before the U.S. Congress, and raising hell in Juneau. For now the ASNA demanded a fair price for the land the government and oil companies had stolen while demanding no further intrusions.[13]

When Edwardsen was able to shrug off his lone wolf status, it was a boost to his cause and the ASNA. He found a partner in Joe Upicksoun, and they agreed on the crucial issues, although Upicksoun used less colorful language to make his point. Together they objected to the drilling and worked to uplift the people to a more autonomous standing. Even as the stealthy oil companies crept in, ASNA stood firm in its conviction for Indigenous rights and environmental justice.

Because Edwardsen was not much of an administrator, Upicksoun took over the duties as president of the ASNA while Edwardsen spent more time traveling, particularly to Washington DC. Upicksoun focused on local matters and politicians, including the influential Nick Begich, who held a prominent place in Congress and had pledged his help in this controversy.[14] This type of alliance was key in getting the word out in the hope of a favorable outcome. Begich had warned that the Native land selections based on ANCSA would be long and drawn out and he anticipated many skirmishes. Meanwhile, Begich played both sides against the middle. When he was with a Native group, he told them tales of how much land they could keep, and when he was with oil companies, he told them how much oil Alaska had—just below the surface.[15]

THE ONGOING DISSENSION between the AFN and ASNA was working at cross-purposes with no relief in sight. Edwardsen and Upicksoun were certain the AFN was moving too slowly, and instead of a cautious approach, the duo believed they should walk into the halls of Congress and demand their land. Upicksoun told Native audiences they were entitled to what was theirs, and they must show the politicians that they were not childlike savages but grown, thinking people who were tired of hearing "we have a better thing for you." He spoke of the evils of any legal settlement established by Western courts: "Your title is going to be extinguished forever. . . . You are landlords and you god damn better look like landlords."[16] Edwardsen punctuated these heated moments by reminding everyone that the State of Alaska was their worst enemy, but it was difficult to sway opinions when the headwinds were blowing so robustly.

In 1968 Charlie Edwardsen was interviewed by reporter Drew Pearson to discuss the current land issues, and he pointed to the former secretary of the interior, Walter J. Hickel, now governor of Alaska, as the centerpiece of their troubles. Hickel, who was a land developer, boasted about his user-state theory, which claimed big corporations could have free reign on Alaska resources, regardless of any past Indigenous title. Hickel ridiculed the notion that Alaska Natives owned anything, further riling up Edwardsen and Upicksoun, but they did not waver. Their commitment was firm as they climbed the craggy cliff of governmental indifference and cavalier attitudes. Meanwhile, initial drilling had already marred the Arctic landscape, and Edwardsen protested the environmental damage. As evidence he pointed to Point Lay, a small village in the North Slope Borough on the shores of the Chukchi Sea. This was an area with the "best polar bear hunting in the world," but the animals were becoming scarce due to overhunting by tourists—the fly-in hunters did not fire a shot—they paid someone else to shoot the animal for them as a trophy. Edwardsen could not condone such disrespect; it went against the Iñupiat way.[17]

More than the polar bear, the marine mammals and aquatic birds were in jeopardy. The Indigenous hunters relied on these resources, and if these big companies were going to come into the north and drill, the people who had lived there for thousands of years should be reimbursed for the loss of their homes, hunting grounds, and sacred sites. Edwardsen had felt at times there was nothing he could do to stop the interlopers: "They'll take oil the way they took gold and there'll be nothing left. The white man makes a killing, and then he leaves." He punctuated his point with the Lucy Alvakana story. She had gone to her usual summer fish camp and found that Sinclair Oil had taken over the site and built an airstrip. It was an affront that Edwardsen could not tolerate: "How long must we sit by while creeping wolves sneak away our territory?"[18]

Edwardsen had tried everything to get his message out, with varying success, but gradually he came to understand the power of the printed word and television. He had gained experience in presentations and writing speeches while working for Speaker of the House Mike Gavel as a page in the Alaska House of Representatives. This experience had also helped him control his stuttering problem. Edwardsen found a solid advocate in Gravel and was impressed with his campaign for more schools in Native communities and his opposition to the land grab by the oil companies. In turn Edwardsen emulated the same manners, style, and language, believing this would give him a leg up against the government's machinations.[19] It was a good education and helped rein in his fervent nature for a while, but Edwardsen still needed to deal with an oil-hungry nation.

In September 1969 Edwardsen could be found pounding the streets of Anchorage, Alaska's largest city, to protest oil leases. He positioned himself in front of the auditorium that was set to hear oil-lease bids that day, and when the television crews arrived, they found a different story from the one they were expecting. There was Edwardsen and several high school students walking a picket line "with signs that declared 'Eskimos Own North Slope' and '$2,000,000,00 Native Land Robbery.'" When the cameras focused on him, he let out a profanity-laced diatribe and made no apologies. No doubt the tape never made its way off the editing floor, but that did not stop the AFN Board of Directors from condemning his behavior and language, quickly adding that Edwardsen did not represent them. Some might have thought it was a genuine breach of Native etiquette, but Edwardsen saw it as the inevitable turf war and defied the AFN censure: "When you have access to maybe two hundred million people who watch the news all over the world, that is a very powerful thing." He wanted to make sure that the United States would associate the Alaska Natives with the nemesis of big oil, regardless or maybe because of the rhetoric.[20]

UPICKSOUN WAS NOW managing the day-to-day business on the home front, while Edwardsen traveled around the country wherever he believed his voice would be most effective. By February 1971 Edwardsen was testifying in environmental hearings held by Secretary of the Interior Rogers Morton, which centered on the approval of the trans-Alaska pipeline. The hearings were televised, giving Edwardsen another platform to get his message out nationally. The oil industry and their experts opened with a slick prepared statement, and the environmentalists followed, crying out for the birds and beasts, while Alaska's Governor Egan fretted and claimed the whole state would go bankrupt without the pipeline. Edwardsen had prepared nothing, and his thoughts were madly swimming in his mind. Finally, he decided to speak from his experience, in hopes of convincing the audience of the moral transgression of pushing aside people who had occupied and thrived in the region for thousands of years.

Charlie Edwardsen belittled the Department of the Interior's superficial gestures—they were following their own agenda, and he was skeptical of these environmental studies, claiming they did not "even know that there are 147 different varieties of birds, which nest on the North Slope." The draft report, he continued, said nothing about the dwellers of the land and users of the waters. He asked, "How can the white men sell our land when they do not own it?" This latter plea was repeated by Walter Cronkite on the evening news that night.[21]

This was not the end to Edwardsen's media fame. He also made the front page of the *Washington Post*, where he was quoted as saying, "Both legally and morally it is wrong for Western Civilization to move in on the North Slope and ride roughshod over us. . . . The Eskimos who live by hunting, trapping and fishing were completely ignored. It is our lives, our culture, our lands that are being invaded."[22] Edwardsen was also sending out an appeal to his own people to make them aware that this was an emergency situation that could not wait and definitely not the time for delicate negotiations. Perhaps to onlookers his protests could have been viewed as mild during this time of violent national unrest relating to civil rights and the Vietnam War, but to the traditional leaders in the northwest region, Edwardsen's methodology was called into question, and he was labeled a radical.

The first one to take affront was Eben Hopson, the esteemed Barrow whaling captain, who had been leading his own group to regain hunting rights, but with a philosophy of treading more lightly. These historical factors remind us that Alaska Natives were never a monolith; each culture was (and is) different, and it was not unusual to have disagreements within the same region. But in the case of Edwardsen, he seemed to have a knack for collecting foes until the unlikely occurred—he gained the support of AFN president Don Wright, a significant figure in the land claims movement. Cliff Groh Jr., an Alaskan state senator and heavily involved in the movement himself, summarized the relationship: "the earnest and reasonable-sounding Don Wright with the more militant spokesman like Charles Edwardsen Jr. and Joe Upicksoun, two intense Eskimos from the North Slope." He added that Wright's "quick smile and something of a fatherly manner . . . made him a skillful mediator of disputes and the ideal Native leader."[23] He was also a calming force in trying times.

Despite Wright's interest in the problems, Edwardsen continued to look toward William L. Paul and his sons for assistance in overcoming the barriers. William Paul Sr. was getting older and living in Seattle, so he suggested his son, Fred Paul, might get involved in this case. In short order Fred Paul and Edwardsen became an interesting and oddly dynamic match. Beyond land claims, which was a strong enough cause, they had both observed the changes in the Arctic environment in terms of stability and wildlife survival. In retrospect they were ahead of their time, and both had noted the effects of global warming and climate change way before these became buzzwords and political fodder.

Edwardsen was frustrated that things were not moving faster. He felt as if his land claims movement was going nowhere, and he frequently lashed out at Fred Paul for failing to understand the problems. In hindsight Edwardsen misjudged Paul, who in reality was a valuable ally with a deep understanding of the scientific hazards of reckless oil drilling, including dangerously heating the permafrost and undermining terrain stability. He was an environmentalist without realizing it, and he influenced others.[24] Besides the Native community, there were other major protests against the pipeline, and environmentalists were unifying against the perceived hazards despite receiving backlash accusations of being un-American.

One story illustrates how diverse the Native community was at this moment. Eben Hopson, who was simultaneously fighting for the right to traditional whaling on the north coast, was an influential speaker on Indigenous rights and Arctic environmental issues, although his tactics greatly differed from Edwardsen. Hopson spoke to a 1970 Earth Day crowd in Anchorage, explaining that Arctic conditions were unique: "Because of the different kinds of soils, the rate of melting ice is different. Some places because of ice content, there will be high amounts of disintegration." He continued on, using a scientific approach rather than a strictly political one, and when he was finished, there was a standing ovation. Two years later Hopson became so enraged over what he determined was Fred Paul's "militant" attitude and his support of Edwardsen that he told Paul "to go to hell." The paradox was that it had been Fred Paul who had written the well-praised Earth Day speech.[25]

While Upicksoun was sounding off about the dangers of oil spills and instability of pipes in permafrost, oil companies were bragging about how rich everyone would be and playing down Native protests.[26] Upicksoun was skeptical: "More than one hundred years ago there were fleets of 150 or more whaling ships up in the Arctic Ocean. They practically destroyed our whales. Who got the profit?"[27] Upicksoun predicted their culture would be changed forever and added, "Society has made sure the Natives are poorly educated. Society should pay the Natives fair value."[28] Edwardsen and Upicksoun realized that the ASNA must be strengthened, and that meant returning to its roots.

In January 1966 the first ASNA meeting had been held in Barrow to start the actions required for reclaiming fifty-six million acres of Arctic land. The borders were determined by using the natural boundaries of the Brooks Range and the Chukchi Sea and the Beaufort Sea to the demarcation line before entering Russian waters. In those early years, the ASNA gathered support from other concerned citizens, who feared the potential adverse consequences of the proposed pipeline and what it might do to the land. Native leaders rose up to defy oil companies by claiming "96 million acres . . . was theirs by right of historic use and occupancy."[29] But how could they make this claim?

To work within the Western legal system, traditional Alaska Native cultures had to be modified for the exigencies without forsaking the ancestors. Charlie Edwardsen had already proved he understood that the bending of norms was the only way to wedge an opening, and he was no stranger to being reproached for a breech of decorum. Regardless, when he stood up to polished politicians, he kept his eye on a bigger prize. The May 1966 issue of the *Tundra Times* carried a statement describing the movement: "Its leaders are young men who are not afraid to speak out. Their utterances are succinct, terse, and to the point. The statements they make publicly are hashed out at meetings, and these sessions are not always sweetness and light but often heated."[30] This was the status into the early 1970s.

Edwardsen was forced to walk a fine line between Alaska Native values and ethics to be a part of Western diplomacy. Yet there were further distractions. As unrest in the Middle East erupted, the nation focused on the domestic oil supply, and Congress was convinced this precious resource could be found in Alaska's Arctic. This put pressure on oil companies, while Alaska Native complaints were merely an annoyance. The ASNA defied the Bureau of Land Management and their assumed authority by requesting an injunction to stop any further selling, leasing, or subletting of Arctic Slope lands or resources until the matter of ownership was decided. Alaska Natives claimed an unextinguished aboriginal title (not terminated by law, treaty, or sale), guaranteeing the continued use of the land. On the other side, oil companies and the consumers believed this matter had been settled after the passage of ANCSA, but questions remained, and the devil was in the details.

When ANCSA was signed in December 1971, the regional corporations were given about forty-four million acres of land and resources, a far cry from the original ninety-three million acres requested, yet, since the legislation had been hurried through Congress, the exact provisions were vague. To Edwardsen's way of thinking, ANCSA machinations had ignored previous precedents, and that was its fatal flaw.[31] He argued that "the Treaty of Cession in 1867, the Organic Act of 1884, and the Statehood Act of 1959 had guaranteed Eskimos the lands that were under their use and occupancy," so they were theirs in perpetuity. Based on this rationale and Justice John Marshall's trespassing premise, Edwardsen asserted that outsiders were violating the law and stealing Native land.[32] His opponents countered with the contention that ANCSA barred any further claims. Given this situation, Edwardsen saw no other recourse but to take the case to court and relied on the 1955 *Tee-Hit-Ton* Supreme Court case, particularly its mention of aboriginal title and trespassers, to back up his claim for Iñupiat possessory rights.

Edwardsen recalled his 1966 letter to William Paul Sr., disclosing his concerns: "We wish to obtain an injunction on the grounds that our people have not adequately been compensated for said land and that by decisions in similar cases, neither the federal government or the state has a clear title to said land,

and therefore cannot exploit such land until either compensation, adjustment, or title is settled by a court decision."[33] William Paul had agreed this was the right way to go about this matter. Remembering these words, Edwardsen armed himself to do battle with the big oil companies that threatened to usurp a wide swath of the northern regions, traditionally used for settlements, summer camps, and hunting grounds, and turn them into oil fields.

He hired Fred Paul to assist him in this legal contest. They loaded their cannons with the Treaty of Cession, the 1884 Organic Act, and the 1955 Tongass Forest ruling, and prepared for the volley, not realizing their enemy was ultimately going to be ANCSA, the legislation that had forced Alaska Natives into corporate America. Despite these obstacles, Edwardsen sued the secretary of the interior "for lands illegally taken from the Inupiat—Naval Petroleum Reserve Number 4, the Arctic Wildlife Refuse, Prudhoe Bay" and for trespassing on the lands of the Iñupiat. The Department of Justice thought the case was "crazy" and moved to dismiss the suit.[34] Edwardsen and his allies could not be deterred and instead increased their efforts to demonstrate that oil leases should never have been allowed.

In *Edwardsen v. Morton* (decided 1973), the secretary of the interior, Rogers C. B. Morton, who had succeeded Alaskan Walter "Wally" Hickel, was charged with overstepping his authority by opening up certain lands for oil exploration that the state had never legally acquired under the Alaska State Lands Act.[35] The act had allowed the selections of lands only if they were vacant, not appropriated, or reserved.[36] Edwardsen declared these same areas were occupied and held by the Iñupiat in aboriginal title, so the oil companies were intruders.[37] That created the conditions where any grants or patents the secretary offered were null and void, according to the Native suit. Moreover, by allowing these intrusions the federal government had breached its fiduciary duties. In effect, "it is clear from the Supreme Court decision in *Tee-Hit-Ton*, supra that federal offices are obligated to protect aboriginal lands against intrusion by third parties until such time as Congress acts to extinguish possessory rights therein."[38] Edwardsen believed the 1955 Tongass Forest case was enough backing, but should there be any questions, he was prepared to offer more detailed arguments.

Before the matter went to court, attorney Fred Paul had attempted to approach the oil companies, specifically ARCO, to see if the matter could be addressed outside of a formal courtroom. As early as 1966, Fred Paul could see into future problems and had sent letters to the oil companies informing the appropriate department heads that the Natives retained aboriginal title to the disputed grounds and that any infrastructure built would be considered an incursion because it was an unsettled matter between all parties. Conversely, the oil companies dismissed the small band of rural villagers and their Seattle lawyer, calling the claims invalid and a roadblock to critical resource development.[39]

After this first legal case, major questions were still not answered to everyone's satisfaction. Had ANCSA extinguished the Native title or not? Secretary of the Interior Morton certainly felt it had, despite the court's finding that the trespass claims were valid and recompense was due based on the Fifth Amendment. Aboriginal title was protected for the time being as well as confirming the federal government's fiduciary responsibility for guarding against third-party intrusion, but Edwardsen did not believe the ruling went far enough. Oil companies had not been stopped, and so he proceeded with further litigation, putting the Department of the Interior on notice and leaving Secretary of the Interior Morton with a dilemma. He could either appeal the 1973 decision that put the blame squarely on his shoulders or sue the trespassers. In the following 1980 case, he chose the latter course.[40]

With steadfast confidence Edwardsen confronted the Atlantic Richfield Company and their proposed activities in northwest Alaska (specifically the North Slope) under charges of trespassing. Edwardsen now had a front-row seat to the court's fickle nature. In *United States v. Atlantic Richfield Co. (ARCO)* (1980), a federal district court turned the tables, holding that *Tee-Hit-Ton* had set the standard for congressional extinguishment of land claims based on aboriginal title. Aboriginal title may exist, but Congress has the right to extinguish these claims based on the "drive of civilization" or the need to provide land and resources to the settlers. In this case it was to drill for oil. Furthermore, Congress could extinguish "unrecognized title" retroactively to suit the narrative.[41] The Iñupiat were not going to leave this unchallenged—there was a moral call to address the absconding of land taken without due compensation. Alaska Natives refused to believe that ANCSA was some nefarious treaty between the government and Alaska Natives. Edwardsen fought on, convinced that, beyond the ANCSA land allocation, traditional resources needed to be protected against unlawful trespassers. He once again invoked the *Tee-Hit-Ton* case, arguing that the government does not have the right to seize land, whether tundra or forest, for its own purposes.

This stood out as a valid judicial premise before ANCSA, and it was believed that it should be upheld. But it was not. In ARCO, ANCSA's execution and meaning were analyzed and in the end shown to have extinguished all claims, even those that came before the passage of the legislation. Further, it was presented that the Fifth Amendment did not apply because the title was unrecognized, once again citing *Tee-Hit-Ton* as the standard. Therefore, the trespassing charges were invalid, and no compensation would be forthcoming. As a finale, it was decided that no property rights were involved, and no Constitutional principles had been broken. In aggregate the *United States v. Atlantic Richfield* summary section 4 of ANCSA was shown to "extinguish aboriginal titles and claims based on aboriginal title," and this conclusion was intended to apply broadly, subsequently blocking any further litigation, including retroactive claims. Fundamentally, at the moment President Richard Nixon signed ANCSA, all pending claims had been extinguished forever more.

Obviously, these findings did not fare well for the Iñupiat or the Alaska Native cause in general, yet the ARCO case was a stepping stone to further recognition. As Alaska legal experts David Case and David Voluck explained, "What is important is that in the basic legal sense, acknowledged in *Edwardsen*, Alaska Natives have historically held their lands under aboriginal title."[42] Relying on the old words of Justice John Marshall, later repeated by Justice Stanley Reed as the majority voice in *Tee-Hit-Ton*, aboriginal or original title was protected and Alaska Natives were perpetually covered under fiduciary responsibility, opening the door to future deliberation when the time is right.

From the beginning Fred Paul realized that the final decision may not turn out favorable for their side, but he did not believe that ANCSA had the power to abolish all Native claims. He prepared an appeal based on the belief that damages were still recoverable for the infringed-on land, despite "the possible but not entirely proven extinguishment brought by ANCSA." Both the district court and court of appeals in the latter *U.S. v. ARCO* had denied justice, according to Fred Paul's analysis: "These courts refused to recognize our distinction between trespass of lands still held by aboriginal title and use of the land after extinguishing of aboriginal title."[43] The courts instead rigidly stood by the interpretation that ANCSA had extinguished all further claims. Paradoxically, the larger Tlingit and Haida land-claims suit, won in 1959, had been based on William Paul's premise that lands were protected and retained unextinguished aboriginal title.[44] The interpretation of Federal Indian Law was perplexing, yet there was no denying that Charlie Edwardsen Jr. had blazed a trail for Indigenous rights, and future drilling companies must first evaluate the Native perspective, as witnessed in current controversies.[45]

Charlie Edwardsen was not deterred by this setback. Historical roots went deep, and it was more than a court battle—it was a call to stem the tide of Manifest Destiny. He contended that he had exposed the "bitter root of truth," dating back to William Seward, the architect of the Russian transfer of Alaska, who had at one time exclaimed, "Go on and build up your outposts all along the coast, even up to the Arctic Ocean—they will yet become the outposts of my own country."[46] Despite the boasts, Alaska Natives have thrived and defended their lands, whether in the court room, on the Senate floor, or in their Native villages. They have made the case for environmental protection and restored their role of stewards to watch over oil drilling in a fragile ecosystem, where infrastructure construction could injure the ice-covered terrain, including prime fishing locations, hunting camps, and even graveyards.[47] The permafrost must be maintained for the general health of the entire region. Those unfamiliar with arctic or subarctic conditions may not realize that, once the frozen layer is removed, the ground rapidly converts to a sinkhole, and anything placed on top of it will fall through like quicksand. This is especially hazardous when using heavy equipment and building infrastructure.

The North Slope dwellers have been put in the position of watchdogs. Although government agencies vowed to follow safety guidelines and "cause a minimum disturbance to the natural environment," irrefutable damage has occurred, particularly to the pipeline and permafrost, without remedy. Understanding the dangers, Edwardsen and Paul had questioned the head of the U.S. Geological Survey, William T. Pecora, about the hazards. Pecora wrote to the interior secretary, Wally Hickel, stating that there had not been adequate testing nor a demonstration of "acceptable fundamental design criteria for below-ground construction in permafrost of a hot-oil pipeline that would be reasonably safe from failure."[48] There remained a chance of the pipe breaking and spilling out oil, but it was already too late—the pipeline project had taken on a life of its own, and there was no stopping it now.[49]

In the final analysis, the oil companies saw no value in fair dealings or environmental protection—the region held the potential for ten to one hundred billion barrels of oil, and the U.S. Senate did not want to see production hindered by aboriginal land claims.[50] Again this was the old story of developing otherwise wasted resources over the needs and traditions of caribou hunters and whalers. For better or worse, Alaska Natives were now game players in the local and national economy and had gained power and respect in increments, dislodging the stereotype of the picturesque Eskimo living in his igloo. Alaska Native corporations were on the *Fortune* 1000 list—in many ways, they had become assimilated capitalists. This culture change generated clashes between the traditional lifestyle and big business, while oil reigned supreme in Alaska and formed the main artery for Alaska's economic growth. The pipeline was completed (aboveground) from Prudhoe Bay to the ice-free port at Valdez, and Alaska residents were not only employed by the oil companies but were shareholders, claiming a dividend every year.[51] Some shunned this apparent rosy picture and instead predicted disaster. Their worst fears were realized in 1989.

In 2005 I discussed this history with Etok, who was an elder by then, yet remained as animated and passionate as ever. He had never stopped fighting with the oil companies, or his own people in some cases, especially if they got in the way of his aspirations. He reminded me that many villages saw oil as a way to end their economic woes, leading to conflict between those who want to drill and others who want the tundra landscape untouched. These disputes are illustrated through the protracted controversy between the Arctic Slope Regional Corporation, the largest regional corporation created by ANCSA, and the Gwich'in Athabascan to the east, who are trying to hold back the opening of the Arctic National Wildlife Refuge to protect the migrating Porcupine caribou herd. This particular issue has been brought to Congress, but testimony did not move the needle. The permafrost continues to melt at an alarming rate, while there is only a faint call for green energy.

As we sat in the Alaska Pacific University cafeteria, surrounded by an untamed forest, lowbush cranberries, and history, Etok and I continued our conversation. This institution, first called the Alaska Methodist University, was founded in the 1950s by Unangan leader Peter Gould. Next to our table there was a plaque commemorating the Alaska signing of the Alaska Native Claims Settlement Act in 1971. As we recalled the old days, Etok smiled, remembering what a feisty character he was back then, but when the subject switched to what was going on currently, he grew somber. He shook his head and said, "I wish things had turned out differently." We sat in silence for a few moments before he added, "I don't know what the old people would say. I don't know."[52]

8 A Whaling Captain and the World

This captain may have been one of the first adventurer whalers, but many more followed him, capturing the animals wherever they could until the stocks were depleted under conditions of great wastage.[1] It took decades for the whale population to recover, significantly affecting the coastal Iñupiat's main food source. In traditional whaling villages, a hunter never took more than was needed for survival, and then only with great reverence and ritual, as their ancestors had done for thousands of years. Whaling was the center of life before the "Yankee" intrusion, which in short order turned the ecosystem upside down, leaving the federal government with an obligation to rectify the worst abuses of the industry, although most of the damage was beyond human restoration. In the historical process, traditional whalers were forced to adapt to outsiders making decisions about their waters and resources, motivating villagers to organize opposition to these intrusions.

Over the course of time, Alaska whalers were used as international pawns in a diplomatic game. This situation came to a head in the 1970s, when Iñupiat subsistence whaling was discredited at the annual meetings of the International Whaling Commission (IWC), the regulatory body that determines whaling quotas from Iceland to Alaska to Japan.[2] The IWC was established in 1946 by treaty to monitor whale stocks around the world, and although membership and compliance are voluntary, the organization holds significant power. Since the northern Alaska villages were isolated from the world, their leaders were neophytes to global hardball environmental politics, but nonetheless they fought against reckless restrictions that endangered their physiological and cultural survival.

Iñupiat activist Charlie Edwardsen Jr., or "Etok," with whom we are now familiar for his fight against Arctic oil drilling, was a frequent speaker on several Arctic topics in contentious forums and public hearings, taking place throughout Alaska. In the early 1960s, Edwardsen railed against the restrictions placed on whalers—they were being punished for the past greed of nineteenth-century whalers. He warned audiences that restricting the native bowhead whale harvest was tantamount to damaging an ancient culture: "Without the whale, there is no Eskimo"—powerful words in response to a multifaceted threat to Alaska Natives' "way of being."[3] In turn these strong sentiments acted as a catalyst to wage war against global powers. Edwardsen never gave up the good fight, and he was not averse to twin causes, but he was stretched thin. While he was attempting to save the fragile permafrost, another Iñupiat leader stepped up to challenge international regulatory powers and to save whaling for his people.

Although this man was known for disagreeing with Edwardsen, they stood together in their knowledge that Native rights were being trampled on and someone had to speak out to local politicians and Congress. Eben Hopson, former Barrow mayor and a well-respected whaling captain, challenged the rules placed on subsistence hunters and dispelled the notion that the Iñupiat did not need to be considered in these vital decisions because they were a dying race and therefore inconsequential. In the face of this disregard, Hopson armed his defense against formidable odds to promote and safeguard Indigenous rights.

THE BOWHEAD WHALE is the giant of the North Pacific Ocean and Bering Sea. In ancient times whale hunters traveled out in their skin boat (*umiat*), seeking the marine mammals that would give themselves to the people so they might sustain themselves during the long, hard winter. These mere mortals, using harpoons fashioned from the materials of the land and sea, were able to capture whales that could weigh up to two tons. There was no doubt this was a gift, and in turn the people showed proper respect to ensure whales would be available in the future. Even as technology progressed, these customs were observed and integrated within the social matrix in the hopes of sustaining the resource. There have been times when no whales would show and other times of plenty—the people modified their subsistence activities in the face of environmental shifts. Regardless of the number of whales harvested, however, the communal and spiritual values of the hunt persisted while communities were bound together in feast or famine, all working together for the greater good.[4]

A lone hunter cannot bring in a whale by himself but instead relies on his fleet to help him with the retrieval and other necessary tasks. It is not uncommon to see the entire village pulling in the animal, each with a designated role, from butchering to distribution. This holistic venture is not complete without ceremonies and rituals, which often extends to inviting nearby villages, all enjoying the bounty and good fortune and thereby cementing good relationships in a somewhat hostile, unforgiving environment.[5] A comparison between Alaska Native spirituality and Western religious traditions might be considered a stretch for some, yet as Eben Hopson explained, there was indeed a blending of the two belief systems: "The whale is the center of our life and culture. We are people of the whale. The taking and sharing of the whale is our Eucharist and Passover. The whaling festival is our Easter and Christmas, the Arctic celebration of the mysteries of life."[6] Upon the arrival of outsiders, however, these deep-seated traditions underwent drastic alterations based on alien policies that did not correspond with realities and certainly were without an understanding of the whaling ethos.

For centuries the whaling captain (*umialik*), keeper of the whaling boat, was responsible for his fleet's welfare, a role that carried over even after the imposition of the U.S. government and its regulations. A whaling captain would not shirk his duties regardless of the season. Cooperation was at the heart of Iñupiat values and integral to social relations in one's village and the surrounding communities. It was these sacred values the people lived by and wanted to keep, even as Alaska resources became more valuable to an expanding nation. To protect the people and the whale hunt, captains became political spokespeople, and along with village councils, they planned strategies for sustaining their traditional activities. This power, however, was undercut when bowhead whale–harvest management was seized from the Alaska Natives and turned over to Western conservation metrics.

While trying to quantify the extant whale numbers, scientists have disregarded history. According to John Bockstoce, an expert in whaling history, "a few Bowheads may have been taken between 1843 and 1847," but the whales were not deliberately hunted until 1848. In one example out of many it was said, "The boys quickly filled his [Capt. Thomas Reyes's] ship and returned to Honolulu." By 1852 an estimated two hundred ships were in the Bering Strait whaling grounds.[7] The whale population was reduced because of greed and wastage, not by Alaska Native whaling methods, yet the scarcity persisted long after the New England whalers had left.[8] The general agent of education and missionary Sheldon Jackson had introduced reindeer herding to the area, but it never caught on, and the crisis persisted until the government became involved in the matter. Based on scientific readings and the presumption that there were too few Native hunters to cause harm, the agents and lawmakers focused on commercial whaling, leaving Native whalers unbothered by regulations.

ALASKA NATIVES WERE not the only whalers in the world. Ancient whaling communities can be found from Siberia to Greenland to the Scandinavian countries to Japan. Despite this long history, in the 1940s there were allegations, without evidence, that whaling was wasteful and primitive, and this controversy was picked up in the global media. The resultant outcry led to a 1946 treaty and the formation of the International Whaling Commission. This treaty, first of its kind and largely written by the United States, originally included fifteen nations, all agreeing to preserve "for future generations the great natural resources represented by the whale stocks."[9] Gradually, the global emphasis on commercial whaling incorporated subsistence whaling, largely based on IWC Scientific Committee reports that concluded subsistence harvesting posed a threat to the whale population.[10] By 1977, in an almost unanimous vote, a ban was placed on Indigenous hunting, and although these findings were challenged, politics drove the issue deeper. Because Alaska whalers were part of the United States, a conflict of interest was involved, and to avoid international confrontation the U.S. representatives abstained from voting on the matter. That show of hesitancy weakened the Alaskan position. The United States, fearing censure from other countries and charges of favoritism, failed to defend Alaska Natives, its own citizens. Communications were primitive at the time, and the whalers did not find out about these restrictions right away, but when they did they vowed to find equity. How could outsiders have the audacity to make rules for them? Their ancestors had plied the waters before the first colonies were set up on the East Coast.

SINCE MEMBERSHIP IN the IWC is voluntary, countries are not legally bound to any judgments, and if a nation opposes the findings or restrictions, it does have the option to ignore such requests, recommendations, or pressures. Yet to do so would go against the reasons for joining the body and could be considered a breach of global cooperation and a blatant disregard for the world's finite resources. Likewise, displaying partiality toward one whaling group over another would certainly have ramifications, throwing the government into a precarious position in the global arena. Additionally, efforts or decisions were thwarted by environmental groups, either advocating for "Indian rights" or the new slogan: "Save the Whales," contributing to more combative behavior and sensationalized newspaper headlines.

In the 1970s the ecology movement had gained purchase on a craggy political mountain, and opposing opinions were circulated throughout the media. Eventually, the controversy filtered into the halls of Congress and was ineffectually juggled about, while the IWC authorities could not help but be swayed by public opinion, resulting in a vote to impose a moratorium on bowhead whale hunting, both commercially and for subsistence harvesters, despite the documented traditional dependence. Now the Native hunter was viewed as a threat to the whale population and depicted as such in numerous rallies across the nation. Civic sentiment was a compelling force and influenced further harvesting restrictions. Naturally, this snowball activity was without any genuine knowledge of the Arctic whalers or their lives but nonetheless was allowed to go on in a perfect storm of political ecology.[11]

Faced with this predicament, the Alaska Iñupiat joined together with their Siberian Yup'ik (Saint Lawrence Island) whaling counterparts to organize the Alaska Eskimo Whaling Commission (AEWC) to represent the coastal villages of northwest Alaska. The AEWC, sensing the urgency, quickly evolved into a cohesive body with the purpose "to bring the hunt within the limits established by the Commission, to insure proper monitoring of whaling activities, to increase the efficiency of whaling techniques, and to provide utilization of all whales taken."[12] The obvious motivation was to show the IWC that they were complying with environmental policy and to tone down the intense rhetoric. In the meantime the first task at hand was to convince the United States to file an objection against IWC sanctions that limited whale harvests for each village, including strikes or attempts. A strike is any time a harpoon (or similar object) is thrown. It can bring down or wound the animal or miss altogether. It is the wounding of an animal that most environmentalists objected to because they considered it wasteful, although whalers acknowledged that unsuccessful attempts had always been a natural consequence for any hunters.[13]

WHALING PROTESTERS, LIKE Greenpeace, condemned whaling but from afar. This particular organization had started in Canada in 1971, and its original game plan was altruistic and generally centered on nuclear-bomb controversies before branching out to other environmental issues. When it ventured into subsistence whale hunting, it was clearly out of its depth, yet remained influential, except in Alaska Native communities where residents had no idea they had been painted as villains.

Others in the scientific and political world came to different conclusions. For example, Patsy Mink was a proponent of equity in this matter and believed in considering both the Indigenous whalers and the health of the resource. She carried a great deal of clout in her role as assistant secretary of state for oceans and international environmental and scientific affairs and with her background as the former assistant secretary of state under Cyrus Vance. To learn more about the controversy, she met with Charlie Edwardsen when he was in Washington DC, and later she traveled to Barrow to hear Eben Hopson's side of the story. With her understanding of the IWC scientific studies, together with the testimony of Native leaders, she became a proponent of realistic rulings that focused on the whalers and their traditions, becoming a formidable ally.

Mink came from the ethnically diverse state of Hawaii, and this may have contributed to her novel approach and understanding of intercultural issues, but she was also aware that her role in the U.S. government could be viewed as a conflict of interest. She turned the matter over to experts who could take a multipronged approach but offered her experiences and knowledge at the same time. In Congress she had worked on the Pelly Amendment to the Fisherman's Protective Act of 1967, requiring the secretary of commerce to report to the president any foreign nationals whose harvesting undermined international conservation programs. Mink filed an affidavit to the effect that the Pelly Amendment permitted the imposition of an embargo against countries whose nationals threaten the effectiveness of international whaling standards. Mink's efforts were thwarted, however, by the final decision that there was no evidence that Alaska Natives had been directly impinged on by a foreign country. She believed it was a misinterpretation of the original legislation, which was intended to protect small whaling villages from a forced adherence to conservation restrictions from other countries, but her argument could not gain traction.[14]

In response the whalers named her former boss in a lawsuit, blaming Cyrus Vance, the secretary of state, for not shielding their rightful interests as U.S. citizens. In the background Mink compiled the testimonies of Edwardsen and Hopson as evidence while campaigning for a strong U.S. Arctic policy that would focus on the needs of all parties, as outlined in the 1972 Arctic Coastal Zone Management Program, charged with monitoring Alaska's long coastline. Mink did not realize this program was closely aligned with the national interests for developing Alaska's coastline, and when local officials discovered their autonomy had been overridden, Alaska dropped out of the program in protest in late 1972.

After reading through Mink's papers, Eben Hopson agreed with her conclusions but wondered if it was too late for the Arctic whalers. What were other Indigenous whalers doing? This question prompted him to start talks with people in Greenland, fully embracing his newly appointed international role. Indigenous in Greenland were a natural partner, with their similar lifeways and historical dependence on whaling. They used the same implements and techniques to harvest the animal and faced the same problems when outside agencies placed restrictions on their livelihood, most notably the IWC. In 1973 Hopson met with Greenland representatives at the World Council of Indigenous Peoples, held in Copenhagen. They discussed the threats to their culture but also shared their views on their responsibility for the health of the resource. Hopson learned much from his visit to Greenland, prompting him to found the Inuit Circumpolar Conference in 1977 to represent Native concerns from Greenland to Siberia, including the Yup'ik, Inuit, and Chukchi (Chukotka), all with similar lifeways dating back thousands of years.[15] There was power in numbers.

CLEARLY, THE WHALING issues were wrapped in layers of bureaucracy and spread out on a wide, disparate spectrum. U.S. representatives were obstructive by demanding a universal approach that negated local problems. Despite concerted efforts by the AEWC through legal channels and diplomacy, the IWC continued to establish unreasonable quotas for the whaling villages without any onsite evaluation or consultation with the whalers. By 1978 the northern Alaska region was allowed to harvest only up to twelve whales, far below what was needed for subsistence.

The whalers were not totally on their own. They had support from a few governmental agencies, such as the National Oceanic and Atmospheric Administration, which in 1978 prepared *A Special Report to the International Whaling Commission on the Bowhead Whale*, recommending an "annual take of at least 27–32 whales for the Northwest whaling region."[16] News of these encouraging documents energized whaling communities to formally oppose IWC restrictions, noting the undue hardship. The AEWC disputed previous Western science conclusions as unrealistic, reiterating that for years whalers had relied on traditional ecological knowledge, passed down by elders generation after generation as opposed to an international body tainted by political goals.[17]

Customarily, Alaska Natives met together to find answers for community problems, and discussions blended expert knowledge with Indigenous wisdom. With this in mind, Eben Hopson, Charlie Edwardsen, and members of the large Brower family went to whaling villages to gather testimony from the people and document their viewpoints. There were a few surprises. Common plaintive questions included: "What would you think if we came down to your country and told you, you could only kill five cows, or five chickens?" Whaling captain Percy Nusunginya reminded everyone that "a whale gives himself to a person that they feel deserves them. . . . You cannot put a number on it." George Ahmaogak fumed, "What this is, is extermination of a culture, without firing a shot."[18]

Meanwhile, without effective cross-cultural communication, the disparity between the whalers and the IWC widened, and the situation was exacerbated when the IWC imposed what was considered preferential treatment toward one country. One glaring incident, out of many, illustrates the point. Japan challenged the Alaska Natives' right to harvest whales in the customary fashion and quantity. As the international debate intensified, however, Japan was also under suspicion. Questions were asked about that nation's ulterior motives in this debate: Did they want to hide their activities? Would disrupting the continuity and authority of the IWC suit their purposes?[19] The Greenland Inuit had even less ammunition to defend themselves in this matter. Hopson had previously heard the Greenland whalers' complaints—they were suffering under multiple restrictions, including salmon-harvest limits, imposed on them by Atlantic salmon agreements. These mutual causes built a powerful bond between the Greenland Natives and Alaska's Iñupiat, as their cultural ambassadors worked to maintain their cultural heritage and fight for environmental justice. These were the ingredients for a strong ideological partnership, along with the mutual conviction that "the Eskimos" received unfair treatment at the hands of international powers, and this must be rectified.[20]

In the midst of these disputes, whaling captain Eben Hopson stood up against the global frenzy to plead the northern whalers' case by defying the IWC and countries, such as Japan, and the unfair global standards. Additionally, he defended Arctic whalers against the charges that they were threatening U.S. reputation in the world. It was obvious that, although the Alaska whalers were citizens, their rights went unprotected, and this lack of commitment angered Hopson, the AEWC members, and northwest Alaska whalers, all feeling a sense of betrayal from their own country.

This political maelstrom was further complicated by the push and pull between the U.S. branches of government coupled with mixed interpretations of constitutional powers, specifically duties, responsibilities, and limits of power.

Despite debates between resource managers and the federal government, Hopson and the AEWC were convinced they must take their grievances to a court of law to establish their standing and rights. Though Charlie Edwardsen and Eben Hopson had previous quarrels, they realized the power in their collective experiences with the U.S. justice system and joined forces against international and federal overreach.

In 1977 Eben Hopson, fellow whalers, and supporters contested the IWC subsistence ban on bowhead whale hunting, arguing it was unjust and unethical, motivating the legal cases of *Adams v. Vance* (1977) and later *Hopson v. Kreps* (1980).[21] Both cases were centered on the same issue, and even as the arguments and facts overlapped, questions were raised concerning the politics of aboriginal hunting and fishing in the global arena. When restrictions were first imposed, the secretary of the interior, Thomas Kleppe, defied the United States' role in this dispute, declaring that the federal government had a long-standing responsibility with the Indigenous peoples, and given the fiduciary relationship, the ban should be lifted. His stance placed him in a vulnerable position to be attacked by his own government and the IWC, but despite those threats Kleppe's position stood as a temporary win for whalers.

In *Adams v. Vance* Native leaders sued Secretary of State Cyrus Vance for failure to object to an international policy that threatened the traditional subsistence cycle, integral to their culture. The controversy created by this legal case was escalated when the Department of State and Juanita Kreps, the secretary for the Department of Commerce supported the ban, largely to keep the peace among whaling nations. Beyond maintaining the status quo, however, Kreps's boss, President Jimmy Carter, also wanted a cessation of whaling. He was in the midst of a self-derived mission to save Alaska's pristine wilderness, and somehow he extended his fervor to the whales without understanding the full circumstances or traditions. As the national controversy heated up, insults were hurled at the Alaska whalers. Typical of the vitriol, one disgruntled citizen wrote to Secretary Kreps, declaring, "I am frankly in favor of the Eskimo disappearing first. . . . There are some things far more important than Predator Man."[22] It is hard to figure out the origin of jingoistic or ethnic slurs, but this statement, among many, were characteristic of public sentiment.

To gain justice Eben Hopson and the AEWC sued Secretary of State Vance on the grounds that he did not fulfill his fiduciary duty by objecting to the prejudicial ban. The court, however, refused to grant the injunction, holding it would be an unwarranted judicial interference in foreign affairs, and raising the political-doctrine question, which specifies that treaties and other international affairs are in the solitary purview of the executive branch. The dismissal of their grievances led the whalers to file another suit, this time against the Department of Commerce in *Hopson v. Kreps*, arguing that limitations on aboriginal whaling were not legally authorized.[23] The AEWC believed they could drive a wedge through the judicial barricade, relying on their past successes for motivation. In the past the AEWC had been effective in its negotiations with the IWC, gaining increased harvesting quotas. To the whalers' surprise the court displayed a new understanding of cultural elements versus international policy and changed its conclusion by defining the ban as an implementing act rather than a treaty document. An implementing act is legislative in nature and binding, but because of its local nature, it does not involve foreign policy or protocol. Therefore, the district court had the authority to decide issues raised under the statute.[24] In the end, after great manipulation, the political-doctrine question was dropped in favor of domestic laws. This meant that whale monitoring or calling for a moratorium on whale hunting fell under judicial scrutiny.[25]

The Department of Commerce and Department of State ignored the ruling and continued the whaling ban on conservation grounds. This noncompliance was further complicated by misinformation, accusing the United States of receiving special treatment, heating up debates, and resulting in a global maelstrom. Once whaling turned into an international quarrel again, the decision-making authority reverted back to the U.S. executive branch. Amid differing opinions on the treaty status and the legality of Arctic whaling, the United States attempted to protect and maintain its leadership role within the IWC by upholding the multinational treaty and past agreements concerning the conservation of the bowhead whale. To do otherwise would show a lack of respect for the international community.[26] That the courts had previously deemed this a domestic matter was of no consequence, and the question of jurisdiction was on the table again.

Law is complicated and can be divided between local norms, state regulatory standards, and federal legislation. In this case it all spilled out to the global arena, forcing Alaska whaling villagers to play by the same rules as the Inuit of Greenland or Japanese whalers, regardless of differences in environmental conditions. The courts were of limited use, particularly when they politicized science. When Western science was upheld as the decisive defense, the Alaska Native position was crushed in *Adams*, leading Hopson and the AEWC to extend their arguments in support of local ecological conditions and the age-old cultural stance, hoping this might sway the court to see that what they considered intangible was in fact reality. Despite the whalers' efforts, the two legal cases, separated by only eighteen months, stood as decided law for the time being, regardless of the remaining quandary concerning the separation of powers between the executive and judicial branches of U.S. government.

The perceived prejudice of the courts could be seen as an affront to environmental justice and a setback for the whalers, but quitting was not an option. The AEWC had gained potency during this period, assisted by unlikely sources. A study, financed by ten oil companies in conjunction with the North Slope Borough, researched the health of the bowhead whale populations. The findings concluded there was a population of about 3,800 bowhead whales, 3,000 more than the IWC Scientific Committee had cited as evidence for the ban.[27] Based on these latest facts, the quota was raised even as the two legal cases were ongoing between 1978 and 1980. Under these circumstances Western science, coupled with Native knowledge, successfully challenged the IWC, but that was not the end of the conflict.

Opposing sides either supported or condemned the IWC sanctions. The AEWC could not understand Secretary Vance's assertion that his hands were tied by the Endangered Species Conservation Act (1969, revised 1973). This act stated that threatened species were entitled to ecosystem rehabilitation and maintenance, intimating that the whalers were destroying the ocean. Vance further referred to provisions under the Marine Mammal Protection Act (MMPA) of 1972, prohibiting the taking or importation of bowheads within U.S. jurisdiction, as his defense.[28] But had Vance fully interpreted all the ramifications and stipulations of this act? There was a clause within the MMPA that protected Indigenous subsistence traditions by allowing the nonwasteful taking of whales and other marine mammals for subsistence purposes or arts products and cottage industries.[29] The MMPA protected both the species and subsistence harvesters, but it was the term *nonwasteful* that was at the heart of the debate. Once again the "strike" was analyzed and characterized as inefficient, although in reality some chance was inevitable in bringing down a whale. But the controversy would not die.

Regardless of these factors, the Iñupiat believed the MMPA and its stipulations should still cover the whalers for subsistence purposes, given the whale harvest had been carried on for hundreds of years. They believed they were being punished for the past greed of commercial whalers.[30] For the whalers the harvest was not about laws or scientific tallies—it was the continuance of their culture, incorporating their traditions physiologically, culturally, socially, and spiritually. Nonetheless, several "Save the Whale" groups, like Greenpeace, continued to anthropomorphize animals and advocate an unconditional, no-take approach as the only viable form of conservation—there was no middle ground. These same groups were also capturing headlines and invited to television appearances as celebrities.[31]

Attempts at compromise could not seal the gap between the Iñupiat subsistence needs and whaling regulations, though there were efforts to create novel agreements. For example, a cash settlement to the whalers was proposed but drew little favor. Another suggestion was to implement a voluntary and temporary whaling moratorium. Authorities were convinced the whalers would need to sit out only one season, while more scientific studies were completed with the hopes that the numbers could be reevaluated, ostensibly in favor of continued whaling activity. None of these plans, however, were satisfactory to the AEWC. In many ways it was not about whaling or science but about the Alaska Native place in the U.S. legal system. In truth there had been no legal or fiduciary change since October 1977, when the acting secretary of the interior, James Joseph, in his capacity as director of Native affairs, wrote to Secretary Vance to outline his objections to this state of affairs, declaring, "Our trust responsibility to this Native American population cannot be ignored or subjugated to other concerns," and it is "the only option which will ensure protection for the cultural and nutritional values associated with the subsistence hunt."[32]

If these principles had been acted on from the beginning, the results would have been much different, but it was apparent that even within the government there were incompatible opinions surrounding the whale controversy, making resolutions difficult. The issues were localized and not global. Traditional whaling was also thwarted because the U.S. officials believed they had to make a show of solidarity. For the whalers this political maze was immaterial—they were more interested in feeding their families during a hard, cold winter. In the years between 1977 and 1980, the political tap dancing continued amid debates concerning scientific knowledge.

Arguments were polarized between the theory of sustainable yield, a maxim of Western science, as contrasted to traditional ecological knowledge. Succinctly, "no one in the IWC or the U.S. government believed that the observations on the bowhead population by Eskimo hunters could possibly be superior to the data gathered by scientists."[33] Treaties, laws, and bans were interpreted on a multinational level, and the Iñupiat understood they were defending their way of life, much like other Native Americans had watched their resources exploited or restricted. Ellen Partridge, an attorney for the AEWC, believed that "whaling must be differentiated from commercial whaling" and evaluated on a more rational basis, without the priority being "how rapidly the stock can be returned to levels sufficient to allow commercial whaling." Alternatively, creative thinking and cultural sensitivity could better address the "unique status and problems of native American cultures" and "foster progress toward a fruitful resolution of issues involving government responsibility, conservation, and human rights."[34]

Alaska Native whalers had an unsteady legal platform in the face of governmental convictions and global dominion, let alone the unremitting and vociferous "Save the Whale" campaigns. In response the Alaska Natives declared their civil liberties had been violated by congressional indifference, the international powers, and the scientific world. To the Native plaintiffs, "liberty" should have been interpreted with consideration for the "competing legal rights and interests of the Eskimos and the Bowhead whale," although these issues "were largely, albeit quickly dismissed" without an equitable examination. The overriding fallacy, therefore, had been the unchallenged rights of a minority "facing a severe limit on an important aspect of their liberty" as guaranteed by the Constitution, which was founded on the principle of protecting minority rights against the potential tyranny of the majority.[35]

An endangered culture observed a country not upholding its own Constitution, rousing Eben Hopson to proceed with another legal showdown centered on the same issues but with the hope of a different outcome. With a fresh set of players in the political arena, the 1980 appeal, *Hopson v. Kreps*, was reheard by the Ninth Circuit Court, a venue familiar with Indigenous legal cases. The political-doctrine question was once again at the crux of the adjudication, particularly as regards to the widening international scope, which included countries with similar whaling histories.[36] Hopson did not discount the differences between countries but disputed the authority of the U.S. Department of Commerce to implement whaling restrictions and questioned the power of IWC policies since they were voluntary, and so it was a matter of ethics that the standard should be set according to the best interests of the Indigenous peoples.

Further, Eben Hopson wanted a larger focus on what he believed were more dangerous hazards to marine life and the oceans due to oil exploration and the building of infrastructure on fragile permafrost. In sum Hopson declared, "For we Iñupiat and the bowhead whale have become the index species in the Arctic. If offshore operations cannot pass muster with both whale and whaler, they must be prevented."[37] The court's conclusion was to maintain the status quo. This meant the IWC had the power to ban subsistence whaling, but if local areas could show prejudice, the district court would hear the case.[38]

After all the jargon and political jockeying, the whalers were only slightly better off, but they had cracked the ice. While the United States held to their conviction that "embarrassment, disrespect, and the possible international consequences" were detrimental to their image, the Alaska Natives carried on their ancient social and cultural ways that assured the well-being of their villages, even if that ultimately meant civil disobedience. Hopson's stood steadfast in his stance that there must be a separation between commercial and subsistence hunting and that the legal cases had presented "difficult questions of statutory interpretation, justifiability, and the scope of judicial review of administrative action in foreign affairs." In the end Alaska Natives had strengthened their political effectiveness through these experiences, both the triumphs and the losses, and had refused to be ignored in the international arena.[39] Alaska Native communities working together achieved these gains.

IN 1982 THE IWC established separate policies for subsistence hunting and commercial ventures, and today whale harvests are regulated according to historical records, traditional use, and need. The IWC Scientific Committee meets annually to set quotas, and steps are taken to meet Alaska Native requirements, culturally and nutritionally, while giving importance to the preservation of the bowhead whale for future generations. This was not an easy fight for the Alaska Natives and their advocates, and some arguments continue to this day, particularly concerning Japan.[40] To meet the threat, the AEWC, as the "oldest and most continuous co-management" resource organization in Alaska, provides its own defense and carries out local scientific tests, reporting to the U.S. representative for the IWC.[41] Co-management between governmental authorities and Native communities has steadily become more important for resolving environmental issues, and although the AEWC does not have a direct voice in the international body, it remains a respected authority for scientific reporting. Local communities recognized they were "integrated participants in management . . . providing knowledge and experience to the process that only they possess . . . [to] train government managers and bureaucrats. It encourages local responsibility for plans and methods and reduces the adversarial nature of relationships between agency personnel and subsistence harvesters."[42]

EBEN HOPSON NEVER retired from his role as a vocal advocate for Alaska. He was a frequent speaker at public hearings and press interviews and traveled to London and Tokyo, giving addresses on the hazards of further oil exploration on the Arctic whaling habitat. He emphasized cooperation, open dialogue, balanced scientific measures, and strong alliances with the federal government. The whaling controversy had been "the first time since before the American Revolution that American Indigenous Peoples have participated in international treaty negotiations directly affecting their aboriginal rights."[43]

This history, dating back thousands of years, demonstrates the link between the Alaska Natives and the environment, socially, spiritually, economically, politically, and culturally, with a mutual legacy extending from Siberia to Greenland. The Western view of science and traditional ecological knowledge are at odds, and it will take humble dialogue to bring the two sides together. At this time the best method of management takes into consideration expanding knowledge, both Western and Indigenous, in a relationship that cannot negate that the bowhead whale and the Iñupiat are inextricably bound, as the species recovers from past commercial exploitation.

In closing it is illustrative to note the words of well-known whaling captain Harry Brower Sr., who had encouraged the Barrow whaling captains to take part in the scientific research that promised an opportunity to find accurate species numbers and assess the health of the whale, while merging Western science with traditional ecological knowledge in a beneficial union.[44] In 1998 these compromises led to Barrow's forty-seven crews harvesting twenty-two whales. Each year after, the number was to be reevaluated based on the villages' history and need, using a co-management approach between the whalers and the governmental agencies, thereby mitigating environmental disputes. Born from a previous exasperating no-win position, the co-management approach is currently used more often in environmental matters between government agencies and Native hunters and fishers with positive outcomes, opening a new door to resource management.

THERE IS NO doubt that whaling is integral to Arctic life, fulfilling physiological, social, and cultural essentials. Harry Bower Sr. (Kupaaq), whaling captain and community leader, summed up the state of affairs: "Whaling gathers the people together in cooperation and celebration; it unifies and invigorates the community. It symbolizes what it means to be Iñupiat, and whaling makes life worth living."[45]

9   When the Raven Flies with the Dove

The Alaska Native Claims Settlement Act (ANCSA) was signed into law in December 1971, and regardless of how prepared the Alaska Natives were for the drastic changes, it still came as a shock. Suddenly the use and tenure of the resources their ancestors had lived with and held stewardship over were divided up and defined by legislation. To assess the cultural trauma, the Alaska Native Review Commission engaged the services of Thomas R. Berger, a Canadian lawyer, who traveled around Alaska towns and villages, talking with Alaska Native residents about the effects of ANCSA. He later wrote a report on this matter for the Alaska Native Review Commission, published as the book *Village Journey*. During the course of his interviews, he found that when these newly minted shareholders realized that ANCSA afforded no protection for their traditional lands and waters, there was a great deal of dismay—some believed they had been cheated. Not only did the corporations divide the people geographically along artificial borders, but a foreign economic system was introduced, in which financial failure would result in bankruptcy. According to Walter Johnson of western Alaska, "The Alaska Native put everything, the land, the money, according to the ANCSA, they put their birthright and everything else into that corporate structure that we hate so much."[1] When traditional lands and waters reverted to the corporations, it appeared to be the first and only treaty between the Alaska Natives and government, manufactured by capitalism and fueled by the continuing colonial servitude of the state. Unbeknownst to Native fishers and hunters, their rights had been extinguished in the process, and in a do-or-die position they must harvest local resources or face bankruptcy. Conflict was inevitable.

All these factors played out in the following story about the Hoonah fishing fleet, illustrating the predicaments between the ANCSA promises, a newly formed state fishery-management agency, and a traditional way of life. When I was there in the early 1990s, I discovered the irretrievable tie between the forest and the fish—it is a symbiotic relationship. Once broken, the entire ecosystem is set up for failure. Yet villagers in Hoonah had to make money from the fish and forest to keep their head above water. Before sharing the demise of Hoonah residents' fishing occupation, I would first like to share an account of a forest in crisis and the environmental justice warriors who continue to protect these resources.

Hoonah, located on Chichagof Island, in southeast Alaska, is surrounded by dense old-growth forest. Outside companies saw this piece of the Tongass Forest as potentially prime timber, and the natural inclination was to cut down the trees, using the most effective method for industry—clear-cutting. Against the pleas of elders, whose predictions were dire, the village corporation, Huna Totem, in conjunction with Whitestone Logging and the regional corporation, Sealaska, cut wide patches from the hills until the once-verdant landscape looked like a giant razor had scraped the earth with a vengeance. Subsequently, that spring the elders' warning came true as the soil washed down into the streams, filling them with debris and robbing oxygen from the salmon. The logging roads, miles and miles of them, had also proven hazardous to the deer habitats, primarily due to erosion. In essence commercial avarice defied age-old stewardship principles.

Many Hoonah residents protested these actions, blaming the village and regional corporations for leaving naked hills that one Tlingit man described as devoid of eagles because of lack of habitat, while another man mourned the loss of salmon streams.[2] Activist and Hoonah resident Wanda Culp was adamant that the "battles for sovereignty have been compromised by ANCSA. They have turned our land over to corporations," and in doing so have broken the rules of nature. There needed to be a better arrangement, but it was a long time coming. Culp believed the hope of the future would lie in the next genera-tion. In the meantime there have been small inroads established through the Hoonah Indian Association, a federally recognized tribal organization. But to this day there are many unhappy Hoonah residents who are not satisfied with the progress or conservation efforts. This was not, however, the first time Hoonah residents had to find a balance between their ancient landscape and the traditional culture.[3] The history of the Hoonah fishing industry illustrates how this community worked together in an attempt to build communication between diverse agencies and meld together in common cause. Amid anger and resentment, human innovation rose to meet the challenge.

WHEN I BOARDED the two-seater bush plane in Juneau to travel across the water to Hoonah, I had no idea how it would change my life. Before I could fully envision my visit to the small Tlingit village, however, I adjusted to the immediate experience of aircraft controls only inches from my face, while the plane maneuvered through the uplifts and slight drops. I had never been on a plane this small. The pilot was jovial and confident, assuring me that it was a great day for flying. About a half hour later, the plane made a turn and threaded through the narrow pass leading to Hoonah, landing on the gravel runway much more smoothly than I anticipated, and taxied to a small build-ing with a sign that read "Welcome to Hoonah."

I was supposed to meet two others here who were also working on the his-tory of Hoonah and its purse seine fleet, but no one was here, so I walked in the only direction that had a trail, cutting through the dense forest for about a mile before reaching the town, unaware until later that there was quite a bit of bear activity during the summer months. On the main street, the business area of the village, the harbor lay in one direction, and in the other, steep hills reached toward the sky with houses of every color lining the ascent. Fishing boats were docked in the waters below, and from this height Hoonah looked like a sparkling jewel.

No one was out, and I had the feeling of complete isolation until two children ran by, stopped, stared at me, whispered to each other, and ran off. I was an outsider. The intense July sun permeated every cell of my being, and I had no idea what would follow next, but as the day progressed, a few people did speak with me, often in harsh tones as they related their grievances and obvious frustration. Others told me stories with twists and bends that lasted for hours, and I learned lessons that I have never forgotten.

HOONAH, LOCATED ON the Alexander Archipelago, is nestled in the heart of the Tongass Forest, the largest temperate rainforest in the world. Tlingit legends relate how the original people of Glacier Bay escaped a moving glacier and were led to the place they would call home for thousands of years. On the eastern shore of Port Frederick and the important confluence of Icy Strait, the Hunas have plied their trade for hundreds of years, making a living through hunting and fishing for subsistence and trade with their neighbors, including other Tlingit villages, the Athabascan, the Russians, the English, and finally the Americans. Like other Alaska Native communities, the people follow a holistic way of life guided by an ancient socioeconomic system and an environment dominated by the seascape and forest.

Commercial fisheries were established in the area between 1880 and 1910, initiating a move from solely subsistence fishing to the Western cash and wage economy.[4] At the same time, canneries were built up and down the Archipelago, including in the vicinity of Hoonah and nearby Icy Strait (about fourteen miles away). Tlingit fishers, already working commercially, modified their occupational emphasis to fish for the canneries while often their wives were "inside workers" at the same packing company. The canned-salmon business was profitable, and along with money came power until some plant owners attained a monopoly on the land, waters, and political affairs, directing the course of events. By the 1920s canned salmon was king, and the industry never faltered during the Depression because it provided a relatively inexpensive form of protein. In addition, economic activity was bolstered by a rise in fish harvesting using industrial traps, quickly leading to the demise of fish runs and the need for conservation measures.[5]

The first long-term Hoonah cannery was established in 1901 and was profitable from the beginning, employing Tlingit men as fishers. World War I brought an increased demand for canned salmon and further strengthened the importance of the purse seine–gear type, the preferred harvesting method for the community and the fleet.[6] In this highly competitive industry, however, this particular gear type was attacked by those arguing it was unfair: the gear type was too effective, and the purse seiners were accused of catching full runs of fish—a similar claim made about the commercial fish traps. Regardless of fishing apparatus, overharvesting occurred, and when it could no longer be tolerated, fishery agents were called on to decipher which fishers were the real culprit in this disaster.

It would be several years before it was acknowledged that the industrial fish traps were the main culprit and responsible for the meager salmon runs, though this was already known among both Native and non-Native resident fishers.[7] Meanwhile, the rivalry between the seine fleet and the cannery-owned traps escalated, and by the mid-1920s trap piracy was frequently reported from southeast Alaska to Bristol Bay (located in southwest Alaska). There were those who claimed piracy was necessary or even justified, and with few patrol agents and stealthy thieves, the perpetrators were rarely caught, while the salmon runs declined at an alarming rate.[8]

Seeking less competitive grounds, Hoonah boat captains studied the movement of the fish runs and out of necessity readapted obsolete gear for the outside fishery, most notably the challenging Inian Island area, located between Cross Sound and Icy Strait.[9] The outside fishery is distinguished from the inside waters by its proximity to the open ocean, a location with known perils. During the 1930s the Hoonah purse seine fleet were masters of these dangerous waters, but they could do nothing about the overharvesting by outsiders. By 1941 salmon in southeast Alaska had diminished to record lows, threatening the local economy and instigating manic rivalry. To adapt, the Hoonah fleet traveled out farther to the south on the Alexander Archipelago, the southeast Alaska Panhandle, at quite an expense in terms of fuel and crew wages. If possible, the Hoonah fishers liked to work in a closer area, either Inian Island or Home Shores.

Inian Island was a special site, with a long history for these fishers and today continues to be marked by totem poles and monuments erected in honor of fishers who lost their lives in these treacherous waters—incidents that have become the stuff of legends. A fisher must have prowess to manage the northern entrance between Cross Sound and Icy Strait because of the turbulent tidal currents that surge through the narrow channels. In fact, there is one site so volatile that it is named "The Laundry." From a young age, boys were taught how to manage these waters and the importance of the correct gear. The Hoonah fleet stuck together against the challenges, and the old-timers agree that the heyday occurred in the 1930s—a time when the Fish and Wildlife Service was too understaffed and ill-equipped to bother them.[10] In a couple of decades, this would change.

BY 1959 ALASKA became a state, and fish traps were abolished—good news for everyone. This had been one of the outstanding reasons to strive for statehood. There were high hopes that state regulation would result in the rebound of the salmon runs that had been overfished since the turn of the century throughout Alaska, but that was not to be. As village elder Jessie Gray described, "We thought when the first traps were gone, all those fish we used to know would be back. They never were. Where did they go?"[11] Several ideas and potential solutions were tossed around by the fledgling Alaska Department of Fish and Game (ADFG), including hiring local residents to watch the creek, which might have been effective since it closely paralleled traditional clan responsibilities, but it was never fully implemented. Regardless of proposals or possible solutions, the fish stocks continued to decrease, along with the general health of the fisheries until the ADFG ultimately closed Icy Strait in 1974 through an emergency order. The hardship on the fishers was immediate, but they believed they needed only to wait it out.

After several years, however, the fishers realized there was no end to the so-called ADFG recovery plan, and they were angry. To assuage the hard feelings, the ADFG held meetings in Hoonah and Juneau to explain why the emergency order was in effect and to assure the residents that they were not prejudicially targeting the purse seine–gear type. But as the closure dragged on, fishers who had for years fished for a living were cut off, and the entire village suffered. In an attempt to supplement the family economy, women worked at the local canneries when the runs came in, but this was not adequate for their needs, and it was about to become worse.

As if things were not dire enough, in 1974 the Limited Entry Act was put into effect as an attempt to curb the number of fishing boats in each district throughout Alaska.[12] As the name implies, now fishers had to apply for a permit to fish in their usual and accustomed fishing grounds, and the openings were regulated by statute and fishery biology. This was more than an insult—it was a gut punch. This legislation might have been well intentioned, but in the long run the ultimate outcome benefited the professional fishers who had ample resources to compete in the waters and enough gasoline to travel to openings, leaving smaller fishers without a chance.

At the onset of the limited-entry implementation, a point system was established that determined the qualifications for permit ownership. One of the ways to earn points was to demonstrate a historical dependence on the resource, but this proved difficult, as several Hoonah captains lacked proper fish-buyer receipts, while other fishers had trouble making sense out of the limited-entry form. In spite of these troubles, in the first round several Hoonah captains qualified for the permits.[13] There were, however, holdouts and dissenters, who refused to apply for permits or licenses, reasoning they were not necessary since they and their families had fished these grounds even before the Russians, and that gave them certain inherent rights, having nothing to do with a piece of paper. They may have been justified in their defiance, but the agencies were not listening, and the salmon were not coming back into the streams and creeks.

This situation went on for several years, with the continuum oscillating between captains with permits and a solid crew, and others defying government orders and fishing in an act of civil disobedience. In the ensuing maelstrom, it did not take long to uncover the fallacies within the limited-entry program, which may be one of the most criticized conservation efforts ever legislated in Alaska fisheries.[14] In despair fishers withdrew from the occupation due to low harvest and the high cost of fishing, breaking up the family business in many cases. Regrettably, there were times that desperate fishers sold their permits to survive, bringing in outsiders with expensive capital outlay and turning the fishing grounds into corporate units. Obviously, these new circumstances had the effect of further shutting out established Native fishers from their home fisheries near Hoonah.[15]

For those holding onto their permits, problems persisted, as they were forced to fish farther and farther out, consuming precious gasoline along the way at the same time that oil availability and price were a point of contention in the international market.[16] Permit prices skyrocketed, and the temptation to sell and make a quick profit was overwhelming.[17] In addition, due to the permit qualifications, especially those based on longevity in the fisheries, there was little hope for young people to enter into the profession, since they lacked the required documented background and history. This was not only a socioeconomic crisis but a cultural one as well, since it detracted from the apprenticeship that had normally been part of the coming-of-age experience for young Tlingit men.

These conditions dragged on through the 1980s, until it became obvious the village was nearing bankruptcy, particularly since the numbers of fishing fleet and captains had been dwindling for years. The Hoonah community was fuming, and they knew that someone was to blame for the hardship. Outrage was directed toward the Alaska Department of Fish and Game and the Board of Fisheries—the villagers cited inept management as the main reason for the problems.[18] Passions escalated to the point that on at least two occasions— one at the Juneau Fish and Game Office and the second during a Hoonah meeting—there were physical altercations between fishers and agents. The breakdown in communication between diverse groups was complete and without remedy. Fundamentally, the causes for schism were based on the oversight agency's lack of knowledge about the specific fisheries, leading to inequitable policies. Hoonah fishers were sure that the fish counters had no idea what they were doing, while the agents were irritated, believing the "Indians would take every last salmon out of the water."[19]

To the Hoonah fishers it was a simple matter, and they mocked the agency's charts and graphs. They had made a living on these waters for centuries, they understood the seascape, and they had watched the ebb and flow of salmon runs and followed the eagles, an avian signal that salmon were on their way. This was the Tlingit way. On the other hand, the ADFG relied on Western scientific methods to manage a resource that had suffered from overfishing and federal neglect for decades. The older fishers had seen cannery scows so laden with fish they had to dump the cargo overboard to save themselves from sinking or capsizing. It was that greed that had led to this devastating position, not the small fishers. Nonetheless, the seasons went by with no hope of finding common ground or reconciliation, although there was a great need for effective communication between oversight agencies and the fishers eking out a living.

Without a livelihood, villagers went into serious debt and were forced onto the welfare rolls.[20] They pleaded to have at least partial openings but were turned down by the fishery management based on estimations of inadequate escapement, which refers to the number of salmon allowed to escape the harvest to return to their natal streams and spawn, therefore guaranteeing another generation of fish. Sometimes openings were announced, and the fleet would get ready, only to find at the last minute the opportunity had been rescinded without cause, creating more frustration among fishers and their families as they railed against the oversight agencies. After ten long years had gone by, it was evident that no resolution was in sight, and many believed the state and federal agencies and their fishery biology were bogus. With resentment and desperation reaching the boiling point, another solution had to be found, and naturally the community looked to the local leaders, who knew fishing and had an understanding of the outside world and how to talk to these scientists. This was their last hope.

One of these men was Capt. John Hinchman, who had testified at several fishery hearings. Talking with him back in 1990, I had immediate respect for his words and knowledge, as he recalled meetings with "fish and game" and told me that the Hoonah seiners "were made to feel like they were criminals." Hinchman had tried his best to smooth the waters, but it was not easy. The general attitude was that their arguments were ignored, and "the government thought they were smarter than the fisherman, than the Indians."[21] Hinchman was convinced there needed to be a strong organization to promote the Hoonah cause if the village was to survive. Against these obstacles they refused to give up—the stakes were too high.

In 1980 the Icy Straits Federation was formed by a group of eleven Hoonah seiners united to defend customary fishing rights. Along with Steven Langdon, an Anchorage-based anthropologist and professor at the University of Alaska, they authored a position paper to submit to the fisheries board. There is no evidence the ADFG took significant action based on this paper, but they most likely did see it, since I saw it in their files in 1990.[22] The Icy Straits Federation disbanded early on due to a lack of cohesion but was followed by another strong fishers' coalition endeavoring to gain purchase on the precarious ledge of fish politics. The Southeast Alaska Seiners Association (SEAS), originally based in Ketchikan, acted as an advocacy group. Regrettably, this group did not work out either. Although all fishers shared the same problems, the Hoonah fishers did not fully embrace this organization because of cultural differences that could not be bridged, although there were sincere attempts to come up with resolutions and produce a united front.

Meanwhile, Hoonah residents had gone from despair to crisis. The village was in financial trouble, with longtime captains giving up their boats because of a lack of profit. For a while they had hung on to hope because SEAS appeared to have the power to overcome obstacles, particularly as they demanded the fishery should be reopened based on what appeared to be healthy runs. With monitoring they could be alerted if anything went awry. This particular report was long and detailed, but in summary SEAS stated, "It now confronts users and the processors as a completely unpredictable hodge-podge of openings and closures.... Harvests are lost to the detriment of returns." The proposal concluded, "More objective analysis for monitoring is necessary.... It cannot be dependent on a biologist's opinion."[23] For fishers who needed to feed their families, the wheels turned painfully slow, and when they saw that an organization as strong as SEAS could not move the needle, it was discouraging.

AT COMMUNITY MEETINGS the elders offered hope by retelling the old stories about how the village had been challenged before by natural resource–oversight agencies. If obstacles had been previously overcome, there must be a way to get through these times. One of these stories concerned the southeast Alaska fishery crisis back in the 1940s, during the war, when the fisheries were taken over by the government, and fish could be sold only to approved canneries. This had the effect of curtailing the fishers' livelihood, particularly when their usual cannery was closed due to consolidation, supposedly for efficiency. The elders continued to retell about the times when Fish and Wildlife agents made incongruous rules that hurt the Tlingit, both commercially and for subsistence purposes. In 1912 one disgruntled Klawock (another Tlingit village) fisher lamented that the "white fishermen came, and then at that time we don't protest, because if we make a kick they always tell us, 'This belongs to the Government, Uncle Sam,' and we were ordered to shut up. Keep out of the way. You get in trouble. And they threatened us with marshals."[24]

It was no secret that the price of Americanism had been the relinquishing of ancient clan-owned waters, beachfronts, and the forest, while Native rights were questioned because of the dwindling Native population caused by contact with Westerners, who brought disease, decimating the population while the settlers staked their claims. Often during the course of history, Native families had been forced to relocate to take advantage of employment opportunities in the new cash and wage economy, especially with the loss of their fishing livelihood. In yet another act of injustice, the Tlingit were accused of abandoning their fishing rights by not objecting to the intruding canneries that had set up shop, not caring whose land or waters they might be on, while freely using the local (clan-owned) timber sources.[25] For the cannery owners, the fishery was a veritable free-for-all, and no one had ownership rights. In a classic case of the tragedy of the commons, the motivation was to fish as much as possible because there was no one to efficiently and fairly monitor the resource.[26]

For many the only recourse was civil disobedience. They went out and fished, daring to be caught. Protesters viewed the Icy Strait and Inian Island closure as another act of dispossession, and this justified their actions.[27] Before the closure local residents estimated there were approximately twenty captains and boats in Hoonah from a population of about nine hundred individuals, and by 1990 there were only eight captains left. The old-timers recalled that, back in the early 1970s, the Hoonah fleet had harvested approximately one-third of salmon caught in the tributary area, and naturally those numbers were way down, but they were convinced they were not responsible for this problem.[28]

Finally, the crisis exploded, threatening to tear a hole in the village socially, economically, culturally, and politically, as both the closure and limited-entry rule intensified an already bad situation. For the small-time operators, the once-cherished permits were worthless because of heavily restricted fishing grounds. Fishing had always been a dangerous business, but now, out of desperation, the fishers took more risks, creating further safety issues. For instance, some openings, often referred to as postage-stamp sites, were called, and hundred of fishers squeezed into an area as small as one square mile, increasing the hazards in an already perilous profession. With accidents, poor runs, and decreased profits, fishers thought it was time to quit.

At first it was only the older fishers who sold their permits and took an early retirement, but when the cost to fish increased in the face of corporate competition, it reduced many traditional fishers to poverty. They had to sell their valuable permits to stay afloat. In other words, they could no longer afford to fish.[29] Those without permits but desiring to maintain their participation in the fishery became crew members, a major socioeconomic and cultural setback for many former captains. After the independence of owning one's boat, spread through generations, a pervasive dissatisfaction arose from "working for someone else."[30]

HOONAH, AS A tight-knit community, was forced to make some difficult choices. The closure effects coupled with other restrictions had crippled the local industry, but their pleas had gone unheard for years. Early on village leaders had sent a letter to the then Alaska governor Jay Hammond stating that limited entry "outlaws the fishing rights of many in our community and this is wrong, unfair, and unjust. They should not be outlawed from making a living to be left to suffer privations and hardships. . . . We feel we have been greatly deceived and misled in the original presentation of limited entry."[31] The governor, however, had his hands tied, and residents, now permanently disenfranchised from this fishery, were left to witness licensed boats from outside Alaska fish in their former territory, and they had no remedy.[32] When Hoonah residents left to secure employment, the village cohesion and kin relationships deteriorated and severely undermined those long-standing factors that had bolstered group strength during disruptive times.

When the Native knowledge of the fisheries was disrespected, this was another assault. As perpetual stewards of the resource, duly recorded in the oral narrative, the Tlingit believed they were well qualified to watch the runs and the health of the fishery. They felt certain that they, even more than the oversight agencies, could monitor escapement, harvest levels, and stream preservation to ensure the survival of the salmon. Howard Gray explained this system in detail and remarked on the effectiveness of the stream watch. He added, "You've got to look where the eagles are, then you will know," a reference to the eagles' preferred prey of salmon.[33]

In this state of crisis, men and women learned how to run the bureaucratic

maze, and they could periodically count on the support of Native organizations. The Tlingit-Haida Central Council, a federally recognized tribal power
with a firm standing in the community and in Washington DC, stepped forward to engage in government-to-government discussions, assisted by their
subsidiary, the Fisheries Development Corporation, which was dedicated to
the rehabilitation and enhancement of southeastern Alaska salmon and provided expertise.[34] Some inroads were met, but for the most part the impasse
was unbreakable. Again there was a call for a Hoonah-centric organization,
leading to the relaunching of the Icy Straits Federation under the leadership
of two important Hoonah skippers, Jake White and John Hinchman. They
presented what they believed was a sound position paper to the Board of
Fisheries, explaining the effects of the closure and how it unfairly targeted
seiners. The were backed by the Alaska Native Brotherhood and the Sitka
Advisory Committee, a citizens' group under the Alaska Department of Fish
and Game.[35] In the combined analysis, the conclusion stood that inappropriate
management techniques had relegated fishing boats into a limited space, the
existing runs were still under threat, and there was a need for proven scientific
techniques to measure sustainable harvest levels.[36] In other words, the ADFG
had consistently been incorrect in their assessment and management strategies.

By the 1980s the monolithic government was accused of wiping out the
small, independent fishers, and disgruntled Hoonah residents pointed to
illegal weirs and other management problems, until finally John Hinchman
brought fishery agents out to Hoonah to show them the hundreds of dead,
floating salmon carcasses in the stream. The salmon had not only been blocked
from their spawning waters but also had been deprived of oxygen because of
overcrowding (too much escapement) and logging debris. In some instances
the fish had thrown themselves up on the creek banks in desperation and lay
there rotting—not even the bears would go near them.[37] These environmental
issues had to be addressed and could no longer ignored.

FROM THE 1930S on, Hoonah fishers believed their particular commercial
fleet had been purposely targeted in discriminatory fashion without legal
protection, not even through ANCSA. Hoonah's village corporation, Huna
Totem, did not retain any territoriality rights in the fishery and could act only

as an advocacy body.[38] All authority was derived from the ADFG and the Board of Fisheries, and this meant that former clan territories were foreclosed. Public meetings were run according to ADFG guidelines and fishers (or their wives) traveled to the meetings at their own expense but believed they were disregarded while the regulatory officials stood by their scientific studies. In all this confusion, there was a wild-card attempt to use the "submerged waters" statute to gain a foothold on the issue, and the village corporation took the lead in this endeavor.

The land surrounding Icy Strait was federally owned before ANCSA, and that included the land under the waters, or what is referred to as "submerged waters." Under the Submerged Land Act, underwater lands were granted to the State of Alaska in January 1960. By virtue of this ownership, access to water became the prerogative of the state, and as time passed, the state's hold intensified. To complete the dominant position, the state constitution vested authorization of Alaska's salmon resources within the joint management of the ADFG and the Board of Fisheries, an impervious wall. Did ANCSA change any of these designations?

In a last-ditch attempt, Hoonah fishers tried to find a hidden loophole in ANCSA, but the results were disappointing. Certain lands were under the authority of the village corporation, but not customary fishing sites, and in fact the legislation had abolished all reserved or implied Native fishing rights.[39] If there was going to be change or a reclamation of rights, it was now incumbent on the Hoonah fishers to take their complaint to the larger regional corporation that represented Native members in southeast Alaska, Sealaska, but this would not be without complications. ANCSA legislation was convoluted, without much respect for cultural history, and Sealaska was still defining its authority structure, overextended in its tasks, and trying to make a profit.

In the end ANCSA was not helpful, especially with additional legislation thrown into the mix. In 1980 President Jimmy Carter, relying on the Antiquities Act, signed the Alaska National Interest Lands Conservation Act, which was set in place to protect Alaska's pristine grandeur, as determined by legislators in Washington DC.[40] The act also reserved federal lands for subsistence purposes but had no clause for Native commercial fishing. Although the subsistence clause would be important to all Alaska Natives in the near future, it was too late for the Hoonah commercial fleet, and the controversy eventually lapsed into obscurity, forcing the Hoonah residents to look for other ways to sustain their economy. This had been their last substantial effort to right what they believed was a wrong.

STEVEN LANGDON, WHO had been working with the Board of Fisheries on social policy, described his experience as "coming face to face with the realities of hardball politics."[41] Those in power brought their own perspectives to the table, yet affected fishers were left out of the hearings, due to the high cost of travel and accommodations, leaving one omniscient fishery-regulation source. Beyond statistics, studies, and escapement goals, the communication system had been ineffective, and Hoonah captains complained that no one listened to their testimony.

For many years John Hinchman, the captain of the *Johnny-A*, had made his home in both Hoonah and Seattle, Washington. From the beginning of the controversy back in the 1970s, he had been regarded as a political activist, especially on the historical Icy Strait issue. He had attended not only numerous board meetings but also less formal meetings with the ADFG. He regularly canvassed the neighborhood to gather support and record concerns. When I was in Hoonah in 1990, I had the opportunity to talk with him on several occasions, and the conversations were lively and informative. He could have held a grudge against the government, but instead he was simultaneously optimistic and realistic.

One afternoon I walked out to his boat, and we talked about the fishers' problems. He summarized it in one word: "communication." He referred back to an old incident when an Angoon fisher had attempted to speak out at the 1979 Board of Fisheries meeting about the Icy Strait closure. His Native tongue was Tlingit, and he spoke English haltingly. After several efforts to express his thoughts and being laughed at by the board members, he raised his voice and said, "I thought you wanted to hear from real fishermen." The board agreed they did want to hear his testimony and that of other fishers. He attempted to speak again, but his stuttering drew laughter, and he left the meeting. Hinchman was emphatic: "That is why the fishermen don't like to attend these meetings. They are treated as inferior." Sometimes, he added, the men stay home and the women fly over to Juneau. Hinchman emphasized his point with a chuckle—"You don't say no to Tlingit women."[42]

The fishers and their families were demoralized, and that increased the communication dysfunction between the board and fishers. There could be no pragmatic dispute resolution until a communication channel was assembled, and that conduit would be difficult, given the fishers' general distrust of all the natural resource agencies. Without respect there could be no compromise, and for the interim the government was wrapped up in Western scientific thinking, leaving no opening for Native ethnoscience.

As Hoonah elder Lily White stated, "They made up their minds, and that is that. We have traveled to Juneau at the request of the ADF&G to make compromises, discuss policies. When we get there they read the rules they have already made. We could say a lot more when we were a territory." She called the current restrictions "granite laws." Jake White, her husband, had been fishing for fifty years and knew every inch of Icy Strait. His irritation was evident as he recounted, "You can't talk to Fish and Game; they won' talk." He asked me if I had ever seen how the meetings were handled, and before I could answer, he continued, "A man gets up with a pointer stick and looks at this big map and says, 'Do you mean this place or that place?' All the time with these places. That is not the problem. All the time with this pointing stick." Hinchman supported the "pointing stick" contempt and agreed that fishery management "are not interested in what the fisherman knows." Further, he was appalled that the Hoonah fleet had been called "creek robbers" by high-ranking ADFG officials, a term of defilement among fishers.[43]

THESE WERE OLD fishers who had worked at Icy Strait for decades, and they could not understand what had happened—nobody told them anything. It was not uncommon for a fisher to remember fishing back during World War I, when the Fish and Wildlife Service was the regulatory body, and continuing to call it such, although most of their dealings were now with the Alaska Department of Fish and Game. The most common grievance heard was that "Fish and Wildlife" were not interested in the fishers' problems. Archie Brown Sr. related, "We spent a lot of money to go to the hearing in Anchorage, but they don't listen. . . . I guess they got our number." He added, "I think there is complete misinformation on both sides." George Dalton Sr., with a long family history of fishing Icy Strait, said, "We call Fish and Wildlife, we tell them what is happening, but they don't care. . . . They're more interested in moving the money fish." Howard Gray summed up the problem as "we don't work together; there is no respect; we've got to work together." In reference to meetings with management, again he stated, "Your voice is no good. We know the fishery, but they have the power, so our voice is no good." He restated this opinion, still prevalent in Hoonah, that management needed to initiate an on-site evaluation of the fishery. "They have got to come here and meet with the people. That would spill the cold water on them."[44]

Don Hotch, a gillnetter from Klukwan, had fished at Icy Strait and was familiar with the problems of Hoonah. He was matter of fact in his assessment: "The biologists need to be local and trusted. We don't communicate well with the biologists. I feel we know more." When questioned about the input of the advisory boards, he replied, "What's the use? They don't listen; there is no power." Hotch stated the adverse effects had escalated in the mid-1970s, which prompted him to write a letter to Governor Wally Hickel, but he never received a reply. He added that the ADFG "go by the paper, not the people who know the fish." Older fishers had spent their life out on the waters and relied on that knowledge, not fish counters, but their statements were "considered hearsay; it is not scientific and has no power behind it."[45]

Hoonah residents received infrequent contact from oversight agencies, although the ADFG countered that they had held meetings in Hoonah several times.[46] The Hoonah fishers did recall one such meeting, when the former deputy commissioner of Fish and Game, Carl Rosier, had traveled to Hoonah to speak. Little came of that meeting, and during the next meeting in Juneau, things heated up. Rosier, already disliked, was physically assaulted by a Hoonah fisher, acting out of frustration. This was not the first record of such a reaction—there were instances of fisticuffs on both sides of the water, Juneau and Hoonah.

Nonetheless, Rosier and other officials defended the agency's position, by claiming they were "going with the best information we have." Limited entry, which was finally shown not to work for any of the Alaska fisheries, was allegedly designed to protect the traditional rural fishers from out-of-state fleets, but never did.[47] The state shielded its reputation by asserting that "There was never a consideration of pushing the small-scale fishermen out. This is what we told them. . . . The small community should be protected." The ADFG also spoke about Indigenous knowledge in this way: "The fishermen feel they do not have an input, but we have trouble quantifying these ideas in a scientific basis, but it does become part of our thought process and relied on. Few management decisions are made in a vacuum."[48] Obviously some statements were political in nature.

Ultimately, the status quo was maintained, and the few fishers who possessed permits continued to fish, often sharing with their less fortunate kin. On Chichagof Island subsistence fishing and hunting was still viable, although heavily regulated. Fishers met in small groups and discussed possible solutions until a new phrase was thrown out across the waters—co-management. This style of oversight had been shown to work in other areas of Alaska, and it seemed worth a try. To be successful, however, the two parties, ADFG and Hoonah fishers, had to come to terms.

WANDA CULP OF Hoonah was outspoken and knowledgeable about her home. She had become an environmental activist at a young age, and when I spoke with her in 1990, the very mention of the fishery and what was happening drew heat. She was irritated by how the fishers had been treated by the government. Then she described the Tlingit way of managing the stocks for a healthy fishery: "There is a reason for everything that is done, even if that might seem ritualistic to outsiders. Fishing is the backbone of the culture, and Indigenous knowledge preserved methods used by the ancestors." She completed her thoughts by saying she believed the closure had been nothing less than "genocide."[49] It was a forceful word but not the only time I had heard this sentiment.

At the same time, one can not be so naive to assume that a fisher's motivation is not to produce a profit. That is natural and a necessity. Years later there were still legendary tales about Joe White and others who were considered highliners, bringing in thousands of fish in one run. But was that so bad when the fish were plentiful? After all, they were not wasted. Before the advent of industrial fishing, the species had been maintained though natural conservation methods with the understanding that in some years the salmon stocks are low, and proper procedures and restraint must be upheld to assure the next year will be better. If these two types of understandings could be blended, such as in the co-management model, perhaps positive aspects could be incorporated, but by the late 1990s and into the next millennium, the village had gone too long without profitable fishing years and were on the verge of bankruptcy.

TO SURVIVE, HOONAH residents developed innovative and dynamic ideas. Through the work of village elders, fishers, Huna Totem, and other residents, a magnificent scheme was unleashed—a novel concept—ecotourism. The old Icy Strait cannery was converted into a museum and now offers tourists a look at how fish were brought to the plants, expertly butchered, and packed when canneries were in their heyday. This business operation also incorporated a mission statement that upholds cultural values and gives credence to the Tlingit way of life. Once the beaches of Frederick Sound were lined with canoes, then piers and wharfs were built for the purse seine fleet, and today cruise ships come to port. Facing an economic crisis, the village reinvented itself, creating a successful tourist attraction. Visitors travel to Chichagof Island to explore the fishing sites and the harbor and walk through the Tongass Forest, thick with spruce, birch, and hemlock. For the adventure-minded, Hoonah boasts of the longest zipline in the world, at 5,330 feet. Those not quite so daring can relax back at the lodge and view the waters—if they're lucky they will see the salmon popping out of the water.

Although fishing activity continues in Hoonah, the village knew it could not support itself on this resource alone anymore, given the restrictions and the loss of captains. According to Dennis Gray Jr., a fourth-generation commercial fisher, one has to "adapt or die." He continued, "Hoonah has always done a good job of transitioning from one industry to the next. We are good fishermen, we were good loggers, and now we are good tour operators." Gray remembers the early plans and the initial doubts, yet they courageously gathered their resources and invested in new infrastructure. Tourist dollars assisted the tax base while introducing large host companies to the village, such as the Disney Cruise Lines. Russell Dick, CEO of Huna Totem, attributes authenticity and community buy-in to the success, adding, "If there is any place we are going to invest our money, it is going to be at home, putting our people to work."[50]

Change is never easy. Hoonah and other areas have regrouped to stay afloat but not without problems. A 2007 forest service report stated that the introduction of tourism to Hoonah acted as a disruptive factor by encroaching on private or historical lands, while the charter fishing fleet competed with the commercial fishers. Though the growth of tourism saved Hoonah from economic bankruptcy, it may have negatively impacted community well-being and the traditional decision-making progress.[51] That remains to be seen, and problems will be worked out on ongoing basis, but the village's resiliency is a testimonial to an innovative nature and the stability of the traditional culture.

Hoonah, Alaska

12. The traditional Tlingit village of Hoonah in southeast Alaska. Courtesy of the Michael Nore Collection.

13. Another view of Hoonah, on Chichagof Island. Courtesy of the Michael Nore Collection.

14. Hoonah's fleet. For decades they depended on the ocean to supply their needs. Courtesy of the Michael Nore Collection.

15. A view of an Aleut (Unangan) settlement on the Bering Sea. Courtesy of the Michael Nore Collection.

16. An Unangan vessel at Cold Bay, in southwest Alaska. Courtesy of the Michael Nore Collection.

17. Alaska Native family at seasonal camp, Kodiak Island, in southwest Alaska, the traditional home of the Alutiiq. This island served as the first base for the Russian American Company, a mercantile fort built to harvest sea otters and send the furs back to Russia or China as part of the Cathay trade. This site also saw many ships from Hawaii. Courtesy of the Michael Nore Collection.

18. Children and perhaps a teacher's aide gathered in front of the schoolhouse, 1905. Courtesy of the Michael Nore Collection.

BASKET WEAVING

19. Demonstration of Native weaving. Courtesy of the Michael Nore Collection.

20. Nunivak Island dancing regalia. This island is located off the coast of southwest Alaska. Besides regular subsistence activities, they have a thriving reindeer-herding industry. Courtesy of the Michael Nore Collection.

21. Fred Paul, son of lawyer and activist William L. Paul Sr. Fred Paul was the attorney who represented Charlie Edwardsen Jr., or "Etok." William Lackey Paul photo collection. Used with permission from Ben Paul.

22. William L. Paul Sr. (*third from the right*). In the 1920s he activated the ANB so that it was a stronger advocate for Native rights. He encouraged other Native groups to form their own chapters to fight for the cause. William Lackey Paul photo collection. Used with permission from Ben Paul.

10 The Day the Waters Died

Walter Meganack, chief of the Port Graham community during the 1980s, looked out at the waters after the disaster. Only hours ago those same waters were teeming with life. He lamented, "We heard the news, oil in the water, lots of oil killing lots of water. It is too shocking to understand. Never in the millennium of our tradition have we thought it possible for the water to die, but it's true." Later on he testified, "We caught our first fish, the annual first fish, the traditional delight of all; but it got sent to the state to be tested for oil. . . . We walked the beaches, but instead of gathering life, we gathered death."[1] The *Exxon Valdez* spill occurred in 1989, but back in the 1960s Charlie Edwardsen Jr., "Etok," had predicted this would happen—it was only a matter of time.

THE ALUTIIQ, a maritime people, traditionally occupied the area from Kodiak Island to Prince William Sound in south-central Alaska. They spoke a dialect of the Yup'ik language also called Alutiiq or (Suqpiaq).[2] Culturally, the western Alutiiq people have affinities to their neighbors on the Aleutian Chain (Unangan), while those occupying areas closer to the southeast Alaska Panhandle have sociocultural ties with the Tlingit, all sharing an orientation toward the Pacific Ocean. Another small cultural group lives mainly in the Cordova area, the Eyak, who are considered proto-Athabascan and included as part of the early migrants of the Na-Dene migration.[3] There are ancient stories about the Eyak migrating from the north and overcoming barriers, such as glaciers, to finally find their homes. Although the Eyak are a small group, they were also involved in the fishing industry and affected by the natural and manmade disasters that befell the region.

In the oral narrative, the waters have always been filled with life, and the Indigenous have made a living, for both commercial and subsistence purposes, though it has never been easy. The region has been subjected to some of the worst adversity known to Alaska, but the people learned to cope and adapt to whatever befell them, whether it was an act of nature or a manmade tragedy. In addition to epidemics and severe assimilative measures, the Alutiiq and their neighbors, the Eyak, dealt with the 1912 Katmai eruption and the 1964 Alaska earthquake (9.2) that required whole villages to relocate under the direction of intrusive governmental agents.[4] Yet, of all the historical disasters, there has never been anything as continually disruptive as the 1989 *Exxon Valdez* oil spill.

How could such a disaster occur? Capt. Joe Hazelwood and his crew had been spending the afternoon at a Valdez bar, waiting for the weather to clear. That evening the tanker, carrying fifty-three million gallons of North Slope crude oil, attempted to navigate through icebergs while the captain was relaxing in his quarters. The ship responded too late to an unmonitored danger and was grounded on Bligh Reef, twenty-eight miles from Valdez. The ship's hull tore open, releasing oil into the ocean, and did not stop until nearly eleven million gallons had fouled the once-pristine waters.[5] It did not take long to uncover that human error was involved in this tragedy.

TO REALIZE HOW so much devastation occurred, it is helpful to understand the ecological setting before the oil spill. The Alutiiq environment was abundant with animals, fowl, and fish, including five species of salmon. Historically, Cordova, the hub of Prince William Sound, was established as a townsite in 1906, motivated largely by the activities and employment related to the copper discovery and the Copper River and the Northwestern Railway, built by well-known magnates J. P. Morgan and Simon Guggenheim, part of the notorious Alaska Syndicate, which usurped every major industry in Alaska to gain control of the resources and keep the profit out of the federal government's hands. Before the inevitable corruption was revealed, valuable resources had been stripped from the land, and the first people, the Alutiiq, Eyak, and Athabascan, had been forcibly removed from their homes to make way for railroads, copper fields, gold dredges, and salmon fish traps.[6] Eventually, this monopoly was broken up, but not before it left its mark, branding Alaska as a colony for industrialists.

At one time a few small fox-farming operations had been employed at the short-lived Katalla oil refinery, but fishing was the most important livelihood, in a pattern that blended commercial and subsistence harvesting in one of the world's best salmon-fishing locales. There were occasional tussles with federal oversight agencies and attempts to regulate fishing grounds, but the fishers found ways to work around what they considered an occupational irritant. Floods, earthquakes, and volcanic ash presented a whole new challenge.

Patricia Partnow, an anthropologist who has written about the Alutiiq culture, explains, "Natural and human disasters figure prominently in the oral tradition of the Alaska Peninsula. Catastrophic eruptions, earthquakes, and tsunamis, as well as epidemics and oil spills, have required the people to adjust often to loss of life and economic opportunity."[7] In 1964 the resiliency of the Alutiiq people had been tested when a 9.2 earthquake rocked south-central Alaska, destroying whole villages in Prince William Sound and surrounding areas. The initial earth movement, as strong as it was, was no match for the destructive tsunami that violently swallowed whole villages, including Afognak, Kaguyak, and Old Harbor, and badly damaged the city of Kodiak. Along the mainland coast several villages were destroyed, and many of them were never rebuilt. Two of the hardest hit villages, Tatitlek and Chenega Bay, suffered additional destruction because of the 1989 oil spill. Their stories are highlighted in this chapter.

THE POSSIBILITY OF an oil spill might have been on the minds of all Alaska residents at one time, but fears subsided as the profits started to support the state and fill the government's coffers. No one could have imagined that on that spring day, a few days before the twenty-fifth anniversary of the Great Earthquake, their whole lives would be turned upside down. Fishers had been gearing up for days, and the marketplaces were eager for fresh Copper River salmon. Suddenly, the radio and television were filled with nonstop coverage of an oil spill in the Prince William Sound. The early details were conflicting, but for a while the outlook was optimistic, yet it did not take long for this naive sanguinity to be crushed, although the "experts" attempted to put on a thinly veiled show of confidence in front of a skeptical and shocked audience.

Any rosy outlook quickly dissolved when we saw photos of the grounded *Exxon Valdez*, followed by more photos of dead, oiled seabirds floating in the waters and sea otters trying to swim ashore with dead pups on their bellies. Within twenty-four hours it was evident that the situation was out of control. Dozens of volunteers poured into the region to help clean waterfowl or provide food for the workers, as the residents witnessed their fishing villages evaporate in a pool of crude oil. Eventually the Prince William Sound fisheries were declared a disaster area. In the panic and disorganization, ill-prepared governmental agencies entered the scene, only complicating the situation and adding to the general confusion.

HOPE LINGERED THAT this was only a temporary problem, but as the months passed by, the traditional fishers had to find ways to keep financially afloat while swarms of people, many tourists, all strangers, descended on their homes from newspapers, trying to scoop a headline to government agents, exerting their authority in an area they knew nothing about. The national news was filled with photos of college students, out on spring break, cleaning oily birds with baby soap, dead baby seals floating in the black waters, and boons (containment nets) being set in place to attempt to control the unmanageable. When the federal government personnel finally figured out they were out of their depth, they went to the locals for help, employing the fishers and their families in counting dead birds or reviving animals that had escaped the worst effects. Simultaneously, government agents interviewed fishers to assess how this had affected each of them and took testimony on the wages of oil and death, while others jammed onto the beaches with less altruistic intentions—to collect souvenirs.

DURING THIS TIME no one was notified of potential widespread toxic effects, how far and wide the oil had spread, or the amount of oil that had spilled. The residents were in the dark for months, and preliminary studies on the safety of the fishing grounds were inconclusive. Fishing families watched their meager savings dwindle, while seals and herring became scarcer as well. The Alaska health bureaucracy assessed captured animals for oil damage and other injuries, even as the oil continued to travel farther out to sea or seep deeper into the beach silt. Clearly, the region had never faced a crisis of this proportion. Ed Gregorioff recalled that they felt they were living in jeopardy, even though "after the oil spill especially they say it didn't affect it [animals and fish] but you could notice year after year this stuff is still disappearing slowly and it ain't going to be long before we ain't going to be able to have any of that stuff anymore. And that makes me feel bad. I like the Native lifestyle. I mean that subsistence lifestyle."[8]

The Alutiiq could not wait for governmental answers. They needed to be aggressive in their approach if they were to see any recovery. It had to be more than politics, though—they needed legal experts, and a potential lawsuit was discussed even in the early weeks after the spill. After noticing that the government was more hindrance than help, the Native fishers and their families prepared a foundation to seek redress. Once again, as in other environmental crises that threatened Native villages, the residents rose to the exigencies of the moment and bolstered traditional councils to represent Native fishers against big oil, summoning an age-old resiliency to survive and live to fight another day.

Alutiiq oral narratives record past cataclysmic events, delineating how the people faced enemies. The latest opponent was incompetent government administrators and oil companies, attempting to put forth a grand public relations image while ignoring, in large part, the plight of the environment and fishers. The continual circle of the ancient past and the current realities underscored the need for adjustments, a necessity since first cultural contact. Roy Madsen from Kodiak spoke about how the "tides and ties of our culture" had previously facilitated modifications and transformations without altering the foundations. Although the people were no longer completely homogenous in their way of life, Madsen believed they were like a bag of "mixed herbs" and able to meet the exigencies of the day, while retaining roots which retain "aspects of the culture of our Alutiiq ancestors."[9] Nothing stays the same; there is always the element of change, yet there was an indissoluble pride in the past—a sentiment that would be tested in this seismic disaster.

Days after the initial spill, the destruction was evident. The game was unseen and the landscape was ugly. Similar to other Alaska Native cultures, the Alutiiq (and the Eyak) are place-based, and now the entire region was coated with black tar and mortality. Outside agencies could not offer answers, and in fact many agents and officials had never been to Alaska before and had no idea about the people, the fishing, the history, or even the appropriate science for developing solutions. Additionally, the air of secrecy, real and imagined, resulted in further distrust, while the fishers and sea harvesters were told to test their foods (by sight or smell) for contamination or to send specimens to scientific labs for testing.

In 1990, almost a year later, a Port Graham resident complained, "I never believe a lot of what is written, and I mistrust the information about contamination," referring to promises that everything was okay. When tests were conducted, the residents were confused: "I never heard back the results from anything. I'm still worried about contamination." From Larsen Bay, over on Kodiak Island, one resident resented the enforced testing and having to do the work for these outside agencies. Bureaucrats were not his priority. He was more concerned about how he was going to feed his family that year.[10]

Again the government could not be relied on, motivating affected households to take matters into their own hands and rely on their own ingenuity. It was nonsense, they believed, to smell things to detect contamination. In fact, it was an insult, increasing the "gap between what official wisdom called for and what the people at risk, acting on wisdom of their own, actually did."[11] The fishers believed that both their political rights and livelihood were endangered, but despite the protest, the government agents stuck to Western science and used agency jargon to falsely reassure those affected and the news media that the damage was not that bad, although the photos spoke a different story.

VULNERABLE AREAS WERE hit hard. The village of Chenega had been thoroughly disrupted after the 1964 earthquake and tsunami.[12] After the oil spill, there was no place for these residents to escape the effects. By 1991 the U.S. Fish and Wildlife Service reported, "Over 1,200 miles of coastline were oiled, extending nearly 600 miles from Bligh Reef to the Alaska Peninsula. The oil entered the ecosystem just prior to the most biologically active season of the year in south-central Alaska." The deleterious effects extended beyond the shoreline; the deer and bears who feed on kelp and tidal pool resources were ingesting oil in a toxic cycle. The driftwood used for energy sources was not only covered in oil, but it had seeped in, rendering it useless. Since undetected dead wildlife never made the final tally, the statistics were wrong along with the estimate of harvestable animals, but beyond these aspects hunters were afraid that many animals were diseased, and they could not trust government assurances.[13] These circumstances applied not only to small coastal villages but to the vast area at large.

Caught in a hubristic bubble, the scientific community would not give up their authority and disregarded traditional knowledge when it was offered, exacerbating cross-cultural misunderstanding and tensions. In desperation concerned individuals called "safety meetings," and, when government agents spoke at these meetings, the fishers heard pep-rally speeches, but they were not buying into the propaganda. While grieving for the once-unspoiled land and waters they had known for years, they were advised to wear rubber gloves and wash off the oil that touched their skin.[14] Yet the fishers saw no progress and asked why. The answer centered on money.

Oil is big business in Alaska, serving as a lifeline to the economy, and the resource is not only protected but also deeply networked into the political matrix. "Native people expressed concern about the objectivity of the analysis due to Exxon's involvement in the testing program. This participation appeared to be a conflict of interest and raised strong suspicions as to the validity of the information."[15] There had been other crises in rural Alaska, where the Natives had felt shut out of the process, and this looked no different. In towns like Cordova, there was more activity, but the smaller villages were easily ignored, with no recourse.

Chenega Bay and Tatitlek were examples of neglect, past and present, and the village similarities are often spoken about together. Following the 1964 Good Friday Earthquake, Chenega Island had slid over fifty feet to the south. Seventy-five lives were lost when the tsunami hit—there was no higher ground to climb to, and those who survived this ordeal were moved to a safer site on Chenega Bay on Evan Islands in Prince William Sound, among strangers.[16] The adjustment was never complete, and the oil-spill repercussions were another hardship to overcome. The same was true for the Alutiiq village of Tatitlek, located in Prince William Sound, the closest Native village affected by the oil spill. One eyewitness recalled how he had "gazed out at the inlet into the intricate winding darkness there of water and rock, and saw a sheen of oil, a long thin shine." Gary Komkoff, the Tatitlek council president, was adamant that the village could not be moved again, declaring that they had lived in a "white town" at one time but never grew accustomed to the place: "We don't like city life."[17] Yet they were forced to do something when "a ribbon of oil had entered the narrows, and in the first days of the spill the fumes had been almost overpowering." One week after the spill, the lack of clear communication was evident when a burn test was conducted without the prior knowledge of the villagers. They found out about it only "when they saw the flash and then smelled the fumes drifting their way"—toxic fumes![18]

THE TRAUMATIZED PEOPLE were faced with hardball politics and the "claims, counterclaims, and denials from various scientific, political, ethnic and economic quarters" did not assuage their concerns. Instead, the alleged perpetrator of the disaster was accused of sneaking in and taking charge with no local input. For a solution there was bold talk of taking the issues to court, leading to a lawsuit—the first of many. The grounds were certainly evident. After two years of coping, a Chenega Bay resident lamented, "We have lived all our lives here. People say that everything is going back to normal. We live here and we don't think so. We are the ones who know. We live off the land. It is still bad and will be for a long time." Some families chose to give up harvesting wild foods because of this uncertainty. In field notes from Larsen Bay in 1992, it was observed that the oil spill "affected the subsistence way of life. For how long is hard to say. It will be in most people's minds all the time. The fear is still here, and it will be here for a long time."[19]

Native councils met to plan a course of action and to learn more about the Western court system, while the public applauded their efforts—television viewers had watched the disaster unfold, including the scenes of oiled and dying animals and volunteers scrubbing rocks. Natives had already won their case in the local public opinion courts, yet in reality this meant coming to blows with the monolith of big oil. Not only was there the Exxon Corporation to take on, but also a state legislature that did not want to rock the boat and cut off their money supply. When the hearings finally opened, the path was bumpy due to intimidated witnesses who could not understand court procedures and protocol. This worked two ways. The court could not comprehend the importance of subsistence on a cultural or practical level. They wondered why the Natives didn't just go to the grocery store, failing to realize there are no stores in most places, and where they do exist, the prices were exorbitant. The plaintiffs persisted, however, and in the words of one Akhiok resident, "Appropriate compensation from Exxon would be some help with the grocery bill. But it isn't the same thing to send food; [that lacks] the joy of going out subsistence hunting and fishing. If that's taken away, your livelihood is gone."[20] Pride allowed no other options such as public welfare.

In seeking redress Alaska Natives, Alutiiq and Eyak, aligned with other non-Native resource users in a class-action suit, acting to strengthen their composite cause. Native fishers recognized they might be taking the chance that their individual problems would not be acknowledged, but they also understood there was power in numbers. Other smaller litigation events were ongoing, but this larger lawsuit took center stage, and its history provides an outlook on Native concerns versus governmental interpretations of the law. The court, with foundations in English common law, was set up to defend big business over small fishers, and with the Exxon Corporation using false statistics and manipulating the scales of justice, an unbiased balance was not to be found.[21] The corporation had the money and expertise to run a subterfuge and counteract any allegations thrown its way—surely more than these fishers, regardless of ethnic background. When all else failed, Exxon listed its do-gooder activities, as if this mitigated damages. The haggling went on for many weeks and included corporate managers quoting statistics that did not fit and Native testimony that did not seem to move the needle.

When all the testimony was included, all parties waited for a decision. In October 1991, over two years past the oil spill, the case was decided, and the damages were calculated, mainly centered on environmental rehabilitation.[22] Eventually, the Exxon Corporation was fined, and the settlement funds went into a trust account to fund restoration efforts and other corollary efforts. One of the more important legal actions created the *Exxon Valdez* Oil Spill Trustee

Council to oversee the monies designated for remedying the worst regional damages, particularly wildlife habitat. This trust fund, amounting to $90 million, was set aside for further cleanup, construction, water studies, and habitat restoration. Yet these programs were one-sided and did not take into consideration local input as part of the decision-making process. Instead, the choice of projects and how the money was spent "reflected the will of the state and federal administration." Even though there were other organizations concerned with the oil spill, nothing affected the Native fishers more than this council, a bureaucratic organization charged with managing funding and deciding what was important. In sum under "the settlement terms scientific studies, capital construction projects, and habitat acquisition" were prioritized by and "reflected the will of the state and federal administration."[23] The battle was extended by these conditions.

IN SEPTEMBER 1994 an Anchorage jury returned punitive damages intended to act as a deterrent to other errant petroleum companies and imposed a $5 billion fine on Exxon Corporation and Captain Hazelwood. After collection these monies were to be used to support or recreate livelihoods and pay for property that had been harmed or lost due to the incident. Although Alaska Native fishers were part of this suit, they were not specifically singled out, and there was no way to determine which individuals were entitled to the settlement. With the confusion the litigation was subject to endless wrangling, initiating several more class-action and independent civil suits against the Exxon Corporation. In desperation, frustration, or exhaustion, other Alaska Native communities settled independently.

Few were content with this decision, particularly the affected Native fishers, believing their subsistence lifestyle had been disregarded.[24] When commercial fisheries were compared to subsistence fisheries, the latter were categorized as noneconomic pursuits. The court deemed that the Native fishers had chosen to live there, although their families had occupied the area for hundreds of years, so in essence they got what they got. Obviously, the courts were working within the Western value structure with a total indifference, bordering on disdain, for Native lifeways and the holistic pursuit of fishing and hunting. In sum, when commercial fishers brought home a paycheck, that was quantifiable, but not Natives bringing home dinner.[25]

There were also complaints based on the lack of inclusive Native testimony.[26] The fishers believed that their families should have been able to tell their stories and have these details entered as evidence. But what happened next shocked everyone. The court entered a summary judgment in favor of Exxon, founded on this noneconomic supposition. The court stated, in effect, that a subsistence way of life is not comparable to any constitutional principles or statutes, and arguments to the contrary failed to prove a special injury, as required to bring a private suit, even for a public nuisance. Public nuisance? This disaster had been judicially reduced to a minor annoyance. Places held sacred and marred by oil, such gravesites and other archeological sites, were insignificant, and in the eyes of Native leaders and fishers it was as if the courts were saying that the oil spill barely occurred and never created lasting damage.

There was a challenge to this summary judgment, and evidence was offered to illustrate a lack of proper and in-depth investigation into the matters. Further details were added concerning standard environmental law, including maritime law. The Alaska Environmental Conservation Act (1971) was cited as relevant to the charges of water-pollution standards. The court, however, could not be budged and stood fast in a conviction that no special injury had been proven outside of the already understood public "nuisance"—one of the few positions that had the potential to expose "criminal and civil suits stemming from the 1989 oil spill." While the Ninth Circuit Court acknowledged that the Alaska Native lifestyle had been adversely affected, it was a question of magnitude and not kind. In other words, the Alaska Native fishers, although shut out of their jobs by contaminated waters, were not a special class but in the same boat, so to speak, as other Alaska fishers and harvesters damaged by the spill. Moreover, the Alaska Constitution reinforced that the law must be applied equally, regardless of race, ethnic background, or other like factors.[27] In sum the court deemed there could not be a "special injury" because subsistence was not an extraordinary condition or pursuit, upholding the summary judgment in favor of Exxon and its legal team.[28]

THESE COURT CASES were delightful fodder for newspaper reporters and subject to great debate in Alaska circles, but in the end the Alaska Natives had not fared well. Naturally, they continued their livelihoods the best they could, despite onerous regulations, but the issues did not die until taken up by the highest court in the land in *Exxon Shipping Co. v. Baker* (2008), nineteen years after the spill. To recap in 1994 the jury had returned a verdict that was purportedly to act as a deterrent against environmental negligence in the future by imposing costs and fines on the Exxon corporation in the amount of $5 billion. In 2001 the court of appeals denied both Exxon's and Captain Hazelwood's arguments, but in 2004 Exxon appealed the judgment on the basis that the award had been excessive, and Exxon Corporation did not accept that blame, instigating a petition to the Supreme Court. During the proceedings there was no value placed on subsistence fishing, which was treated more like a casual hobby, nor was there one dime considered for emotional damage.[29] This was a game that favored the wealthy. Environmental justice was allusive and inconsistent. In the end the penalties were reduced from $2.5 billion (from the original $5 billion awarded) to $500 million.

The Alaska public, let alone the incensed fishers, were stunned by the penalty reduction. This was an insult! Anger and protest filled the air against the prejudicial treatment and corporate favoritism. The flames were fueled by the rationale for the decision that was based on an indistinct maritime law from other international cases that did not come close to this disaster and a formula that concluded that Exxon Corporation had already paid punitive damages that should stand for compensation in a 1:1 ratio. These decisions were based on the fact that subsistence fishing had a value of zero, despite expert testimony.[30]

In the Supreme Court's five-to-three decision, written by Justice David Souter, the original award was based on the court's determination that this award more closely fit maritime common law, despite the outcry from national environmental groups and legal experts. The three dissenters—Justices John Paul Stevens, Ruth Bader Ginsburg, and Stephen Breyer—gave insight into what was flawed in this decision by deeming that maritime law was not part of the court's purview and should be left to Congress and that, in this particular case, the blatant negligence by Exxon should have been considered for full recompense to the victims. Justice Ginsburg called the fine reduction egregious. Because of the drastically reduced amount, many *Exxon Valdez* victims believed the corporation went unpunished and that they did not receive a fair recompense.[31] Succinctly, as in the words of one Cordova fisher, it was "a giant cold slap in the face."[32] Years later this Supreme Court case was deemed one of the ten worst Supreme Court decisions in the body's history.

In the end every qualifying fisher, Native and non-Native, was awarded about $15,000 for damages, and even Alaska's state government thought this was unfair but later dropped its district court appeal in 2015, when the principals recognized their arguments were going nowhere. Notwithstanding exhaustive testimony in trials and field studies, the Prince William Sound area remained devastated even after recovery efforts. Quantifying the lasting effects have been the source of many studies, symposiums, and Alaska Native meetings with conflicting views, but in the end the plaintiffs were hard-pressed to present their case to Western courts. Many did not even have the travel expenses to do so, and even if they did have funds, the process was exhausting, with the so-called experts flip-flopping in their opinions on what had occurred and the amount of damage.

For the region this had been a massive change. Suddenly, fishers had to deal with lawyers, politicians, and government officials, while Exxon was working a clever public relations angle, even employing some of the locals to work on the oil-spill restoration. There were a few out of the injured parties who took jobs with Exxon and were accused of working for the enemy. In sardonic terms the business interests suggested the financial cost of the disaster had been mitigated by this employment generated for the spill efforts, churning up the perpetual conflict. The long drawn-out legal process resulted in little satisfaction, even though there were some environmental improvements and cash settlements. For instance, the heavily criticized trust fund had financed the Alutiiq Cultural Center. For the majority, however, they continued to decry the day the waters died.

Regardless of in-fighting and jockeying for control, villages did work together, and many consolidated their efforts to make a difference. Some repairs could be made, while others are undergoing treatment to this day. In this major catastrophe, communal forces were a source of political strength when they were needed, and although the situation was not fully amended nor adequate justice found, there were moments when unified energies broke through bureaucracy and Western courts. "People depended upon each other and upon nature's environment. . . . Human survival depended on cooperation and social relations. . . . The importance of community was vital to societal norms and patterns that developed. . . . Without these moral assumptions the society would disintegrate into a disordered collection of individuals."[33] That is village power.

Today, in the midst of climate change, there are more human-caused environmental disasters, and many places, similar to Prince William Sound, have never got back to business as usual. If one digs deep enough, there is still oil below the surface, and the herring runs have not returned to prespill numbers. Riki Ott, author of *Not One Drop*, took a long, hard look at the *Exxon Valdez* mishap and confirmed that the ecosystem has never fully been restored to good health, and the fishers are hard-pressed to make an adequate living. She largely blames the Supreme Court decision, which did not go far enough, and compares the final award to "ExxonMobil feeling this sting like an elephant feels a mosquito bite." Further, she added that the legal system needs alterations to provide equity "to reflect a shift in priorities from economics to human rights and community values."[34] Other reports indicate that villages have reduced access to their customary ocean base for subsistence, and fishers see no relief efforts. Plainly, as activist Sylvia Lange affirms, any attempts to return to normalcy are merely cosmetic. The scars remain and so does the question: What price are we paying for fossil fuels?[35]

11 Grandmother to Water Guardian

From time immemorial the Ahtna Athabascan have lived in Interior Alaska's Copper River region. Their seminomadic lifestyle included an annual journey to fish camps each year to harvest and put up salmon for the winter, a time when the whole family was together to remember stories and pass on life lessons to the next generation. Young people learned the values of sharing with others and a respect for life within a legacy founded on enduring unwritten laws and mores that have stood the test of time and guided the people through hardships or times of plenty. This cultural bedrock held true through the Russian era, gold-seeking intrusions, and the early settler period. By 1959 the Great Land had become a state, impacting Alaska Natives and their way of life to a greater extent than any other social transformation before this time. Federal and state government authorities expanded the extant territorial natural-resource laws and regulations, imperiling Indigenous customs and subsistence resources. Many of the new rules defied logic, as in the following Ahtna Athabascan clash that pitted Western science against traditional ecological knowledge.

As with many disputes between rural and urban Alaska, neither party understood the sociopolitical stance of the other. Katie John, a traditional Athabascan elder, wholly believed her people's customary fish camp was part of her home. Contrary regulations made no sense. She did not need to speak loudly to command respect, nor was she naive. When the elders' warnings about strangers became a reality, she fought back by defying discriminatory laws, eventually leading to direct conflict with the regulators, attorneys, legislators, and politicians. She had never thought of herself as a guardian, but when the task presented itself, she took up the mantle, and in treasuring the past she fought for the future.

KATIE JOHN TRACED her roots through Mentasta, and even more specifically Batzulnetas, an ancient communal fishing site in the Copper River region. Her father, Charley Sanford, had held a hereditary leadership role in the Batzulnetas village, and his influence extended to nearby villages. His grandson, Fred John Jr., recalls that he was a spiritual man and well regarded in the region, as he traveled as far as the Yukon for trading purposes.[1] The Upper Ahtna villages of Mentasta, Batzulnetas, and Suslota are rich fishing grounds and have supplied families for generations, with enough to share for those unable to do their own hunting and fishing, a tradition that ensured community health. Each May the people gathered in anticipation of the salmon runs. Fishing and preserving food were cooperative affairs, uplifting Ahtna life. The Headwaters people had fished along the Tanada Creek and Copper River for decades and passed on the skills and technology to the next generation, following ancient laws based on respect for the environment and natural conservation measures. When friction came to the region, it was caused by state regulators dismissing ancient ethnoscience, while the Ahtna Athabascan could not believe in a world without it.[2]

Katie John shared her wisdom, letting the landscape be her classroom. She recalled that her own schooling had not involved pencils or paper. Lessons taught by her mother and grandmother were used in everyday life, and she generously shared her knowledge with her fourteen children and six adopted children. The Ahtna's ecological consciousness did not include finite measurements or statistics but rather the promotion of a wholesome relationship with humans, animals, fish, the waterways, and the land. Each generation's task was to guard over this legacy so others may experience this cultural wealth, and given these factors, it is simple to understand how the Natives rejected the imposition of oversight agencies and restrictions on seasonal activities.

In 1964 the Alaska Department of Fish and Game deemed the salmon runs were low in this region and required conservation measures. Consequently, the Johns' traditional fish camp was shut down. Despite the hardship, the people managed the best they could while believing these actions were unfair, until the crisis reached an inflection point. The Ahtna realized nothing would change unless they spoke out, and after thirty years of living in limbo and being denied both fishing access and ancient rights, Katie John and Doris Charles, another revered elder and Katie's longtime friend, combined forces. Both women spoke English as a second language, and state bureaucracy was another entirely foreign language, but they were fueled with outrage based on the affront to their homeland and strangers telling them when and where they could fish.

The women sought venues for speaking their minds, and one can only imagine these unfamiliar arenas must have been intimidating, but the women were supported by the community. They looked for meetings or other social events where they might be heard, even if they had to travel some distance. One can only imagine their determination as they traveled north over 250 miles to have their issues heard by Fish and Game officials in hopes of making a case for overturning "government policies regarding the division of salmon among subsistence, commercial and sport fisheries," all with different rules and disorganized rationales.[3] Once the meeting began, they tackled the scientific terminology that had no basis in Ahtna reality, with terms like *escapement goals* and *sustained yield*. The two cultures were on a collision course, and neither was going to give in.

The women might have guessed this would be a protracted fight, and in the meantime harvesting food sources must continue even if that meant outright civil disobedience. With limited access and use, Batzulnetas had lost some of its former prominence as the economic and spiritual hub of the Upper Ahtna people, particularly after the people relocated to Mentasta to be nearer the schools, but the cultural foundation remained intact despite the disruptions brought on by the fishery regulations. The sacredness of the site was never in question and always maintained by the culture bearers, who visited the old fishing camps to make sure the gravesites were well taken care of, along with other significant markers that served as the history of the people. They often brought young people with them to help and took the time to share the old legends, renewing their bonds with the land and waters even in the midst of controversy.

As we have previously seen, Western government, politicians, and scientists held conflicting definitions on how the resources should be used and managed for maximum benefit. Agencies even quarreled among themselves, but consistently the harvesters' ideas were disregarded, and there was no mention of Native stewardship. Instead, it was more like two different worlds—one belonging to the takers and the other to the caretakers. These tense and fragile conditions lasted for years, while the Natives were shut out of their customary fishery.[4] The people adapted, but the injustice was unbearable, and the Native leaders could not let it go. Filled with frustration, Katie John and Doris Charles attended as many meetings as possible, reiterating their point of view about the fishery closure, but nothing changed. It appeared as if these issues must go before a court. This venue was foreign, and the plaintiffs would have to depend on the promised scales of justice, despite language barriers, confusing scientific charts, and limited political allies in high places. It was a courageous move.

The women were assisted by Native American Rights Fund attorneys, and when they agreed to represent the Ahtna, by extension they were speaking for all Alaska Native people who encountered this maze of issues, including state and federal regulations, often at odds. One of these attorneys, Robert Anderson, was struck by John's strength: "She had an innate leadership quality that affected everybody around her. She was an inspiration to work for."[5] To prepare for the inevitable showdown, the women and their attorneys learned the exact parameters of current legal status and regulations, including reserved lands, navigable waters, and the water-rights doctrine.

Naturally, these expressions were foreign. Navigable waters are those waterways that can be traversed by vessels, although the type of vessels is open in its definition. The stipulations and applications stem from the U.S. Constitution, specifically the Commerce Clause (article 1, section 8), which protects water bodies for ship travel and cargo delivery. The water-rights doctrine stated that the person or group who first used the water was entitled to its continued use, although it gave preference to agriculture or business pursuits. Subsistence alone did not fit because it could not be quantified monetarily. One can imagine how Katie John and Doris Charles might have been perplexed when they looked at their fishing site and Mentasta Lake, knowing this place was never going to see ship travel or agricultural pursuits.

Summarily, navigable waters favored commerce, and the water-rights doctrine sheltered those engaging in profitable pursuits, leaving Native lifeways without a slot. Ahtna plaintiffs were baffled by how a simple matter had been bound by red tape—that it was prejudicial in their eyes was an understatement.[6] For Alaska's unique circumstances, there needed to be a legally defined foundation and precedent that addressed subsistence activities, and that was the moment when the Alaska National Interest Lands Conservation Act (ANILCA) played an integral role. Even after ANCSA was settled, there was a stipulation that certain lands must be set aside as permanent undeveloped wilderness or otherwise protected areas for conservation purposes. This requirement was implemented when President Jimmy Carter signed ANILCA, and consequently, about eighty million acres of land were reserved as national-interest lands. Almost immediately there were problems with this legislation, because it divided prime hunting areas, fishing grounds, and sacred cultural sites, leaving questions about use and ownership between Natives and non-Natives.[7] The most controversial issue concerned the so-called D (2), named for the position in ANILCA legislation, which referred to areas set aside for public parks, wildlife regions, and scenic rivers. These designated locations were also traditional hunting and fishing sites—now off-limits.

Subsistence rights must be decided—there was a renewed sense of urgency—and the answer was also found within ANILCA. The legislation had a subsistence preference clause, establishing that Native hunters and fishers had first-user rights, increasing the inevitable jurisdictional competition between the state, federal government, and Native corporations and setting up a turf war. As if there were not enough opposing forces, the ecology groups clamored for Alaska to remain unblemished in perpetuity, with no fishing and hunting.[8] The naive activists, living in Tennessee or California, had no idea of Alaska realities and could be ignored, but the federal government could not be pushed aside.

When Alaska became a state, the federal government enacted the Alaska State Act, which allowed the nascent government to select lands. The final selections were often prime Alaska Native subsistence lands or sacred lands, and no legislation had addressed aboriginal title. In addition, powerful sports-lobby groups and independent Alaskans were against any federal legislation, because it appeared to tighten the federal yoke on what they believed was fair access to their land and other resources. Matters worsened when it was mandated, through ANILCA, that rural Alaska residents (not necessarily Natives) were to be given a priority status for subsistence fishing and hunting on public lands before commercial or sports activities, although the details for implementing this priority were vague and left water bodies or fishing grounds in contention. Alaskans, imbued with a frontier spirit, demanded impartial and equal treatment—rural preference seemed biased. And the debate entered round two.

As if there were not already enough controversy, a tumultuous dichotomy between the federal government and the state government was exacerbated based on divergent philosophies and expected fiduciary responsibility. The state government, referencing the Alaska Constitution, believed it was its duty to apply the law, benefits, and resource access uniformly among all Alaska residents, while the federal government acted as an umbrella for minority rights in tandem with a long-established trust relationship toward American Natives.[9] Katie John and others named in the eventual lawsuit found themselves caught in the middle of these legal and constitutional divisions, while the natural resource agencies added to the chaos.

While Fish and Game regulators were assessing what was best for the resources, factions intensified "between those who argued that the cornerstone of any democratic regime is the principle of individual rights and those who take the view that at least some political rights . . . belong to a community or culture."[10] Newspaper headlines were ablaze with accusations of the unfairness to hunters and tourists, while others argued that the first people of Alaska should have the right to their traditional fishery. Typical was one such headline that read: "Grandmother Katie Prevails over State of Alaska on Subsistence Fishing Rights."[11] The legal drama tested the tenets of the Alaska Constitution and its judicial interpretation pitted against the U.S. Constitution and its minority protections. As events unfolded, the question was posed: Who has the ultimate power to regulate resources? All the while the Ahtna Athabascan could not understand what all the fuss was about because the "truth" was plain to see—their village had fished at this site for generations, and these imposed restrictions only muddied the waters. To the Ahtna plaintiffs, this was like watching two ptarmigans facing off with raised feathers and menacing beaks, but in the end one bird was going to have to walk away. For the time being, however, Katie John and her fish wheel remained blocked from harvesting fish as the long winter approached.

IN 1985 A lawsuit compelled the state to open the Batzulnetas fishery and to modify existing policies to permit a limited fishery with a subsistence preference, but in 1989 the ruling was challenged in the Alaska Supreme Court through *McDowell v. Alaska*. This lawsuit was based on the principle that all Alaska residents, regardless of ethnic background or traditional resource use, are allowed equivalent access to harvesting sites. Special privileges for rural subsistence fishery were struck down because such actions would be contrary to the Alaska Constitution and discriminate against urban Alaskans. *McDowell v. Alaska* stated, "The grant of special privileges with respect to game based on one's residence violates provisions of Alaska's constitution that guarantees all Alaskans equal access.... However, the court upholds the state's rights to grant subsistence users priority and further requires that criteria other than just place of residence might be constitutional."[12] In a state where almost all the lands are located in rural areas, this was difficult to administer, and in real terms nothing changed. Katie John and her family maintained that they were morally allowed to continue fishing, but when they attempted to do so, they were harassed by Fish and Game agents and forced to conduct their activities covertly in an act of civil disobedience.

A political hornet's nest had been stirred—one side wanted a state constitutional amendment to establish a rural preference clause to align with federal requirements, and the other side wanted the federal government out of their business. In response the federal government used its full force, warning they would halt state management on federal land if there was no compliance. Often the Old West mentality characterizes the Last Frontier, and right on cue Alaska residents rejected special treatment for any group or more government tentacles in their life. In 1992 the issue was once again fought out in the courts.

In *McDowell v. United States*, the scene was set for contentious testimony. At the conclusion the federal district court upheld ANILCA's rural preference, deeming the circumstances met the equal-protection standards under the U.S. Constitution, and since the fundamental power to delineate the legal users resides with Congress, states' rights were unimpaired in this particular case.[13] All this haggling and semantic splitting no doubt employed many lawyers and lobby groups, but it did nothing for Katie John's family and their traditional fish camp, so she renewed her fighter spirit and returned to court.

In 1994 the legal case titled *Katie John v. United States* exposed several jurisdictional issues for the Native plaintiffs but also for non-Natives living in rural communities. Both groups were dependent on local resources. At the conclusion of these proceedings, consideration was given to two new categories: non-Native rural residents and urban Native residents who could prove that subsistence was part of their history. The federal district court ruled, "For purposes of Title VIII (ANILCA) public lands include all navigable waterways in Alaska and that it is consistent with the Congressional purpose and policy of ANILCA that the Secretary [Bruce Babbitt] regulated subsistence fishing in navigable waters."[14]

Since the Ahtna fish camp was on federal navigable waters, the U.S. constitutional protection was justified, and in additional analysis it was concluded that Title VIII "acted as a treaty" to restore hunting and fishing rights that had been extinguished by ANCSA. That was a huge victory. Katie John's fishing spot was now protected under a federal canopy, upholding minority rights and using these circumstances to override states' rights. Ironically, the confusion over navigable waters located in traditional Native land worked in the Athabascan's favor, but a large segment of the non-Native population would not stand for this conclusion, even if did not affect them directly. Based on a jingoistic argument, a growing faction believed their rights had been stomped on and demanded an appeal.

When the issue was heard again before a judicial body, additional clarification was reached through *State of Alaska v. Bruce Babbit*, when the federal district court ruled (in consolidation with the *Katie John* case, sometimes called Katie John II) that, even though Congress had not spelled out everything for the Alaska circumstances, the policy and purpose were clear in intention.

The secretary of the interior rather than the State of Alaska possessed the ultimate authority to manage fish and wildlife on federal public lands under ANILCA.[15] But the turbulence persisted, and Alaska was divided by support or opposition to rural preference, while the U.S. Supreme Court refused to consider further appeals.

Ignoring all the commotion, Katie John, Doris Charles, and the residents of Mentasta resumed their traditional fish camp activities by putting up fish for their families, believing everything had finally been settled. But in reality the issues had not been resolved, and the controversy hung in the air, until Katie John found that she still needed to defend her way of life and fishing rights against the critics. The nature of her fight was made clear during a 1996 discussion before the Board of Fisheries in Cordova, located in the Prince William Sound area, about fifty miles along the Copper River Highway. In a heated argument, the commercial fishers disputed the *Katie John* ruling. Many at this gathering did not realize that Katie John was sitting in the crowd listening to the fishery reports and the grumbling of the commercial fishers. Later she commented that these folks had twisted the history, because it was actually the newcomers, all the way back to the gold seekers who had intruded on Ahtna land. It was their activities that should be controlled as a moral imperative. She was careful with her message, knowing the power words have once spoken, yet offered a compelling message as she defended her fish wheel: "The Copper River . . . this is my life, this is where I was raised from the fish. The fish is our life. That's the way it's been for a long time ago. We don't waste them. We take care of our food." She then questioned the chain of events that had led to this moment: "We had big salmon, that kind of salmon we used to have, just wanted to find out what happened," turning the matter of proper conservation back to the fish managers. In essence Katie John was convinced these oversight agencies should be offering her some answers.[16]

IN 2000 THE Ninth Circuit Court of Appeals reaffirmed the federal government control over state-owned subsistence hunting and fishing areas adjacent to or within federal lands. After the court reviewed the evidence, the conclusion was cemented: federal control had more legal backing than the state, based largely on the tenets of ANILCA. Faced with this news and after deliberation, the State of Alaska initially declined to appeal the case to the Supreme Court, but the battle lines did not disappear. Many Alaskan residents were angry and accused the federal government of exceeding its limits and debasing individual rights, including access to resources that many felt were held in common by all citizens. This hot topic filtered into a series of Alaska governor races, with questions concerning the extent of federal control, resource rights, and potential unequal treatment of Alaska's citizens. Governor Walter Hickel boasted that Alaska would secede from the union, while Steve Cowper, later governor of Alaska, likened the situation to an absolute nightmare, as commercial and sports fishers cried favoritism.[17]

By this time Walter Hickel, author of the prodevelopment user-state philosophy, was the governor of Alaska, and he predicted the resolution had two ways to go. It could be either a peaceful Alaska or one torn apart by bitterness and violence.[18] In the middle of this tempest, Katie John stood her ground, with an agenda based on feeding her family and nourishing a healthy community—an atmosphere that had been undermined by restrictive laws. The controversy stayed current, but the final legal case was upheld, despite impassioned words at fishery board meetings and in newspaper editorials. When Tony Knowles was elected governor, he was confronted with an issue that Alaska residents would not let die. He had inherited the calls to appeal the *Katie John* decision, and he agonized over trying to do the right thing. He understood he must govern for all Alaska residents but was sympathetic toward cultural survival and saw it as a genuine right. In real terms he found himself in a no-win situation. Depending on what choices he made, he would alienate one or more of Alaska's polarized constituencies. In the beginning he had announced his intention to contest the *Katie John* ruling in 2000, which he called his "clear responsibility," placing him at odds with the Native community, while the sports hunting groups called him a hero.[19] But Katie John would not give up the good fight, and she understood what her "clear responsibility" must be as well.

Governor Knowles was torn in two from the beginning. He did not know if he wanted to pursue the case in the Supreme Court to make a statement about states' rights or if he wanted to settle the matter on a smaller scale. Public opinion was already vilifying him for his hesitancy, and he was concerned that his actions could come back to haunt him or that he might appear inconsistent if he changed his mind. From other corners Native American Rights Fund attorney Heather Kendall-Miller did not mince words: "If Knowles appeals, the Native community will forever walk away from him, and he will have no political future in the state."[20] This was no idle threat.

Alaska has the highest percentage of Indigenous peoples per capita when compared to any other state, and the Native vote was important to any politician. The Alaska Federation of Natives, an organization formed in the 1960s to seek land claims, was a significant body, and their endorsement was widely sought by those who wanted to score big at the ballot box. Several pundits and Native leaders were convinced that Knowles had been elected to his position in part by the endorsement of the federation, but now he was facing backlash from both sides. Opponents of rural preference were crying foul and intimating that if the governor did not follow through on his initial promises, he was kowtowing to special interests. Taking these factors together, the governor had to consider whether he followed the mandates of ANILCA, appeased the fishing and hunting sports groups, or acted out of ethical concerns for Alaska Native cultures. To add to his woes, the federal government had made good on its promise (or threat) to take over the management of Alaska's federal lands because of Alaska's failure to enact a constitutional amendment, guaranteeing rural hunting and fishing preference. What would be his next move? Should he appeal?

Governor Knowles had come to office on a strong platform of shaking off the state's colonial status in the hopes of regaining an authoritative stance over the land, waters, and resources in opposition to the perceived domination of federal authorities. Yet to be successful, Knowles needed Native support, but what he was proposing went against those priorities. As the Dena'ina Athabascan attorney Kendall-Miller emphasized, "If the state takes the appeal, it would be seen as an act that is directly hostile to the Alaska Native way of life."[21] Katie John understood Knowles's political dilemma and figured the governor's mansion in Juneau was no place for him to make an important decision. Although she was a fierce fighter, she also had a kind heart and believed she could show him the right path through hospitality, so she invited him to her home. Knowles accepted and went to Batzulnetas to get a firsthand view of the issue, including the importance of the salmon water bodies to the people. After meeting with Katie John, Knowles recalled the elder in these terms: "Her strength was apparent as she described how she had raised and fed 20 children . . . in the old customary and traditional subsistence practices that she learned from her parents." Kendall-Miller confirmed this point: "She was determined that her children and grandchildren would carry on those practices as well."[22] The cultural preeminence of Ahtna family values, extending to the next generation, could not be ignored or deferred.

In real terms Katie John had offered the governor an education in Native ways that transported him away from the political pressures and the restrictive confines of Western legal tradition. There was an uncompromising authenticity when on the waters. Firsthand teachings worked well, because afterward the governor remarked, "I learned more that day than is written in all of the boxes of legal briefs in this long lasting court battle."[23] And it was enough information for Governor Knowles to roll over his thinking and make some tough choices for the future of Alaska.

Knowles weighed history and established standards in an effort to bridge the great dissension between the law and Native rights. Later he said his decisions had even surprised himself. Upon returning to Juneau, he called Katie John to inform her that he would not pursue the appeal. Knowles acknowledged that "we must stop a losing strategy that threatens to make a permanent divide among Alaskans. I cannot continue to oppose in court what I know in my heart to be right."[24] From a political vantage point, this was a daring move for the governor. Many were stunned by his shifting gears, but in the end his attitude had been permanently changed by going fishing with Katie John.

THE LEGAL BATTLE did not stop here. In 2005 Native American Rights Fund attorneys pursued the case further, representing Katie John as she challenged the federal government's definition of boundaries, protected waters, and the relationship to ANILCA lands. For example, an upstream designation would allow the Athabascan to fish in a more favorable location, and John emphasized this area had to be protected since it was important for spawning salmon and the continued lifecycle. This was the people's usual and customary site for finding the richest salmon. Moreover, John also brought up the fact that many Alaska Natives owned homesteads, and these pieces of land and accompanying waterways were not included under the current regulations, whether state or ANILCA.[25] Waterways located on homestead lands should rightfully be the property of the owner and protected as such.[26] When John went back to court in 2005, she did so because she believed the previous rulings had been too limited and neglected genuine title to places that were homes and hunting and fishing areas. In her view federal agencies should have sheltered those Alaska Native allotments as public lands with the appropriate legislation.[27] Yet nothing was immediately resolved, and instead this particular debate was left in abeyance.[28]

KATIE JOHN DIED in mid-2013, but Alaska continues to remember her courage and tenacity. Ahtna corporation president Michelle Anderson recalled, "She lived what she believed. If not for Katie John and her fighter spirit, we would not have the subsistence rights we are still fighting to retain today." Current Alaska senator Lisa Murkowski described Katie John as a piece of Alaska's soul and went on to say, "She was unafraid to challenge any bureaucrat standing between her Native people and their opportunity to fish, whether that was the State of Alaska . . . or a National Park Ranger."[29] She showed the Alaska Native population they possessed political brawn and could take their case all the way to the Supreme Court. Today Katie John stands as an icon for the Alaska Native subsistence cause and the traditional way of living, and her legal efforts have evolved into an ideological fortress for the protection of hunting and fishing rights for future generations based on a reverence for Indigenous values. Her legacy was formally solidified when the state legislature designated May 31 as "Katie John Day."

12 Fishing for Fines on the Kuskokwim River

A mixture of outrage and anguish rang out across the tundra that June day. Women ran out of their houses to see what was going on, gathering along the banks of the Kuskokwim River. Akiak fishers were out harvesting salmon to preserve for the winter, to give to the elders, and to share at celebrations—the fish cops stopped them. Many may not have been aware of fishing restrictions, and for those who were aware, it didn't matter. One young man had been out on the waters with his grandfather's net. He treasured it, and it was even more special because he was fishing for the elders. That is the way it is—the young ones take care of the old ones.

Within moments the Fish and Game agents had cut the net and spilled out the catch into their boat, slashing through the fisher's heart. He cried out that he was fishing for his *apa*, his grandfather: "What have you done to this net? Ah man, you didn't have to do that to the net. That's my grandfather's net." In this confrontation the fish cops had all the power, as they cut the net strands with military precision, which was all too appropriate, for this was a fish war.

EVERY YEAR THE villages in southwest Alaska watch for the changing seasons, and each cycle is respected and revered for its bounty. Summer is the time for fish camp, when families gather together to put up fish for the long winter. The elders recall years when king salmon were not plentiful, and caution was observed to sustain the people and the resource. That was the life cycle, the Yupiaq way, maintained through the good years and the bad ones. This natural law of conservation had been carried from generation to generation through oral literature and necessity. There are no fancy grocery stores in southwest Alaska villages, and the people are dependent on the land and water, yet it is a rich existence that revolves around a holistic worldview. Spiritually, the animals give themselves to the people if proper reverence is shown, and in this socioeconomic world villages along the mighty Kuskokwim River flourish when successful hunters and fishers share with other families, thereby preserving the genuine wealth of the people.

These ancient traditions were maintained for thousands of years, until federal oversight agencies arrived with their science and legal measurements to quantify moose, caribou, fish, and other animals that the Yup'ik and other Native peoples have never distinguished by finite numbers. When the U.S. Department of Fish and Wildlife and later, in 1960, the Alaska Department of Fish and Game (ADFG) applied their facts, data, and restrictions on this immemorial system, the troubles escalated between Alaska Natives and the government in a continuance of a long and embittered past that was all too familiar.

For many years Alaska's natural resources went undiscovered, and in fact the territory was often neglected. The land, seas, and coastline are massive, and there was no patrol bureau that could manage the expanse. Through the Russian period, the ten-year military sojourn, and even into the civil government times, the fish, timber, and precious metals were unencumbered by a bureaucratic thumb or other restrictions until the Bureau of Fish and Wildlife stepped in and began the enumeration of animals and plants according to Western guidelines. That is not to say there were no previous disturbances to the natural balance. Before 1867 there had been a number of interlopers and entrepreneurs benefiting from the wild, unregulated territory, but it was nothing like the U.S. governmental agencies and sanctioned resource barons, whose activities greatly impacted these sovereign people by imposing their own political and legal systems. There were many newly arrived businesspeople who considered tapping the bounty as an immutable right, and there was no one to stop them. It took Alaska becoming a state to shine the light on the out-of-control industrial fishing, timber cutting, and mineral extracting.

In 1960, when the Alaska Department of Fish and Game took over fishery management, the agents wanted to establish their presence and authority, which included inserting the "new science" and discounting Native ethnoscience. It did not take long for the fish cops to build up a reputation for a prejudicial and ad-hoc management style, generating crises and butting heads with Native fishers in ecological conflicts. Policies were created in an office setting and based on computer models that diverged from the realities on the waters and the needs of the villagers, who had lived on *nuna* (the land) for generations, passing on the wisdom and lore to the next generation. Despite the interference, traditional leadership remained strong and able to resolve predicaments though the maze of statistics, escapement counts, and conjectures about the future.[1] In an air of superiority, the ADFG refused to compromise, similar to what the Hoonah fishers had encountered in the 1970s.

IN JUNE 2012, based on projected low escapement, the ADFG announced a temporary closure for king salmon harvesting on the Kuskokwim River. There had been closures before, affecting the people's fishing needs, but this time it meant that Kuskokwim fishers would face additional hardships because they would not be allowed to put up fish for the winter. The people had depended on king salmon for decades, and families would go without, including the elders who had been promised fresh fish. The closure was poorly publicized, but for those who had heard about the restrictions, there were the usual grumblings and objections but no panic because the closure was only for seven days. The fishers resolved to wait it out, although they opposed the ADFG assessment that salmon stocks and escapement numbers were low, but they realized they were powerless against this emergency order, and it was better not to further roil the waters. The brief respite did not stop the fishers from readying their boats and stowing gear, anticipating the upcoming fishing season. They waited for word of the opening for seven long days and then found out the closure had been extended. This was too much! The carefully preserved threshold of tolerance disintegrated into shards.

Not only was civil disobedience advocated, but there was talk of outright violence. The elders, as ever-present leaders, stepped in with their sage words and reminded the angry fishers of the Yupiaq way and the ancient law. Aggressive behavior would hurt the entire village, yet practicing nonconfrontational manners under these inequitable conditions was unbearable. Who were these agents daring to tell us about the river? Then, perhaps noting the foreseeable suffering, the elders reversed their initial words and urged the fishers to go out and get those king salmon for their families in direct violation of the state's mandate. The fishers were to observe strict caution. Yes, the elders wanted peace and realized the trouble these actions might bring, but this was an emergency and ultimately a moral imperative.

The Yup'ik fishers were aware of past civil disobedience episodes. One of the most outstanding examples involved the protest against the 1916 Migratory Bird Treaty with Mexico and Canada, which had made it illegal to hunt birds in the spring, based on conservation measures. This restraint caused hard times for people coming out of a long winter with dwindling food supplies—spring had been the prime time for Alaska Native hunting. Yet the treaty stated that fall was the only acceptable hunting season to preserve migrating birds, many of whom had already flown south. Civil disobedience against these restrictions was on full display when duck hunters, including Charlie Edwardsen Jr., harvested birds out of season. Afterward they turned themselves and the birds in to authorities, overwhelming the system to the point that all poaching offenses were ignored, and the hunters were told to go home. This event was referred to as the great duck-in, and news spread throughout Alaska, with the help of the *Tundra Times*. Years later, along the Kuskokwim River, the fishers possessed a similar rebellious spirit, compelling them to strike out for environmental justice.[2]

In many ways the nature of the protest was comparable to what had occurred among the Pacific Northwest tribes, who believed that the treaty signed by Governor Isaac Stevens in 1854 guaranteed them a certain percentage of the salmon and steelhead trout before other users.[3] Billy Frank Jr., of the Nisqually Tribe, had risen to what would become a legendary role by way of the 1964 fish-ins on his property at Frank's landing. His protest cast a light on broken treaties and promises that circumvented "the right of taking fish at all usual and accustomed grounds and stations . . . secured to said Indians in common with all citizens of the Territory."[4] In the rush to open land for settlers, tribal rights had been ignored, while the villages were surreptitiously moved out of the area to make more room for the inevitable settler colonialism. At the signing the governor had assumed the "Indians" would never have enough leverage to cause concern. Pioneer spirit would override any of their complaints, but it was only a matter of time.[5]

That is the way it unfolded in the Pacific Northwest, until the fisheries were in critical distress. To gain access to a limited harvest, more treaty tribes staged more fish-ins, and the protests were no longer in Oregon but had spread to Washington state. Numerous arrests were made until the Native fishers had their day in court. They were backed by celebrities such as Dick Gregory and Marlon Brando to add more news coverage to the "Indian plight" and, correspondingly, the arrests turned into a public relations nightmare for officials. These disputes were ended in the 1970s, when it was decided that tribal fishers had the same right to fishery access as sports and commercial fishers. This fight and the victory inspired other Native fishers, including those in Alaska.[6]

Mike Williams, fisher, hunter, Iditarod dog musher, author, and influential leader in the southwest Yup'ik village, lives in Akiak. For many years he had admired Billy Frank Jr. and his efforts. After several conversations with him, Williams attempted to adapt that philosophy to Alaska fishing limitations. Since there were no treaties in Alaska, the problem had to be approached from a different angle. Minor impromptu protests had occurred before without resolution, but in 2012 it appeared that the long-awaited showdown was at hand. Fishery agents had already anticipated the resistance and waited for the right moment to make an example of the closure opponents. In the past a blind eye may have been turned, but this time the agents were armed with reports documenting the depleted salmon runs, and they were ready to crack down, leading to the scene where fishers were arrested, their nets destroyed, and their harvest confiscated, while women on the shore screamed at the fish cops.

This incident continued to deteriorate when the fishers were castigated in the courts, largely due to lack of knowledge about judicial procedure and legal language. U.S. laws are not easily translatable into subsistence fishing needs, and the court's terminology was worlds apart from the Yup'ik view in scope, meaning, and priorities.[7] When the hearings opened, the fishers pleaded innocence—they said they were unaware of such laws, and they were not criminals. It was a practical matter. They needed to provide for their families, and manufactured numbers were not more important than the directives from the elders. In the end the Yup'ik fishers could not convince the court that state and federal officials were wrong for seizing twenty-one nets and 1,100 pounds of salmon from them as an enforcement measure. Arguing was futile—the decision appeared to be preconceived, and there was no recourse. Instead, the fishers regrouped to figure out how they could avoid jail time.

IN THIS PARTICULAR episode, most of the attention was focused on the fishers from Akiak, a small Yup'ik village along the lower Kuskokwim River in southwest Alaska. Historically, the Moravian missionaries were the first major non-Native group in the area and had built a school, church, and eventually a reindeer station. Regardless of the newcomers, most customs remained the same out of necessity, and this included harvesting fish for those who could no longer fish for themselves, while the young looked toward the older ones for guidance. That is why when Akiak chief Ivan M. Ivan declared that the ADFG practices were wrong, the fishers listened. He remarked, "This enforcement practice toward our tribal citizens is totally inhumane, as the elders have stated. It is violating our basic human rights as first peoples of this land and first protectors of our resources."[8] His words illustrated that not only had their right to fish been usurped but also stewardship duties, which are part of the holistic circle of life. Fishers' duty is to harvest for their family's needs and protect the resource for future generations. With governmental interference, however, the role of caretakers had been taken from the Native fishers and placed with agencies, who in truth struggled to understand the Kuskokwim River. The agency's actions also placed limitations on the people's sovereignty, which they believed was their inherent right.[9] Above all, any mismanagement of the king salmon runs was blamed on outsiders, who had broken the rhythm of the land and waters and the proper code for living, socially, economically, and spiritually. This, in the view of the Akiak fishers, was the real threat to the continuance of healthy fish runs.[10]

THE FISHERS WERE angry that they were treated as criminals. The seizure and waste of salmon stung. The community was greatly impacted by the loss of fish and imposed fines, generating a food-security emergency with no relief in sight. This was a region with some of the lowest incomes in the nation, and fishing was their job. The resentment was strong, based on the belief among the Yup'ik that this incident could have been nipped in the bud if the ADFG and federal authorities had not ignored the previous and almost unanimous vote by the Kuskokwim Management Working Group, an advisory citizens' group for the ADFG, which had resolved to open the fishery after the seven-day closure. If this had been heeded, there would have been no problem, but the delay was too much to cope with, "and tribal leaders across Alaska called the government decision to extend the river closure by an additional five days a violation of trust and a threat to sovereign fishing rights."[11] Again Akiak chief Ivan M. Ivan was adamant that this crisis demanded the fishers and villages rise up in protest and use all their political clout to turn this around.

By working at the local level, the Tribal Council gave their word that they would work to protect "our resources and our land as we have done for over 10,000 years."[12] "We have done this because there were many people from the river who stated that they did not have any fish yet hanging for drying on their racks." This was not sports fishing or the dreaded catch and release that some Natives have compared to playing with food, but instead survival. Ivan added, "The elders have directed their fishermen to fish without any fear of breaking laws. It is just common sense that they have been taught by the great teachers before others showed up."[13] And before commercial fisheries and canneries arrived, the Kuskokwim River had flowed from a time before human memory, teeming with salmon and stretching from the Bering Sea, 702 miles to the headwaters of Mount Denali. The question centered on who or what force was responsible for the resource depletion, but at this time these deep questions had to be put aside for immediate crisis, including a court trial.

In October 2012 the alleged violators pleaded their cases in a packed and emotional Bethel courtroom. In back-to-back cases, Alaska state court judge Bruce Ward ruled against three Alaska Native fishers whose defense had been that they did not realize the closure had been in effect at the time. The judge was not impressed with this defense, condemning them with "reckless ignorance" for not consulting the latest news to learn the fishing status. The conflict escalated because of the judge's misunderstanding of rural conditions. Communications and media access were problematic, and posted restrictions were not without challenges. Several fishers spoke and understood English only as their second language, and some of the elders did not use English at all. As the cross-cultural encounter grew more hostile, the fishers rebelled against the court system that tried to define their lives in foreign terms.

The three initial fishers were found guilty of fishing violations and received fines ranging from $350 to $500, which the judge considered a light fine, but in an area where the median income is considered poverty level by government standards, this was a great expense. The money was needed to maintain efficient fishing gear and net repair, including the one that had been destroyed by the fishery agents in the incident. The fishers were also subjected to probation, which acted as a degrading paternalistic gesture and a further erosion of cultural esteem.

The defendants' attorney worked to strike a bargain, and in the end the state reduced the charges to violations, taking the offenses out of the criminal system, but not before national attention had been drawn to the ethics involved. By decriminalizing the offenses, it also made Judge Bruce Ward the sole authority on the guilt or innocence of the violators, not a jury of their peers, and the judge held everyone accountable for state regulations, whether they were knowledgeable or not.[14] In this instance agency science prevailed over Yup'ik customs, history, and needs, yet there was hope this situation might be approached from a different angle to arrive at a more equitable conclusion. The question was if the court had adequate knowledge of Fish and Game rules, Native culture, and the realities of the ecosystem.

The court case brought up some complicated points concerning subsistence rights. In 1980 the Alaska National Interest Lands Conservation Act (ANILCA) was signed into law after years of wrangling about the specifics. Within this act, in addition to protecting natural areas of wild and scenic rivers and wildlife refuges, there was also a clause protecting Alaska Native subsistence rights, as we have seen in the Katie John case. Title VIII of ANILCA replaces aboriginal hunting and fishing rights that were extinguished by ANCSA, thus supporting Native endeavors, but creates an inconsistency between the federal government's fiduciary responsibility toward minorities versus states' rights. Back in 2002 these very contentions and arguments were outlined during a Committee on Indian Affairs meetings, when Loretta Bullard of the northwest Kawerak region declared, "Nothing—not the US Constitution, not the 1867 purchase of Alaska from Russia, not the Statehood Act, not ANCSA, and certainly not ANILCA, gives the majority urban society in Alaska the moral or legal right to destroy the very foundation of our culture."[15] To the Yup'ik, fishing was more than harvesting salmon; it was integral to the culture, and oversight agencies could not see this with their blinders on. There was also distrust of the officials and their fish-counting techniques, plus charges of favoritism toward non-Natives.[16]

As regards ANILCA, Mike Williams did not believe the protective elements of the legislation have been effectively applied to the Native fishers' case. He based his reasoning on the history of government involvement and further stated that Alaska Native sovereignty is innate, and this aspect was not being upheld on the waters or in courts, which created a vital need to recognize aboriginal hunting and fishing privileges.[17] In brief the Yup'ik community wanted state constitutional amendments that restored their apparently lapsed sovereign rights.[18]

Mike Williams and other fishers had allies. The Alaska Federation of Natives president Julie Kitka wrote to the then governor Sean Parnell asking for clemency for the fishers, but all appeals were referenced back to the courts.[19] In other words, Alaska's executive branch indicated this matter was out of their jurisdiction and only within the purview of the judicial system, avoiding a conflict of interest between government branches. These inactions and decisions followed a long trend that had started over one hundred years ago for either overriding or ignoring the rights and claims of Indigenous peoples. The court may have thought the matter was concluded, but the fishers did not.

Mike Williams continued to speak out about the discrimination Native fishers experience throughout the Yukon-Kuskokwim Delta, and he was not alone in this fight. Harry David of Tuntululiak had been fishing when troopers pulled his boat over. He was accused of having a net with the wrong size mesh. His defense: "My nieces and nephews were looking forward to eating fresh fish. I didn't know I was breaking the law." Another fisher from the same village, Adolph Lupie, didn't make any more headway when he testified, "I thought I had the right to fish out there until I got the citation. Subsistence is my way of life. It's the Yup'ik way of life."[20] For the Native fishers' defense, this was an existential crisis, and two opposing systems were on a collision course. During the proceedings the violations were compared to driving rules, and Lupie responded that villages do not have stop signs. To many onlookers this was a classic case of the dominant culture imposing their environmental laws on Alaska Native villages, traffic laws and all.[21]

As time dragged on without resolution or fresh fish, anger simmered, and the accused fishers were determined not to give up. Yet doubts started to creep in about resolution methods and what direction was best. All were positive, however, that citations and court appearances would not discourage the Yup'ik fishers from living in their customary style as part of their traditional cosmology and Yup'ik religion.[22] Mike Williams called fish camp their church. Religion or spirituality can be defined in many ways, and it is not only a matter of attending church or a synagogue but rather the ethics and principles embodied within a people that give meaning to life. According to Yup'ik mores, the group is more important than the individual. Those lucky in their harvesting share with the community, and these principles had been obstructed by fish cops and the natural-resource regulation system.

THE FREEDOM OF religion, as defined by the Alaska and U.S. Constitutions, turned out to be a strong defense. After attorneys presented the fishing case under this new scrutiny, the Alaska Supreme Court was called on to look at First Amendment rights, the fishers' protest of the closure, and the validity of the arrests on religious grounds. Ultimately, the convictions were appealed based on the justification that the Yup'ik fishers have "a spiritual right to fish for king salmon when restrictions are in place based on a free exercise clause of the Alaska Constitution." It was, therefore, the state's responsibility to manage the salmon in a way that did not infringe on this right. The final ruling was based on the wording in the Alaska Constitution, specifically article 1, section 4, which states, "No law shall be made respecting an establishment of religion or prohibiting the free exercise thereof." For a time it looked like clear sailing, until Judge Ward, though appearing sympathetic to the religious appeal, concluded that state management supersedes any constitutional interpretations. What? How could this be? This meant, in essence, that fish counters were more important than the state constitution. Seeing that the legal path was strewn with boulders, the defendants searched for precedents.[23]

Several former cases were used to support an Indigenous religion defense, but the most emblematic was based on an Athabascan hunter, Carlos Frank. In 1979 he had been accused of transporting a moose over restricted grounds. He had killed the moose for a memorial potlatch, a ritual community affair that honors deceased members of the village one year after their death. This had been going on for hundreds of years and surely much longer than ADFG regulations for moose harvesting and transportation. The lower courts upheld Frank's conviction, but when it went to the Alaska Supreme Court, the charges were dismissed because the court deemed that the moose harvest was comparable to Christian sacraments.[24] Specifically, the Athabascan right of hunting the moose was valid based on the American Indian Religious Freedom Act (1978), which protected sacred sites, rituals, and consecrated objects. This legal case set a mighty precedent, leading to a 1994 state constitutional amendment to include the transport of goods or other materials for religious purposes as defensible under the law.

The Yup'ik fishers did not see any difference between that case and theirs, despite the argument that a potlatch event is a one-time affair, where the annual subsistence harvest is a continuing need. The fishers remained convinced that government regulations interfered with their social and religious freedoms and looked to the wording in the American Indian Religious Freedom Act for support in taking fish, concluding that Indigenous customs were "an integral part of their culture, traditions, heritage and practices, forming the basis of Indian identity and value systems."[25] According to these principles, if the government impeded on subsistence fishing, they were infringing on religious rights.

As in so many different situations, there was confusion in definitions, philosophies, and cultural belief systems that persisted, making the waters roil. If the judicial system had taken the time, they would have more fully understood these differences. Religion was not necessarily about church attendance or Bible readings but rather a holistic cosmology or *ellam yua* (the way of the universe). The creator provides king salmon for the people in a natural cycle—to ignore this generosity is an affront. Based on these ancient precepts, an amicus brief from the American Civil Liberties Union was filed, explaining this situation as an example of "collaborative reciprocity between hunter and game," integral to the changing seasons. Without this balance life becomes irretrievably disrupted, and it may have already begun. The elders spoke of how the landscape had changed in recent years, and the Kuskokwim River was no longer the same because of environmental transformations that were out of their control. In one man's words, it was not their fault that "global warming had killed their God."[26]

During the trial it was said that "if Yup'ik people do not fish for King Salmon, the King Salmon spirit will be offended and it will not return to the river."[27] This philosophical premise extends to the stewardship role and parallels what anthropologist Ann Fienup-Riordan noted many years back. The oversight agencies manage fish as if they are a finite resource, but to the Yup'ik they are infinite, as long as the proper ritual is maintained. If not, they will hide themselves from the fishers. These differences are what Fienup-Riordan calls diverse "cultural logic." There is little hope of bridging the gap between Western science and that of the Yup'ik when the former denies that "nonhuman persons must be shown respect." Regardless of the pressures put on the Native people by government agencies, they resisted by "not dismissing their rich tradition as noninstrumental in their daily lives."[28]

BACK TO COURT they went, believing that if the judge understood that subsistence fishing was part of the Yup'ik religious system, they might have a chance, although many remained doubtful. Finally, the court of appeals concluded that subsistence activities might be considered a religious or spiritual component of the culture but was unconvinced it had the power to overturn the prior conviction. At this point the fishers were weary and frustrated. They decided to cut their losses and not pursue action in the Supreme Court. In the meantime another solution had appeared on the horizon that could effectively solve the problem between the southwest Alaska fishers and the oversight agencies, but it took a while for both sides to meet in the middle to chart a course of action.

Meanwhile, even after the fines had been reduced and some restrictions lifted, the Yup'ik fishers' attorney, James J. Davis, claimed that Judge Ward had erred because the fishers should have been given priority in those waters, and other fisheries in the area were not being monitored and therefore contributed to the problem with unabated wastage.[29] In the interim the legal matter now involved sixty fishers who had joined the protest. The best that Assistant Attorney General Laura Fox could do was assuage the defendants by reassuring them that the state's cross-appeal had been filed and would act as a placeholder for future arguments.[30] Although not resolved, this initial courtroom drama stood as a landmark case with ramifications for all Alaska Natives in terms of subsistence needs and cultural foundations.

For the younger Native fishers, this might have been their first tussle with the law, but it was certainly not foreign to Alaska Natives. Yup'ik anthropologist and professor Oscar Kawagley recalled the times when similar decisions had to be made by the traditional elders' council. The Yupiaq way of knowing is based "on an alliance and alignment . . . to maintain the delicate balance." This is no less important than the scientific readings of the Fish and Game Department in determining the health of salmon runs or the need for increased escapement. Kawagley used Akiak as an example to explain that in the past elders had been concerned about getting "enough king and chum salmon for the winter . . . while comments about needing enough dollars for the winter were never heard." The priorities were solid. When they were thwarted, there was the option of civil disobedience, even though it might turn out badly. In the past "a number of fishermen are usually caught fishing during closed times for areas and jailed. The entire situation was unfortunate for Native subsistence hunters and gatherers because they often have to break federal and state laws and regulations to make a living."[31] For decades rebellion was inevitable to put up fish for the family and community for the winter.

Little had changed since those times, and oversight agencies refused to budge or give up any authority. In turn common ground could not be found while oversight agencies managed resources under strictly scientific measures, frequently extrapolating from past runs or computer readings. Conversely, the Yup'ik believe the salmon are infinite if proper respect is shown toward the entire environment. To be fair, however, even the conservation-minded fishers can overstep their own conscience in a state of emergency: "The hunter's legal obligation to limit kills is often in direct opposition to his moral obligation to provide for his family and treat his prey with respect." Fienup-Riordan describes that "people living along the Yukon River have been subject to laws regulating the salmon fishery for many years" and have developed ways to circumvent the system. At times the fishers ignore the restrictions or work around the seasonal rules. Above all, they distrust resource managers, because for years there has been a "lack of prior enforcement of regulations, resistance to change, basic unfairness of regulations that prohibit hunting" or fishing, as the Native fishers struggle with situational ethics.[32]

This background was well-known in Kuskokwim River communities, and they did not see a path of vindication for the current criminal charges. They looked for other answers. In the meantime Mike Williams had been in further contact with Billy Frank Jr., and their discussions centered on the possibility of co-management between the government agencies and the fishers. This plan had been working in Washington state for several years. When it was decided that the legal route was not viable, the Yup'ik fishers met with the oversight agencies and ultimately formed the Kuskokwim River Inter-Tribal Fish Commission in 2015. It was founded on co-management principles, which opened the lines of communication, a condition vital for managing the resource with equity, In unison they are fighting against the greatest threat to the fish population: climate change. The warming of the Arctic and sub-Arctic has grave consequences for the fish stocks, with no solid solution in sight. Williams speaks about the current conditions and remarks that the fishers have limited their harvest because of adverse water conditions. For several seasons it has been recognized that the salmon were not coming back in the same numbers. In addition to the warming waters, there is the problem of intercept fishing, which does not allow an adequate escapement from the Aleutian Chain area to the lower Kuskokwim River.[33] Despite these major obstacles, the fishers are working with, not against, regulatory agencies and have signed a memorandum of agreement with the U.S. Fish and Wildlife Service for co-management of the resource, with all parties having a seat at the table. During the summer of 2022, I contacted Mike Williams, and in glowing terms he expressed his satisfaction with the co-management strategy and held high hopes for this alliance and the future.[34]

As a further update to this ongoing predicament and the health of the fisheries, I close this chapter with the news that in November 2022 Yup'ik political leader and former state congress representative Mary Peltola was elected to the U.S. House of Representatives as the sole representative for Alaska. Her victory could not be foretold but was likely boosted by her campaign slogan, upholding Alaska fisheries and families—that is something Alaskans can get behind. As the former executive director of the Kuskokwim River Inter-tribal Commission, she has had much experience with the issues and brings this knowledge to Washington DC to fight for the rights of all Alaskans. She has also brought to light the environmental damage that has occurred in the state and, with her effective and passionate communication skills, has made it clear that these environmental problems are not only in Alaska but part of a global emergency that demands immediate attention.

Epilogue

THE AFTERMATH

For thousands of years, Alaska's Indigenous people lived in an exceptional ecosystem, adapting to the climate, terrain, fauna, and flora. There were times of starvation, yet other periods that were so prosperous that the expanding population motivated groups to migrate to formerly uninhabited regions and adjust to a slightly different landscape or seascape. Others were forced to find another place to live because of the natural disasters that frequent the Pacific Rim of Fire. This was not a new phenomenon: massive earthquakes, volcanic eruptions, great flooding, wind erosion, fires, and more have been recorded as far back as the oldest-known legends and myths, often serving as cautionary tales. Nothing, however, was more shocking to Native societies than the first Europeans: the Spanish, French, Russian, and English, followed by the Americans, all demanding deference based on their supposed superiority. Ultimately, these intrusions led to environmental injustice. While entrepreneurs and speculators engaged in schemes intended to reap the bounty from deep in the ground, in the waters, or in the forests, Alaska Native leaders attempted to stop or ameliorate the destruction of their homelands, only to face Western regulations or a biased courtroom. Other manmade intrusions were more subtle.

Climate change has proven to be a challenge, and its effects can be seen on hills, in creeks and tidal pools, or in the forests, often hastened by industrial extraction. The destruction is occurring at a faster rate in the Arctic and sub-Arctic as compared to other areas of North America. As only one example, Shishmaref, located in the Chukchi Sea about twenty miles south of the Arctic Circle, with a population of about five hundred people, has been experiencing the results of ecological alterations since the 1970s. As respected elder Caleb Pungowiyi reported, "Alaska Natives have noticed substantial changes in the ocean and the animals that live there," affecting subsistence. He remarked that the birds have been disappearing from the island simultaneously with the massive erosion of the shores brought on by historical storms. The climate conditions in Shishmaref have detracted from the people's ability to read the ice and other weather indicators, "leading to travel and safety issues."[1] The hunters and sea travelers have had to adjust their ancient scientific knowledge and techniques because of these dramatic shifts. The adverse conditions are not localized and can be found throughout Alaska, varying from swiftly melting glaciers to horrific storms, causing thousands of dollars in damage and the loss of life.

Shishmaref is not the only village falling into the sea. In southwest Alaska, Akiak, the site of many fish wars, is sliding into the Kuskokwim River. Residents are urgently moving their houses, caches, or other storage units back from the newly exposed and eroding ledges. Further north Kivalina residents, many who had been involved in the Project Chariot debacle in the late 1950s, helplessly watch their shores being washed away by unprecedented storms that batter the coast. Villages have little recourse and are not receiving adequate assistance. State and federal legislature disregard the problem while continuing a political tap dance to placate (and subsidize) oil companies. To remedy the situation, villages are rallying community support and banding together to defend their homes and to raise awareness of the dangers. Often the state government's answer to impending doom is to encourage Alaska Natives to move to urban locations, but that type of uprooting would strike a blow to traditional cultures, even if it was affordable. This can no longer be society's answer.

Some dangers have been less publicized, as in the case of unexploded ordnance on the Aleutian Chain that has never been removed, albeit promises to the contrary. The federal government admits the cleanup project is thwarted because of a lack of funds and its rank as a low-priority project. When the Unangan and Japanese Americans reached an agreement on war reparations, part of the stated goals was to clean up these hazardous materials, but the government has never made good on that promise.[2] Moreover, there is another parallel crisis. Few know that on Amchitka Island "the largest underground blast ever undertaken" was detonated in a wildlife refuge, despite the potential ecological consequences from the seismic impact and long-range leakage.[3] This had been yet another experiment by the Atomic Energy Commission to conduct testing, believing no one lived on the island and without considering the collateral damage. Upon hearing of these experiments, the Alaska Conservation Society, which first gained its political footing in the Project Chariot era, publicized that an induced 7.9 earthquake had rocked southwest Alaska, causing widespread damage. These reports sent scientists scrambling to the Amchitka site to test for nuclear leakage. The government pronounced it was safe, but skeptics continued to look for potential disasters lurking in Alaska.[4] Authorities could no longer hide behind science and had to address environmental problems. The military and government agencies were ordered to scrutinize the region more carefully, but this did not reassure Alaska Native communities—they kept their guard up.

ACCORDING TO J. Hopson Jr., part of the greater Hopson whaling family and a leader in the Alaska Eskimo Whaling Commission, the relationship with the International Whaling Commission is smoother than before, and the number of whales harvested is adequate. Strikes and other pertinent data are seasonally reported to the commission and are within the acceptable range. Hopson also noted the growing Alaska Eskimo Whaling Commission partnerships with other government agencies, such as the National Oceanic and Atmospheric Administration.[5] Hopson stressed that subsistence practices cannot be obstructed without harm to the people and to "the fiber of our culture." Chair George Noonguuk, from Savoonga on Saint Lawrence Island, stressed, "Food security is in the ocean, not the grocery store."[6] Overall, though, the whalers do not worry about International Whaling Commission mandates because there are bigger concerns. There are fewer and fewer whales, possibly caused by the rising temperatures in the Bering Sea coupled with increased acidification.[7] Increased conservation efforts are necessary to maintain the marine biosystem, and due to drastic and unpredictable ocean changes, there is only room for cautious optimism.[8]

The waning whale population makes one think about Sheldon Jackson's grand scheme to bring reindeer and European herders to northern Alaska to ameliorate the losses because of greedy New England whalers in the nineteenth century. Although the reindeer project did not work out as hoped, there are still thriving reindeer farms and ranches in northern Alaska, Saint Lawrence Island, and Nunivak Island. Some family-owned businesses are able to ship reindeer products across the world, boosting the economies of these Native villages. Who knows? You might have Alaskan reindeer sausage on your pizza one day.

AFTER THE ATHABASCAN successfully stopped the excavation for a mammoth dam in their backyard, they were forced to turn their attention to another threat to their way of life. For decades, the Gwich'in, located in the northeast corner of Alaska near the Canadian border, have depended on the Porcupine caribou. The herds migrate out of Canada each year to calve on the icy plains of northern Alaska, and Athabascan hunters harvest male caribou when the animals come roaring across the Arctic range to find their favorite grazing areas of abundant lichen, muskegs, and peat lands. There is, however, a long-standing push to open these same lands for oil exploration, and the Gwich'in are convinced this will cause harm to the boreal caribou. In addition, there is no proof that oil exists in this area—it is only a hunch. Nonetheless, state legislators, in collaboration with Alaska's two senators, are focused on Alaska's development, believing crude oil is necessary to sustain Alaska's economy. Today this fight is at a standstill because of the changing shape of oil companies, alternative energy solutions, and the lack of eagerness to build expensive infrastructure on a literal pipe dream. But it is posed to come up again because we still live in an energy-hungry world.

At this juncture the Gwich'in of Fort Yukon, Arctic Village, and Venetie are in a type of cold war with their Arctic neighbors on the North Slope, with few breaks in the ice for rapprochement.[9] The Arctic Slope faction is convinced that finding more oil will allow the creation of good-paying jobs, while Gwich'in counter that exploration has the potential to incur irreversible injury to the animals and landscape. Others take a middle ground and explain that the dispute "is a response to the need for work, and you have to consider that is legitimate. The people are trying to save their own people." Others, acknowledging the complexity of the debate, conclude that the controversy will "pit region against region, making it hard for the people to have unity."[10]

Although no actions have been taken, the arguments persist and can be heard from Washington DC to northern Alaska. In congressional testimony, Dana Tizya-Tramm, chief of the Vintut Gwitchin First Nation in Old Crow Yukon, was adamant that any oil drilling will disrupt the caribou migrations and would be a case of cultural genocide. Bernadette Deminetieff of the Gwich'in Steering Committee declared, "We are caribou people," and taking this resource away from the people will destroy their identity and their human rights.[11]

TO THE SURPRISE of many, including the board of directors of Native corporations, the Alaska Native Claims Settlement Act (ANCSA) has survived, and business is booming. The twelve initial regional corporations and the initial two hundred village corporations struggled at the beginning while their profits were eaten up by the necessity of buying expertise, but after the initial bumps and pitfalls, some of the divisions are exporting fish, timber, value-added products, and more. This has not been without its internal strife. There is bickering between management and shareholders, much of it on a cultural basis, including the way environmental standards are ignored, as readily observed in overfishing or clear-cutting forests until the waters are without salmon runs and the hills are naked and eroded, similar to Hoonah. On the flip side, Native corporations recognize that if they go bankrupt, which was what some of the non-Native legislators were hoping for, they would lose everything. In the ultimate conundrum, the ancient stewardship has given away to the forced commercial harvest on former subsistence lands to meet the burden of a capitalist economy. ANCSA remains contentious, culturally and financially—some have cried out that the Native birthright was auctioned off, while others demand that the corporations be diligent and support their shareholders.

In answer to these charges, the Native entrepreneurs claim they can continue to financially grow without losing any cultural elements or environmental responsibility. As proof of that conjecture, they point to the corporations' heritage foundations, which, according to the mission statements, honor the ancient way of life that was damaged by assimilation methods, acculturation, and untoward adaptation. In 2021 the fifty-year anniversary of ANCSA was marked amid honest discussion concerning the problems the legislation has produced, but there was full agreement that Native communities are vital socially, culturally, economically, and spiritually.[12] In the future, however, these same powerful corporations will need to do more to combat the existential threat of climate change and work with the Alaska senators and Congress to develop local energy sources less dependent on crude oil.

Several Native corporations, both regional and village, are engaged in ecotourism, and these efforts minimize environmental issues by stewarding the land again, respecting the culture, and supporting local economies. On the Pribilof Islands, the first ecotourism business was established in the 1970s. The no-frills retreat gives tourists a prime view of life in this isolated area. Larry Merculieff emphasizes that strict rules must be obeyed by all guests, or they will quite literally be kicked off the island. Merculieff credits the success of the business to the women, who he says really know how to cook and offer hospitality to the guests.[13] Besides being treated to the local fare, tourists receive a rare glimpse into Alaska island life and the traditions of the Unangan. The same is true for Saint Lawrence Island (Siberian Yupik), where the guides take great delight in showing guests just how close they are to Russia. Hoonah also remains successful. Boats travel out to Chichagof Island and explore the old cannery that was operating in the early part of the past century and walk through the dense Tongass Forest or down to the docks. If lucky, they might see a salmon popping out of the water.

ALASKA AND ITS environment have been increasingly the subject of congressional discussions, either for their militarily strategic location or as the canary in the mine for climate change. In addition, Alaska issues have been heard by the U.S. Supreme Court, and one of the more notable cases was a challenge to *Katie John*. The conclusions were relitigated to once again decipher the legal definition of navigable waters, specifically how they are governed by the state and federal government. Who has ultimate dominion? In 2019

Sturgeon v. Frost brought up the questions surrounding Conservation System Units protected under the governance of the Alaska National Interest Lands Conservation Act, which included a discussion about public lands and federal regulation standards. The settled law of *Katie John* was threatened, but the Supreme Court "held that the National Parks Service (NPS) did not have the authority to regulate navigable waters in Alaska's CSUs." This was a victory for subsistence rights. There is no telling if it will go uncontested in the future, but this legal test reemphasizes there must be more cooperation between the state and federal government, particularly in respect to the Lands Conservation Act protections, or else the subsistence issue will continue to be an "intractable problem."[14] For the time being, the Ahtna Intertribal Resource Commission has entered into a Memorandum of Understanding with the Federal Subsistence Management Program, similar to the one that the Kuskokwim River Inter-Tribal Fish Commission has with Fish and Wildlife Service, although from time to time the state threatens to reopen these proceedings based on perceived equality issues.[15]

COMMUNICATION IS ONE of the biggest problems in the resource wars, especially between diverse groups. There are hopes that by increasing the co-management approach, more cultural brokers will have access to scientific data and multiple interpretations of material. Success rates vary. In the past, group-building strategies did not work in southeast Alaska fisheries, based largely on differences too large to overcome, but in southwest Alaska there is another story. After the Yup'ik fishers dealt with heavy restrictions coupled with climate-change issues, they found a middle ground and are working together in a productive atmosphere. Still, unfortunately, the fishers in certain areas have not been allowed to harvest enough fish for their families, frequently reaching a crisis point. In a true sense of community, however, other villages donated a portion of their harvests to help the villages that could not fish because of unhealthy runs.

Communities continue to rally around to support one another in the still-befouled waters of Prince William Sound, a bitter legacy from the *Exxon Valdez* oil spill. The profound governmental intrusion cannot be emphasized enough. People grew weary of hearing, "We are the government. We are here to help you." The trustee council encouraged desperate people to sell off a chunk of their land for development to boost the sagging local economy, pitting traditional Native fishers against the government and their own Native corporation. The project entailed clear-cutting a fifty-acre tract on the east side of the Eyak River, incensing a faction that opposed any further marring of the landscape and fought to stop clear-cutting of what they regarded as a historical Eyak village with a burial site. In *Eyak Traditional Elders Council v. Sherstone, Inc.* (the timber company), the elders presented their case. Donna Platt, an Alaska Native from the region and lifelong fisher, testified that this land use would permanently scar the forest and the culture. Although she understood the necessity for developing resources to financially stay afloat, she pleaded for long-range planning that included guidance from those who lived there and had been environmental stewards. The arguments, however, were not enough to sway the court, and the Eyak elders' council lost their case to the lumber company and the Eyak Native corporation. In the final analysis, Platt compared this defeat to the 1930s Dust Bowl era, when starving families sold what was left of their farms to survive. The corporation had won, but they had not conquered the Alaska Native spirit. Undaunted, the fishers continue to harvest the famous Copper River salmon today, although not in the numbers of yesteryear.[16]

Recently, there has been another western Alaska disaster caused by the effects of drastic Arctic climate change—this event illustrates the insufficiencies in science and public policy. In the winter of 2022, a fierce typhoon hit western Alaska, destroying homes, food caches, and sometimes entire villages. Typhoon Merbok was produced by the phenomenon of suddenly warming Pacific Ocean waters hitting the frozen tundra, and even the National Oceanic and Atmospheric Administration was caught off-guard and failed to predict the destructive power. Many of these areas, previously battered by earlier storms, have not recovered, and the subsistence harvest has been halted indefinitely, leaving a grave food-insecurity emergency. Further, the urgent situation has been exacerbated by the lack of practiced knowledge and cultural insight. When the Federal Emergency Management Agency (FEMA) arrived on site to help the survivors, the agents knew little of the terrain or residents. If this was not bad enough, when the victims received applications for federal assistance, they could not read the forms. FEMA had hired a California agency to print the forms in the Native languages, but elders and linguists, like Gary Holton, could not make out the string of foreign words. After careful analysis Holton discovered the scrambled letters had been lifted from an archaic source—a folklore text from Far East Russian that had been printed in the 1940s, using an outdated language system called Rubtsova, never seen in Alaska. To the already vulnerable Alaska Native communities struggling to survive, this governmental error was demeaning and inexcusable.[17]

THE ALASKA NATIVE story continues to center on the land and waters and on the struggles with the resource extractors. The legacy of government wardship, extreme assimilation efforts, and a strangling paternalism lingers, although these forces never conquered cultural identity. Villages in Alaska carry their values, ethnoscience, and way of life, refusing to transpose themselves into small replicas of model "white" communities. Along the way Native leaders honed their tools and learned how to work in Western court systems to their advantage. Moreover, as the leaders built political finesse, they learned how to rally movers and shakers, including presidents, Congress, benevolent groups, and political parties.[18] Along the coast, into the interior, and down the Pan-handle, there was a drive for continuity, serving as a stabilizing bedrock with the ability to absorb the shocks coming from a resource-hungry world that was enraged that Indigenous people would stand in their way. In response Alaska Natives nurtured their "societal norms and patterns" and formed collective political bodies.[19]

Manifest Destiny, a cheerless trope for land dispossession and Indigenous removal, was the end game in the pursuit of taming the howling wilderness. As history illustrates, this campaign to seize lands in the name of Americanism meant that Native Americans could be removed to reservations through "signed" treaties in a foreign language. Alaska never had genuine reservations or treaties, but that did not stop the newcomers from taking land, timber, or fish. In turn Alaska Natives summoned their warrior spirit to fight for Yup'ik *nuna* (land) or, in southeast Alaska, Lingít Aaní (Tlingit land), halting further federal and state government land grabs. Inch by inch Native organizations built political clout and demanded their rights. Although Alaska Natives were not a monolith, they shared the same basic values concerning the natural world, and this was enough to bind them together against the onslaught of international companies, Congress, courts, and unequal constitutional readings.

For centuries laws had been made by non-Natives, and it was a mammoth venture for these villages to protect their interests. In a perplexing world, the powers-that-be vacillated between developing the lands and waters or keeping Alaska in its untouched form if it suited their needs. It was difficult to find genuine environmental justice, but in the mix warriors, like Katie John, did not use angry words or blame, yet had the courage to make their case known—they could not be conquered. In 2021 Fred John Jr., son of Katie John and Fred John Sr., received a notice from the State of Alaska. Decades before, Katie John had applied for five acres of land at Mineral Lake above Mentasta in Ahtna Territory through her Bureau of Indian Affairs Native Allotment.[20] In 1963 the State of Alaska had decided it wanted that land, so high-powered lawyers and motivated bureaucrats fought against John's claim. On a summer day, years after Katie John had left this temporal world, her son read the letter from the state, which acknowledged they had recently lost another similar case, so they would not contest the Johns' allotment request. Fred was disappointed and questioned the worth of this news, since his mother was gone.[21] Disappointment and discouragement were to be expected, yet there could be no denying this had been a small gain for justice. She had been a trailblazer.

Katie John is among others, such as Flore Lekanof, Alice Petrivelli, Gabe Stepetin, Charlie Edwardsen Jr., William Paul Sr., Fred Paul, Richard Frank, Eben Hopson, Elizabeth and Roy Peratrovich, Sinrock Mary, Howard Rock, Sadie (Neakok) Brower, Harold Napoleon, George and Jesse Dalton, Marie Smith, Lily and Jake White, Nora Marks Dauenhauer, John Hinchman, and *so many others*, who fought for the rights of their people and were victorious. May they never be forgotten.

NOTES

1. Although reverence for nature and not wasting anything are parts of Native American cosmology, that does not mean there are not instances of greed or overharvesting among Indigenous tribes, bands, or clans, especially for those who harvest commercially or are frustrated by oversight agencies and the regulations they deem discriminatory. For an alternative viewpoint, see Krech, *Ecological Indian*.
2. Quoted in Berger, *Village Journey*, 51, 52.
3. Although the term *Eskimo* is no longer widely used, the Iñupiat and Yup'ik were referred to as such in old explorer or missionary journals.
4. "Proto-Athabascan" refers to the original Na-Dene migration between twelve thousand and fifteen thousand years before present. The Eyak show characteristics in their language that are related to the Dene language common among the Athabascan, Navajos, and Apaches, with some links to Tlingit.
5. A tribe is a certain social system linked by lineage with a hereditary leader. Before the Americans there were no tribes in Alaska. The Yup'ik social system was composed of patrilineally extended families, many of them nomadic. On the Aleutians there were matrilineal lineages with a headman, but it did not equate to the modern day meaning of tribe. The Athabascan societies were divided by bands and held distinct regions, whether Han, Gwich'in, Koyukon, Ahtna, and so on. Among the Tlingit there was an elaborate clan system that defined the culture. The word *tribe* was not used until the mid-twentieth century and then only so the government could have an understanding of a group of people that was as familiar as the Crows, Lakotas, or Apaches, for example.

6. The Tsimshian were originally from British Columbia. They migrated to southeast Alaska in 1887 and formed the Metlakatla reserve, established by presidential order. It stands as the only reserve in Alaska today. Although the language differs, the Tlingit, Haida, and Tsimshian share common cultural traits and patterns and are part of the greater Pacific Northwest tradition.

7. Sid Harring, personal communication, February 2010; Harring, *Crow Dog's Case*, 17.

8. Larry Merculieff, personal communication, September 19, 2021.

9. Wenz, *Environmental Justice*, 5.

10. Echo-Hawk, *Courts of the Conqueror*.

11. Laguna, *Under Mt. Saint Elias*, 57. I was fortunate to have several discussions with Frederica de Laguna, or Freddy, as we called her, and she always emphasized that the government's portrayal of Natives was far off from the realities. Juneau, 1990.

12. Romanus Pontifex created the text in 1455, and it was issued by Pope Alexander VI as the papal bull *Inter caltera* in 1493. It was further pronounced by Pope Alexander VI to give church approval for the colonization of other lands by Europeans.

13. For more information on this important topic, see Felix Cohen, *Handbook*; and Deloria and Lytle, *American Indians*.

14. Taylor, *American Colonies*, 188; Marks, *In a Barren Land*, 19.

15. J. Paul, *Without Precedent*, 401.

16. Miller, *Native America*, 85, 86.

17. Usner, "Savage Feast."

18. Robertson, *Conquest by Law*, 122.

19. Miller, *Native America*, 47.

20. English common law was the foundation for all of the country's colonies, including America. The law is based on custom and precedent. One can imagine the problems this caused in situations that had no bearing on former English circumstances, particularly the acquirement of Native American lands. This would be a major problem for Chief Justice John Marshall, who looked at English common law and then created his own law.

21. Miller, *Native America*, 96; Taylor, *American Colonies*, 64.

22. J. Paul, *Without Precedent*, 2.

23. *Marbury v. Madison* allowed any law or executive mandate to be struck down if it violated the U.S. Constitution. What this did in effect was increase the power of the judiciary. An excellent work on this subject can be found in Sloan and McKean, *Great Decision*.

24. Johnson v. McIntosh, 21 U.S. 543 (1823) at 591, quoted with commentary in J. Paul, *Without Precedent*, 401.

25. There is a history of broken or fake treaties where language barriers curbed the full meaning of what the tribal representatives signed. In the Pacific Northwest, Governor Isaac Stevens tricked the tribes into signing a treaty promising a certain percentage of fish that never came to be challenged until the 1960s and 1970s, by the Belloni and Boldt decisions. Sohappy v. Smith, USDC D. Oregon No. 68-409, often referred to as *US v. Oregon* 1968 or the Belloni decision; US v. Washington, 384 F. Supp. 12, 520 F.2d 679 (1974), commonly called the Boldt decision.

26. Jackson's "Annual Message," December 6, 1830, quoted in J. Paul, *Without Precedent*, 413.

27. Stephanson, *Manifest Destiny*, 75.

28. White, *It's Your Misfortune*, 74. With the Indigenous land question, it must be remembered that African slavery was also an issue at this time and had been since Jamestown. These dual issues were the subject of newspapers, political campaigns, and church services.

29. Echo-Hawk, *Courts of the Conqueror*, 7. Echo-Hawk is of Pawnee heritage and has served as an activist in many legal matters.

30. Gilio-Whitaker, *Grass Grows*, 150. Kivalina is located in northwest Alaska, on a long barrier island. The people support themselves through whaling.

1. FISH CAMP TO PICNIC BENCH

1. Nora Marks Dauenhauer explains the Tlingit social system in this way: "Tlingit occupants of a given geographic area, regardless of their moiety or clan, are known collectively as Ḵwaan. The moieties are named Raven and Eagle. Raven is sometimes also known as Crow, and Eagle as Wolf.... Each moiety consists of many clans ... the house where people lived or once lived, and this was part of their identity.... They may be related by marriage or be part of an extended family in some other way.... The father's clan of an individual is just as significant as that of the mother, but it functions and is recognized in a different way from that of the mother's clan." Dauenhauer and Dauenhauer, *Haa Kusteeyí*, 5–9.

2. Joseph, "History of Aukquon."

3. Joseph, "History of Aukquon," 8–9. Four hundred years old is perhaps modest. There is evidence that the village site could have been up to nine hundred years old. See Thornton, *Haa Leelk'w Has Aani Saaxu*, 65.

4. *Auke Bay Breakwater.*

5. Veniaminov, *Journals of the Priest Ioann Veniaminov.*

6. Kowee was not only a notable Tlingit leader but also a Native police officer and acted effectively between different ethnic groups to bridge any disputes or conflicts.

7. Swanton, *Social Conditions.*

8. Krause, *Tlingit Indians*, 68, 76. Aurel Krause was at the Auk village in 1879 on his way to the Auke Glacier. He was a contemporary of John Muir. Krause's firsthand account is valuable in that it is accepted by both Native and non-Native scholars. The temporary Auk village was on the beach, and canoes were readied to go fishing at any moment.

9. Wages were not always paid in paychecks. Sometimes they were paid in scrip for the company store.

10. Several sources give the distance as between fifteen and eighteen miles, including Juneau historian and outdoor adventurer and guide Brian Weed, who states that by canoe the best one can expect is about two miles an hour. This makes it obvious that the Auk Bay miners could not make that journey every evening after an eight-hour shift. Brian Weed, interview with the author, Juneau, March 2018.

11. Glass, *Cruising in Alaska Waters*.

12. Mitchell, *Sold American*, 127. Taku is another Tlingit Kwaan.

13. The exact wording of the 1884 Organic Act can be found in U.S. Congress, *Senate Compilation*, 25.

14. President Theodore Roosevelt to Secretary of the Interior Ethan A. Hitchcock, April 15, 1902.

15. Muir, *Travels in Alaska*, 118, 132.

16. Although Theodore Roosevelt firmly believed that the land belonged to the "white race" as opposed to the "squalid savages," he also thought these men and women could rise to the same level as the "white race." One of his other famous sayings was that he did not believe that the only good Indian was a dead Indian but did believe it true for nine out of ten. This particular comment was from a speech that Theodore Roosevelt delivered to the Lowell Institute in Boston in 1892. His other remarks come from 1901, when he was president. "Teddy Roosevelt."

17. Higginson, *Alaska*.

18. U.S. House of Representatives, *Water Transportation Report*, 41.

19. Flory, *United States of America*, 27.

20. There are numerous references from government officials about the Murphy clan destroying clan property, but since they were never charged with this crime, it appears this testimony is suspicious.

21. Although this was most likely a Raven clan, the word *Crow* in the documents is often used.

22. During the course of the trial, several legal precedents were cited to support the conviction that to use the Organic Act, occupation must be continuous from 1884.

23. The Homestead Act was originally passed in 1862 and allowed a qualified man to own 160 acres of land for farming. This act did not apply to Alaska until 1898,

when it was signed into law by President William McKinley. Few areas in Alaska are suitable for farming, and "Indians" could not own land unless they could prove they had severed their tribal connections.

24. The United States v. Murphy et al., 41 U.S. 203 (1842).

25. Charles Folta mentioned the importance of Alaska's industrial progress several times during the course of this case and also in general during this period.

26. One of his more notable cases took place in 1929, when he presided over Ketchikan Irene Jones's school desegregation case. After being presented with irrefutable evidence, he had ruled that Ketchikan schools had discriminated against Native children, which was exceptional for those times. Petition to the court in Irene Jones v. R. V. Ellis, Ketchikan School Board et al., 8 Alaska 146 (D. Alaska 1929), in "School Desegregation."

27. *United States v. Murphy et al.*

28. Limerick, *Legacy of Conquest*, 27.

29. "Aboriginal title" refers to the papal order that maintained that any people "discovered" by the European explorers kept the title to their land by virtue of being there, as outlined in natural law. *Terra nullius* is Latin for empty land.

30. Goldschmidt and Haas, *Haa Aaní*. The report was first issued in 1946 and titled "Possessory Rights of the Natives of Southeastern Alaska." This is a much-needed copy of the original, which was preserved in hard-to-read microfiche. It contains numerous firsthand accounts and interviews, including several people from the Auke Bay Recreation area legal case.

31. Banner, *How the Indians Lost Their Land*. Banner's book is only one source that outlines the topic involved with definitions of appropriate land use in the western regions of the United States.

32. *United States v. Murphy et al.* The orthography is taken from the court record. Thomas Thornton also calls him Auk Jim without any known Tlingit name and spelling.

33. *United States v. Murphy et al.*, 7, 8.

34. Although naval power exerted its authority in this situation, traditionally all of Juneau was Áak'w property, while the Taku clans owned nearby Douglas Island. Susie Cropley Michaelson was considered an important member of Tlingit society and sometimes designated as "big woman" to note her influence.

35. *United States v. Murphy et al.*

36. Rakestraw, "History."

37. *United States v. Murphy et al.* at 31.

38. The Indian Citizenship Act was not passed until 1924. David Case and David Voluck are experts on Alaska Native law, and in terms of the Organic Act and its

various interpretations, they stated, "The better analysis is that the Organic Act merely preserved the status quo as to aboriginal title under the 1887 treaty without determining the precise property rights of individual Natives or non-Natives." *Alaska Natives*, 52.

39. *United States v. Murphy et al.* at 10.

40. The mention of fences and posts was not only for boundary limits but for "improvement" on the land. When the plaintiff's attorney was arguing against Murphy's ownership, he used this defense, citing Hinchman v. Ripinsky, 3 Alaska Rpts. 557 (1910).

41. Chief Justice Marshall decided what is commonly called the Marshall Trilogy in the 1820s. They include *Johnson v. McIntosh, Cherokee Nation v. Georgia,* and *Worcester v. Georgia*. Based on English common law, these decisions evolved into a legal canon that defined the relationship of the United States and the Native tribes and nations.

42. Testimony from *United States v. Murphy et al.*

43. *United States v. Murphy et al.* at 90, argument by attorneys Grisby and Foster. The reference to "calculated toward the Natives' advantage" originates from what is considered an "Indian Canon" and applied in many legal cases, including those of Justice John Marshall. It states that the law must be liberally construed to protect the weak, defenseless wards of the nation, in this case American Natives.

44. Tongass National Forest Act, 35 Stat. 2226 (1909).

45. *United States v. Murphy et al.* at 88.

46. Eric Morrison, former director at the Douglas Indian Association, interview with the author, Douglas, February 10, 2018.

47. Goldschmidt and Haas, *Haa Aaní*.

48. "Q and A."

49. For more on this case, see "Feds Recognize Indian Point."

2. ALEUTIAN SHORES TO SCORCHED EARTH

1. Cueva, "America's Territory."

2. Laughlin, *Aleuts*, 20.

3. Black, *Russians in Alaska*, relates the chronology of Russia's first discovery but also a softened view of the Russian occupation. I have always admired her use of firsthand Russian documents, but she and I went around and around about the Russian era with two distinct points of view.

4. The most inclusive text of the complaints and issues can be found in Commission on Wartime Relocation, *Personal Justice Denied*.

5. The Unangan were not originally located on the Pribilof Islands. They were forcibly taken by the Russian fur traders to hunt fur seals for mercantile interests. For further insight to this period, see Veltre and McCartney, "Russian Exploitation."

6. Garfield, *Thousand-Mile War*.

7. Commission on Wartime Relocation, *Personal Justice Denied*, 19, 333.

8. *Aleut Evacuation*.

9. *Aleut Evacuation*.

10. Commission on Wartime Relocation, *Personal Justice Denied*, 338–39.

11. Mobeley, *World War II*, 106. Notice the word *internment* rather than *evacuation* in his subtitle, *Southeast Alaska Internment Camps*. This term was prevalent in government reports as well.

12. Alice Petrivelli speaks in "Alice Petrivelli." See also "Alice Petrivelli Interview."

13. Segall, "Bill to Preserve." Elders talked about how the notorious Funter Bay was a sacred place and needed preserving. The first grave was dug less than a week after they arrived.

14. Carter, "Aleut Relocation," 72.

15. Sheador, "Abandoned North." This is only one of many sources that describe the dangerous artillery left on the islands.

16. Commission on Wartime Relocation, *Personal Justice Denied*, 17, 23.

17. Commission on Wartime Relocation, *Personal Justice Denied*, 17, 23.

18. D. K. Jones, *Century of Servitude*, 107, 108; D. Purvis, *Ragged Coast*.

19. D. K. Jones, *Century of Servitude*, 108.

20. Commission on Wartime Relocation, *Personal Justice Denied*.

21. Eric Scigliano, "The Other Internees: The Untold Story of the Aleut WWII Exile," *Anchorage Daily News*, Q17.

22. D. K. Jones, *Century of Servitude*, 112.

23. Commission on Wartime Relocation, *Personal Justice Denied*, 348.

24. Torrey, *Slaves of the Harvest*, 130.

25. See Robertson, *Conquest by Law*; and Wilkins and Deloria, *Legal Universe*.

26. Aleutian Pribilof Islands Association, *Aleut Relocation and Internment*, 25, 27. The APIA is a tribally recognized organization that merged from the Aleut League, formed in 1966.

27. *Aleut Evacuation*.

28. Torrey, *Slaves of the Harvest*, 110.

29. Torrey, *Slaves of the Harvest*, 110.

30. Torrey, *Slaves of the Harvest*, 134.

31. Beech, "Refugees from the Pribilofs," 20, 21.

32. Wrangell Institute has a varied history. Tlingit historian Gil Truitt praised the school that he attended in the 1930s in several personal conversations that took place between 2007 and 2012. Alternatively, Ahtna elder Fred John Jr., who also attended the school, later recounted some of the worst abuses of any Indian boarding school, including being referred to as a number.

33. Japanese religions are based on many gods. In Shintoism, a form of nationalistic religion, the emperor, or sun god, reigns supreme, and this blind allegiance was one of the factors in Japanese aggression.

34. For more on this story, see Golodoff, *Attu Boy*; and Breu, *Last Letters from Attu*.

35. Commission on Wartime Relocation, *Personal Justice Denied*, 357.

36. Mason and Hudson, *Lost Villages*. Not many know the saga of the "Lost Islands," which were never repatriated again because of the expense to the government. People were forced to build communities with strangers. Attu was not populated again, even after the surviving POWs returned from Japan. Gewalt, "Attu."

37. Commission on Wartime Relocation, *Personal Justice Denied*, 359.

3. SEALERS TO SLAVES

1. Torrey, *Slaves of the Harvest*, 51.

2. Larry Merculieff informed me that the elders had told him about the complaints of the time, but little was recorded and what was lives only in carefully guarded oral narrative. Personal communication, December 2021.

3. Williams, *Bering Sea*, 12.

4. *Fur Seal of Alaska*.

5. Torrey, *Slaves of the Harvest*, 105.

6. "International Fur Seal Treaty."

7. Bureau of Fisheries reports (1926), cited in D. K. Jones, *Century of Servitude*, 74.

8. Ralph Baker, Junior Administration Assistant, Division of Alaska Fisheries, Native Canteens of the Pribilof Islands, October 20, 1941, quoted in D. K. Jones, *Century of Servitude*, 68.

9. Torrey, *Slaves of the Harvest*, 122.

10. Aleutian Pribilof Islands Association, *Aleut Relocation and Internment*, 14–15; D. K. Jones, *Century of Servitude*, 78; Indian Citizenship Act, Pub. L. No. 68-175 (1924).

11. Merculieff, *Wisdom Keepers*, 76.

12. Rogers, *Economic Analysis*.

13. Commission on Wartime Relocation, *Personal Justice Denied*, 358.

14. Commission on Wartime Relocation, *Personal Justice Denied*, 359.

15. Larry Merculieff, "The Pribilofs: An Alaska Trail of Tears," *Tundra Times*, April 27, 1983.

16. Merculieff, personal communication, January 21, 2022; October 2021. Merculieff was born in the 1940s.
17. Merculieff, personal communication, October 2021. Merculieff also told me that the old timers who started these grassroots meetings would fool the guards by saying they had to get together to plan a play to put on for the managers and all.
18. Torrey, *Slaves of the Harvest*, 142–43.
19. Brinkley, *Quiet World*, 342–44.
20. Torrey, *Slaves of the Harvest*, 123.
21. Merculieff, "Pribilofs."
22. "Pribilof Islands Survey Reports: Observations and Recommendations," October 28, 1949, reprinted in D. K. Jones, *Century of Servitude*.
23. The ICC was established to hear Indigenous cases and was able to adjudicate several key Native American claims and grievances before being terminated by President Dwight Eisenhower.
24. NOAA, "Subsistence Taking."
25. Labor unions were suspected of being under Soviet control. Although that was not true, many of the leaders during this period had an affiliation with the American Communist Party.
26. The Ice Curtain was another name for the Iron Curtain of the Cold War era. It referred to the unseen barrier between the Soviet Union and the United States. Détente was not possible until the Nixon years.
27. Mel Monson, who has relatives on the Pribilof Islands, tells the story of having to go to the islands to visit his uncle in the early 1960s because the government would not allow him to leave the island. Personal communication, June 2020.
28. D. K. Jones, *Century of Servitude*, 148; Merculieff, personal communication, December 18, 2021.
29. Torrey, *Slaves of the Harvest*, 155; Merculieff, "Pribilofs."
30. Merculieff, *Wisdom Keepers*, 92; Merculieff, "Pribilofs."
31. Merculieff, *Wisdom Keepers*, 147, 148
32. Merculieff, *Wisdom Keepers*, 149.
33. Merculieff, *Wisdom Keepers*, 91, 92.
34. NOAA, "Subsistence Taking."
35. Case and Voluck, *Alaska Natives*, 267.
36. D. K. Jones, *Century of Servitude*, 155.
37. Senate testimony, quoted in Torrey, *Slaves of the Harvest*, 154. See also "The Aleut: Past Tense and Future Present, an Interview with Gabe Stepetin," *Tundra Times*, September 15, 1979.
38. Merculieff, personal communication, September 19, 2021.

39. Merculieff, *Wisdom Keepers*, 96–97; Merculieff, personal communication, October 2021.
40. Case and Voluck, *Alaska Natives*, 268.
41. "U.S. Pays Restitution."
42. Merculieff, personal communication, September 14, 2021.
43. D. K. Jones, *Century of Servitude*, 75, 115.
44. Merculieff, *Wisdom Keepers*, 186.

4. HUNTERS TO REINDEER HERDERS

1. Mowat, *Siberians*.
2. Some Yup'ik villages in southwest Alaska, including Bethel, Aniak, and Akiak, were under the direction of the Moravian Mission. There were also reindeer reserves on the Alaska Peninsula among the Alutiiq.
3. The word *Eskimo* has fallen into disuse because of the derogatory history behind the classification, although it is not uncommon to hear such things as "Eskimo Dance" or "Eskimo Ice Cream." Unless in a direct quotation, the terms used here are *Iñupiat* for northern Indigenous people and *Yup'ik* for those in the southwest.
4. Chance, *Eskimo of North Alaska*, 13–15.
5. S. Jackson, "Report on Education," 957–58.
6. S. Jackson, *Report on Education*. This is but one of many references that carry the same missionary sentiment that the introduction of Western principles and values would save the Indigenous.
7. S. Jackson, *Report on the Introduction of Domestic Reindeer*, 31.
8. Vorren, *Saami, Reindeer, and Gold*, 14–15.
9. Vorren, *Saami, Reindeer, and Gold*, 17.
10. Previous literature refers to this ethnic group as Laplanders or Lapps. These Indigenous northern Europeans entered northern and southwest Alaska and the Alaska Peninsula through different methods.
11. Olson, *Alaska Reindeer Herdsman*, 9.
12. Hunters would never boast about killing an animal. If the proper respect was shown, animals would give themselves to hunters. This is a deeply held cultural conviction that persists to this day. Spencer, *North Alaskan Eskimo*, 265–66. The myth of Alaska Eskimo dependency started with Sheldon Jackson's early descriptions of the happy, carefree Eskimo. In his 1890 education report, he wrote, "The Alaska Eskimo is a good-natured docile, and accommodating race." "Report of the General Education Agent," 1287.
13. S. Jackson, *Fourth Reindeer Report*, 84–85.

14. Taliaferro, *In a Far Country*, 168–69. This was not the only time that Charlie was asked to give up his reindeer for starving non-Natives, reinforcing a pattern for himself and other Native herders.

15. Fortuine, *Chills and Fever*, 215.

16. Ray, "Making of a Legend."

17. Ray, *Eskimos of Bering Strait*, 32. Ray stated she saw the mention of the trial in the notes of A. J. Becker, who was the court reporter at Nome. When asked if he was willing to send a transcription to a contemporary, he said he would do so for a $75 fee. Apparently, however, the trial was never transcribed for "Mary's protection." These were the notes found at the Swedish Evangelical Church Archives in Unalakleet. Before her death Ray expressed interest in writing the biography of Mary Antisarlook, but today that work has gone unwritten.

18. Burch, *Inupiaq Eskimo Nations*. Of interest in this study of territories is the assumption that some reindeer herders may have transgressed on another territory or "nation," adding to the confusion and fighting.

19. Brooks, *Reindeer Queen*. Sinrock is an anglicized version of Sinuk Point.

20. Fjeld, "Alaska Sami," 6. This is part of a long-range museum display that began in Alaska and was carried across the country. Faith Fjeld, personal communication, December 2012.

21. According to Dorothy Jean Ray, it was difficult to discern what Sheldon Jackson was thinking at this time or his level of desperation. He made a promise he could not legally go through with, but it did not matter since he had no takers. Ray, *Eskimos of Bering Strait*, 206.

22. "Political ecology" has nebulous and malleable definitions, often connected to political economies or financial means. In this use it refers to the power that some people or agencies possess so that they can manipulate the landscape and policies. Paul Robbins has extended the explanation by including "environmental change to political and economic marginalization" that focuses on "new activism." *Political Ecology*, 15.

23. Missionary journals, government documents, and school reports all emphasize that Native reindeer are the property of the government, missions, or school reserves and used for a tool of education.

24. Spencer, *North Alaskan Eskimo*, 147–48.

25. Olson, *Alaska Reindeer Herdsman*, 23.

26. Ray, *Eskimos of Bering Strait*, 231.

27. In the 1820s the Supreme Court was confronted with what to do about the American Native tribes and their relationship to the nascent U.S. government. Chief Justice John Marshall derived the theory of domestic, dependent nations, which

meant a limited government-to-government relationship, but the Natives were of lesser status, signifying that Natives were "wards" of the government, which had a fiduciary responsibility for their welfare. As the government bureaucracy grew, so did this "ward" relationship. Beyond this relationship, however, the Alaska Native status has also been affected by the lack of treaties and reservations. In effect, the government-to-Native relationship had to be created anew.

28. Olson, *Alaska Reindeer Herdsman*, 12.
29. Johnshoy, *Apaurak in Alaska*, 140.
30. Beach, *Saami of Lapland*, 51.
31. As early as 1905, Special Agent Frank C. Churchill reported to the secretary of the interior that the church-run reindeer business was inefficient, finally resulting in the firing of Jackson. Churchill, *Reports on the Condition*.
32. Taliaferro, *In a Far Country*, 5.
33. Lopp, *Reindeer Industry*.
34. Olson, *Alaska Reindeer Herdsman*, 11.
35. Lopp, "Lapps and Finns Coming."
36. William "Tom" Lopp brought up the idea of a Native corporation on several occasions and even had the backing of the Reindeer Service at one time, but the actual implementation would have been fraught with troubles, from social structure to the lack of government funding. After 1940 the reindeer business did form corporations, but it was a much different world then, and the reindeer business was much smaller. See Lopp, *White Sox*.
37. Olson, *Alaska Reindeer Herdsman*, 45–46.
38. Carl Lomen was the mayor of Nome at one point, but even when not in official capacity, he wielded a great deal of power.
39. Olson, *Alaska Reindeer Herdsman*, 45–46.
40. United States v. Lomen and Company, 8 Alaska Rpts. 1, 4–5 (D. Alaska 1923). Even though Gudbrand Lomen bought reindeer from the Teller Mission before it was legal, the charges could not be conclusively proven. This would be the first of many of Lomen's transgressions that were overlooked.
41. Rainey, "Memorandum."
42. Olson, *Alaska Reindeer Herdsman*, 40.
43. Committee of Territories, *To Provide for Administration*. The use of the term *national property* is highly significant.
44. Olson, *Alaska Reindeer Herdsman*, 12.
45. Vorren, *Saami, Reindeer, and Gold*, 85.
46. Mona Eben, originally from Unalakleet, tells how her father was in high demand at these trading events because he spoke both Iñupiaq and Yup'ik. Personal

communication, November 2020. Although there is no direct data, there might have been a few Athabascan herders in attendance, although their main vocation centered on caribou hunting and herding. These traditions and regional harmony were kept through a gathering called Kivgiq, where invited villages came from all around and shared their dances, songs, crafts, and stories. The ritual has been reborn in the northwest region in the past ten years.

47. Among Iñupiat whaling crews, there were often meetings to verify individual markings on whaling tools that clarified ownership. This tradition might have been duplicated at the reindeer fairs.

48. Shields, "Superintendent's Report."

49. U.S. Bureau of Education, *First Reindeer Fair*.

50. William T. Lopp, *The Eskimo*, January 1917, 3, 6.

51. Johnshoy, *Apaurak in Alaska*, 24, 144–45.

52. "Reindeer Herding."

53. Olson refers to the Manitoba Expedition, which was planned and executed by Sheldon Jackson. See Vorren, *Saami, Reindeer, and Gold*, 45–47.

54. "Reindeer Herding," episode 2. The small herd numbered about eight hundred, according to Palmer Sagoonick.

55. Willie Hensley, personal communication, October 24, 2017.

56. Lantis, "Reindeer Industry in Alaska," 32.

57. In the early 1900s James Wickersham worked with the northern Athabascan, who were fighting the usurpation of their land. The result was the establishment of the Tanana Chiefs Conference. Wickersham also later worked with the Alaska Native Brotherhood and William L. Paul Sr., who in turn worked with Delegate Anthony "Tony" Dimond to create the Alaska Reorganization Act of 1936. This sole delegate represented the Alaska territory until it became a state in 1959.

58. Atwood, *Frontier Politics*, 367. The famous Byrd Expeditions were supplied by the Lomen Corporation with clothing and accessories made by the Iñupiat.

59. Wickersham, diary entry, March 14, 1931. Native Americans were made citizens in 1924, but that does not mean the legislation was faithfully enforced.

60. Wickersham, diary entry, March 13, 14, 1931.

61. Wickersham, diary entry, March 14, 1931.

62. *Hearings of the Reindeer Committee*.

63. Olson, *Alaska Reindeer Herdsman*, 51, 53–53.

64. Demuth, "More Things." For more cases of Lomen infractions, see Willis, "New Game," 296, 298, where she reports from the "Minutes of the Cape Reindeer Company," which also experienced the other end of the criminal actions.

65. Lopp and Dimond, quoted in Taliaferro, *In a Far Country*, 354.

66. Olson, *Alaska Reindeer Herder*, 65; Stern et al., "Eskimos, Reindeer, and Land."

67. Nash, "Recommendations."

68. Nash, cited in Stern et al., "Eskimos, Reindeer, and Land."

69. The use of the word *Indian* was all inclusive for government use, although a false application of the term in this case. Nash, "Recommendations," 3.

70. Willis, "New Game," 278, 282.

71. The Indian Reorganization Act had been converted and developed into the Alaska Reorganization Act by Delegate Anthony "Tony" Dimond and Tlingit attorney William L. Paul Sr., who were both instrumental in facilitating the implementation in conjunction with the Department of the Interior.

72. Lipps, "Eskimo Villages."

73. "An Act to Establish Subsistence for Eskimos and Other Natives of Reindeer Industry in Alaska," 81st Cong. Rec., 75th Cong., 1st Sess. (1937) at 9486.

74. U.S. House of Representatives, *Congressional Record*, 2120 (includes all quotations from the representative plus references to Dimond).

75. "Act to Establish Subsistence."

76. "Reindeer in Alaska," July 1937, in U.S. House of Representatives, *Congressional Record*, 9473–74.

77. Anthony J. Dimond's biographer, Mary Childers Mangusso, explains that Dimond was frustrated with his role as a nonvoting delegate and what he considered Congress's unethical behavior. There were limits to his patience. "Anthony J. Dimond."

78. In the Great Ohio River Flood, hundreds of mules and other animals were lost. Farmers were looking to Congress for assistance.

79. "Reindeer in Alaska," July 1937, in U.S. House of Representatives, *Congressional Record*, 9479.

80. "Act to Establish Subsistence," 9480.

81. Paul Brooks, "Last of the Lapp Herders," *Alaskan Daily News Magazine*, December 5, 1982.

82. "Acquisition of Reindeer and Other Property," Reindeer Industry, 25 U.S.C. § 500a (2012), Title 25 at 500a.

83. In 1912 the Guggenheims joined with J. P. Morgan to mine copper in the Athabascan territory. The Kennecott Corporation, now internationally famous, was started along with a railroad system to transport the copper. The existing Eyak people were moved out of the way to make room for the copper mine, the railroad, and, ostensibly, progress.

84. Lomen, *Fifty Years in Alaska*, 282. Those few who still have reindeer farms in northern Alaska complain that wolves still are a problem.

85. Vorren, *Saami, Reindeer, and Gold*, 137, 93.

86. Willis, "New Game," 278.

87. Blackman, *Sadie Brower Neakok,* 75.

88. Blackman, *Sadie Brower Neakok,* 75.

89. Hensley, *Fifty Miles from Tomorrow,* 175.

5. BALEEN TO BOMBS

1. Maniilaq was an ancient prophet from the region who predicted the coming of non-Natives and technology to the area.

2. Chance, *Eskimo of North Alaska,* 44.

3. The Ice Curtain referred to the invisible line between the United States and the Soviet Union. The Iñupiat on the Diomede Islands were less than three miles away from the Russian border.

4. Lawton, quoted in Mitchell, *Take My Land,* 14.

5. O'Neill, *Firecracker Boys,* 33.

6. Edith Turner, "Native Reaction."

7. O'Neill, *Firecracker Boys,* 39.

8. Meinhardt, *Legacy of Project Chariot,* 2.

9. O'Neill, *Firecracker Boys,* 86.

10. Coates, *Trans-Alaska Pipeline Controversy,* 121. Peter Coates transcribed this remark from the original speech, and his book illustrates how the Project Chariot question was one of the methods that Alaska Natives used to build political sophistication in the Western world.

11. O'Neill, *Firecracker Boys,* 155, 81; Dan O'Neill, personal communication, September 2021.

12. O'Neill, *Firecracker Boys,* 59.

13. O'Neill, personal communication, August 2020.

14. O'Neill, *Firecracker Boys,* 129, 138, 136.

15. Ross, *Environmental Conflict in Alaska.* The soil was found to contain at least two known dangerous elements.

16. Coates, *Trans-Alaska Pipeline Controversy,* 125.

17. O'Neill, *Firecracker Boys,* 88–89.

18. Hensley, *Fifty Miles from Tomorrow,* 101–2; Willie Hensley, personal communication, May 2018.

19. Hadleigh-West, *Project Chariot,* 53.

20. Hadleigh-West, *Project Chariot,* 53

21. Teller, in a public relations speech, quoted in O'Neill, *Firecracker Boys,* 159.

22. Meinhardt, *Legacy of Project Chariot,* 8.

23. The Bikini Atoll on the Marshall Islands was the site of underwater bombing from 1946 to 1958. Expert scientists found that there was a direct link between the experiments and later cancer cases. Bordner et al., "Background Gamma Radiation."

24. Meinhardt, *Legacy of Project Chariot*, 8.

25. There is little information on the Nevada tests' effects on the local population, but there are more articles and documentaries concerning the effects in Utah. See LaDuke, *All Our Relations*, especially the chapter titled "Nuclear Waste, Dumping on the Indians," where she concludes that the "Indians" received the worst part of the waste debates but refused to be victims (111).

26. O'Neill, *Firecracker Boys*, 83, 85.

27. Virginia "Ginger" and Cecelia Hunter were Women Airforce Service pilots during World War II and fell in love with Alaska. After the war they made a home in Fairbanks and ran a wilderness lodge. This increased their interest in the region's natural bounty, and after teaming up with Mardy and Olaus Murie, they formed the Alaska Conservation Society in 1961. Together they were responsible for setting aside lands that made up the Arctic Wildlife Refuge and then turned their efforts toward Project Chariot and the Rampart Dam project.

28. Human geography is the study of people and places focusing "on how people make places, how we organize space and society, how we interact with each other in places and across space, and how we make sense of others and ourselves in our localities, regions, and the world." This definition can be greatly expanded with case examples, and there is an opportunity to do this in the twelve Alaska cases offered here. Fouberg, Murphy, and Blij, *Human Geography*, 8.

29. O'Neill, *Firecracker Boys*, 102.

30. The press was aware of the events, mostly by the stories of Teller, but the project remained rather hushed still until the entire story was uncovered by Dan O'Neill in the 1990s.

31. The AAIA was originally founded in 1922 in Maryland (now headquartered in New York) to counteract what they believed was bad American Indian policy and to help the Indigenous preserve their way of life. They continue to represent Alaska Native issues, and Mike Williams of Akiak is one of the newest representatives.

32. Morgan, *Art and Eskimo Power*, 172–73.

33. Brooks and Foote, "Disturbing Story," 62.

34. O'Neill, *Firecracker Boys*, 186–87.

35. Coates, *Trans-Alaska Pipeline Controversy*, 118.

36. Reprinted in O'Neill, *Firecracker Boys*, 249.

37. Inupiat Paitot, "Statement and Policy." Dena Hash, the Athabascan organization, joined forces with Inupiat Paitot.

38. *Senate Hearing on Environmental Justice.*

39. Dimitra Lavrakas, "Point Hope's Suffering, Anger Pour Out over Experiment," *Anchorage Daily News*, October 17, 1994.

40. Rosanne Pagano, "Cancer-Plagued Point Hope Gets Radiation Sensor," *Anchorage Daily News*, August 31, 1995. Some lesions have been spotted on the bowhead whales that have been harvested.

41. "Barry Commoner."

42. Gregg, "Teller Misled Alaskans," 98.

43. Ross, *Environmental Conflict in Alaska*, 108.

44. "Are Point Hope's High Cancer Rates Linked to Project Chariot?" *Anchorage Daily News*, October 28, 2012.

45. Lavrakas, "Point Hope's Suffering"; Huntington and Quankenbush, "Walrus Near Point Hope."

6. BOREAL FOREST TO FLOODPLAIN

1. The Kennedy quote was originally spoken in Los Angeles on July 15, 1960, upon his accepting of the Democratic presidential nomination. It is quoted in Limerick, *Something in the Soil*, 80.

2. Haycox, *Frigid Embrace*, 89–90.

3. Howard Rock, "Native Groups Unite: Inupiat Paitot, Dena Nena," *Tundra Times*, June 17, 1963.

4. Treaties had stopped in 1871.

5. Naske and Slotnick, *Alaska*, 197; Grabinska, "History of Events."

6. Berry, *Alaska Pipeline*, 37.

7. Richard Frank's case is discussed in Howard Rock, "Natives Talk Politics," *Tundra Times*, July 23, 1963. See also "Alaska Natives and the Land." Frank's story and testimony are recorded on Project Jukebox, University of Alaska.

8. "Remembering Richard Frank," *Fairbanks News-Miner*, September 21, 2021.

9. "Rampart Villages Turn in Maps, Denoting Land Use," *Tundra Times*, September 23, 1963.

10. Kennedy, "Remarks of Senator."

11. Gruening, *Many Battles*, 496.

12. Gruening, *Many Battles*, 49.

13. R. Nelson, *Make Prayers*, 246.

14. Naske and Slotnick, *Alaska*, 288.

15. Willis, *Alaska's Place*, 205; Gruening, *Many Battles*, 497, 498.

16. Walter Hickel was selected by President Nixon to fill the position of secretary of the interior. Hickel was reluctant to leave Alaska for this position, and he

faced opposition. He was attacked as being an antienvironmentalist, which he denounced. The Sierra Club was squarely against his appointment, based largely on his actions during the Rampart Dam proposal. He finally left the position based on his stance on Vietnam and the president's role, citing the Kent State shooting as deplorable. He came back to Alaska and built an empire. See Hickel, *Who Owns America?*

17. "User-state" refers to an independence of the state from the federal government and its regulations. In this case all Alaska resources would be managed by Alaska. With the hold of the federal government, that was never going to work in Alaska.

18. Justice Marshall used those same words to define the "Discovery Doctrine" and how it applied to Indigenous peoples.

19. Greg Palast, "The True Cause of the Exxon Valdez Catastrophe," *Anchorage Daily News*, March 25, 2021, 9.

20. Willis, *Alaska's Place*, 106.

21. "Egan Speaks Out," *Fairbanks Daily News-Miner*, September 14, 1964.

22. Gruening, *Many Battles*, 500.

23. O'Neill, *Firecracker Boys*, 271.

24. Udall had been called to Alaska on several urgent ecological matters.

25. Daley and James, *Cultural Politics*, 117.

26. *Tundra Times*, February 17, 1964, 8, quoted in Daley and James, *Cultural Politics*, 131.

27. Fred John Jr., personal communication, June 8, 2021.

28. Daley and James, *Cultural Politics*, 126, 128.

29. *Tundra Times*, December 23, 1963, 6.

30. *Fairbanks Daily News-Miner*, February 22, 1964.

31. "Native Groups to Meet Leaders," *Tundra Times*, July 6, 1964.

32. Dena Nena Henash meeting, June 1962, quoted in Mitchell, *Take My Land*, 28.

33. Daley and James, *Cultural Politics*, 115.

34. *New York Times*, March 8, 1965, quoted in Ross, *Environmental Conflict in Alaska*, 131.

35. Spurr, *Rampart Dam*, 49.

36. Norwood, "Rampart Dam at Perspective."

37. *Yukon Flats*.

38. Gilio-Whitaker, *Grass Grows*, 60, 62.

39. Haycox, *Frigid Embrace*, 90.

40. American Friends Service Committee, *Uncommon Controversy*, 175; Ulrich, *Empty Nets*, 189.

1. Mitchell, *Sold American*, 182.
2. Gallagher, *Etok*, 17. "Eskimo" can sometimes be considered a derogatory reference, but it is in common usage even in the village. One problem with the term is that it does not distinguish between the Yup'ik of southwestern Alaska and the Iñupiat of the northwest region.
3. Hensley, *Fifty Miles from Tomorrow*, 197.
4. Gallagher, *Etok*, 118 The Browers were well-known in the greater Barrow area. The settlement was started by New Yorker Charles D. Brower (1863–1945), who arrived on a whaler and stayed to start a family and eventually his own whaling company.
5. D. Purvis, *Drive of Civilization*. The Tlingit-Haida Jurisdictional Act was approved in 1935, with the final decision in 1959.
6. Mitchell, *Sold American*, 382. Bill Paul Jr., son of William Paul Sr., completed his thesis in 1939 at the University of Washington School of Law, proving that Alaska was still owned by the Natives by right of occupancy. F. Paul, *Then Fight for It*, 93.
7. Letter quoted in Gallagher, *Etok*, 120–21.
8. The Treaty of Cession was the agreement between Russia and the United States at the time of sale in 1867. Hubert Howe Bancroft was a prolific writer of western U.S. history and for a long time was the only source of comprehensive regional history, although he relied on local witnesses who may not have been completely reliable. His works are now housed at Berkeley Library in California.
9. Gallagher, *Etok*, 121.
10. Etok, *Bitter Root of Truth*, 3.
11. Charlie Edwardsen Jr., personal communication, June 2005.
12. "Statement of Charlie Edwardsen, Secretary-Treasurer, Alaska Native Housing Committee," April 1966, quoted in Gallagher, *Etok*, 147.
13. Edwardsen, personal communication, May 2002.
14. Nick Begich won the seat in the U.S. House of Representatives in 1970 over Frank Murkowski, father of Alaska's current senator Lisa Murkowski. Begich ran again in 1972 against Don Young. Unfortunately Begich's plane went down, and he was presumed dead. Don Young took his place and has been the sole Alaska representative since that time. Although Begich's tenure in the House was only two years, he was known for his assistance to Native causes.
15. Berry, *Alaska Pipeline*, 189. My conclusions are derived from living with the situation and hearing stories for many years. The Native factions were not easily fooled and did not trust politicians. It would have been interesting to see what Nick Begich's next move might have been.

16. Berry, *Alaska Pipeline*, 157.
17. Edwardsen, personal communication, November 12, 1999.
18. Gallagher, *Etok*, 170–71.
19. Gallagher, *Etok*, 125.
20. Mitchell, *Sold American*, 356–57.
21. F. Paul, *Then Fight for It*, 271–72.
22. "Native Alaskans Speak Out," *Washington Post*, February 14, 1977.
23. F. Paul, *Then Fight for It*, 274–75.
24. Paul family, personal communication, July 2021.
25. F. Paul, *Then Fight for It*, 230.
26. Permafrost is frozen ground that has remained frozen for over two years and can be below the surface of the ground soil or ocean. The permafrost can be from two inches to several miles below the surface. In a bitter irony, the permafrost is melting and creating not only instability in the area but also emitting methane into the air and contributing to more aerial toxins.
27. Upicksoun, quoted in F. Paul, *Then Fight for It*, 244.
28. Upicksoun, cited from the *Anchorage Daily News*, in F. Paul, *Then Fight for It*, 245.
29. Daley and James, *Cultural Politics*, 146–47.
30. Daley and James, *Cultural Politics*, 146.
31. Miller v. United States, 159 F.2d 997 (9th Cir. 1947).
32. Gallagher, *Etok*, 122. The duck-in event was in reference to the act of civil disobedience from both the Yup'ik and the Iñupiat when they took ducks out of season to prove their points about subsistence.
33. Gallagher, *Etok*, 121.
34. Gallagher, *Etok*, 260.
35. 369 F. Supp. 1359, District of Columbia, 1973.
36. The Alaska State Lands Act involves the new state's selection of federal lands up to 103,000 acres. This became a point of contention when the state (through the BLM) began selecting lands for its own use and enrichment, which turned out to be traditional subsistence lands and even sacred sites such as burial grounds.
37. See the Supreme Court case of *The Cherokee Nation v. The State of Georgia* (1831), one of the so-called Cherokee Trilogy.
38. Edwardsen v. Morton, 369 F. Supp. 1359 (D.D.C. 1973). The third-party clause was originally from the Marshall Trilogy.
39. Mitchell, *Sold American*, 315.
40. Case and Voluck, *Alaska Natives*, 75–77, 76.
41. United States v. ARCO, 435 F. Supp. 1009 (D. Alaska 1977), aff'd, 612 F.2d 1132 (9th Cir. 1980).

42. Case and Voluck, *Alaska Natives*, 77.

43. Case and Voluck, *Alaska Natives*, 77, 294.

44. See Tlingit-Haida Central Jurisdictional Act, U.S.C. Title 25, the conclusion of *Tlingit and Haida Indians of Alaska v. U.S.* (1959).

45. In the most ironic terms, there is now a battle between the North Slope corporation members and the Gwich'in Athabascan over the opening of the Arctic Wildlife Refuge for exploratory oil drilling. The North Slope wants to see if there is more oil, while the Athabascan want to protect the migratory caribou herds.

46. Etok, *Bitter Root of Truth*, 3.

47. F. Paul, *Then Fight for It*, 292.

48. Berry, *Alaska Pipeline*, 106, 121.

49. See Ott, *Not One Drop*, for a detailed analysis of what the experts knew about the dangers before any infrastructure was in place.

50. Berry, *Alaska Pipeline*, 203.

51. The permanent fund acts like a dividend that is dispersed each year to qualifying residents of Alaska.

52. Edwardsen, discussion with the author, Alaska Pacific University, Anchorage, April 2005.

8. A WHALING CAPTAIN AND THE WORLD

1. Bockstoce, *Whales, Ice, and Men*, 21. Other sources for gaining a greater understanding of the background and controversy include Wohlforth, *Whale and the Supercomputer*; Boeri, *Ice Whale*; and Hess, *Gift of the Whale*.

2. Hopson, "Eben Hopson."

3. Statement by Charles Edwardsen Jr., cited in Mason, "Bowhead Whale Controversy," 363, 371. The statement is from the draft of an "Environmental Impact Statement," where the major emphasis was placed on the overall well-being of the Iñupiat if whaling must be ended due to restrictions imposed by an international forum and global concern over the fate of whales in general.

4. Hess, *Gift of the Whale*, 11.

5. The spiritual manifestation emphasizes the close relationship between the whaling captain and the shaman. Through special songs and amulets, the whale was discovered, captured, and butchered with respect and traditions. With the waning of the shaman's role and the introduction of Christian ceremonies, the "whaling cult" was altered to become an indigenized Christian ritual. Chance, *Inupiat and Arctic Alaska*.

6. "People of the Whale," 7.

7. Bockstoce, "Preliminary Estimate."

8. The dwindling population of whales led Jackson to introduce reindeer herding as a means to ward off Alaska Native starvation.

9. Preamble to the 1946 Convention from the International Convention for the Regulation of Whaling, 62 Stat. at 1716. By late 1976, in addition to the United States, there were seventeen members, including Argentina, Australia, Brazil, Canada, Denmark, France, Iceland, the Netherlands, Japan, Mexico, New Zealand, Norway, Panama, South Africa, the Soviet Union, and the United Kingdom.

10. The Scientific Committee was an integral part of the IWC from the beginning and responsible for setting quotas and evaluating testing. It did not have an Alaska Native member.

11. Part of the study of political ecology centers on environmental and resource issues that are influenced or decided by political arguments.

12. "Hopson v. Kreps," 247.

13. Blackman, Sadie Brower Neakok, 207.

14. U.S. House of Representatives, Enhance the Effectiveness.

15. The Yup'ik occupy southwest Alaska but also coastal Russia. The Inuit occupy northern latitude settlements from Russia to Alaska through Canada and to Greenland, with a common origin, language, and culture.

16. "People of the Whale," 7.

17. "Traditional ecological knowledge" refers to the ability to understand the environment based on the proximity, daily use, and Native lore of the fauna and biota. For years the Alaska Natives have lived by the waterways, tundra, mountains, and more in all seasons, imparting a certain wisdom that translates into knowing the resources and identifying trends. These abilities have also been called ethnoscience. More and more oversight agencies are working together with Indigenous knowledge for increased environmental awareness.

18. Hess, Gift of the Whale, 13.

19. The Japanese were mainly for-profit harvesters, and "the British charged that this was why Japan had defeated the quota—to force the Americans to defy the IWC and thereby destroy it." Wohlforth, Whale and the Supercomputer, 231–32.

20. Whale and Dolphin Conservation, "Whaling in Greenland."

21. Adams v. Vance, 570 F.2d 950 (D.C. Cir. 1977); Hopson v. Kreps, 622 F.2d 1375, 1377, n.1 (9th Cir. 1980).

22. J. R. Stallings to Secretary Juanita Krebs, December 2, 1978, quoted in Dorsey, Whales and Nations, 248.

23. In the Hopson v. Kreps case, other plaintiffs included Lloyd Ahvakana and Elijah Rock suing the secretary of commerce, Juanita Kreps; Richard Frank of NOAA; and Terry Leitzell, assistant administrator for fisheries in the National Marine Fisheries Service.

24. Case, *American Laws*, 283.
25. Case and Voluck, *Alaska Natives*, 207.
26. Case and Voluck, *Alaska Natives*, 269.
27. *New Study*, 7. Since the question of oil was already paramount among the whalers, who were growing in political strength, this was no doubt a public relations move by the oil companies.
28. Mason, "Bowhead Whale Controversy."
29. Marine Mammal Protection Act of 1972, 16 U.S.C. at 1361–84 (Supp. 3, 1974).
30. The Endangered Species Act of 1973, 18 U.S.C. at 1531–43, allowed the secretary of the interior to authorize certain species to be protected because of their numbers, based on scientific data. The bowhead whale was almost immediately put on this list. The Marine Mammal Protection Act of 1972 protects all marine mammals but does allow subsistence harvest for those approved by the secretary of state, who also is responsible for any international negotiations deemed appropriate. Hoffman and Kim, "Science or Slaughter?"
31. Freeman, "Political Issues."
32. Mason, "Bowhead Whale Controversy"; Plaintiff Exhibit B, re: Adams, Hopson v. Kreps 462 F. Supp. 1374 (D. Alaska. 1979).
33. Hess, *Gift of the Whale*, 5.
34. Mason, "Bowhead Whale Controversy," 386.
35. Mitchell and Reeves, "Alaska Bowhead Problem."
36. In addition for these countries differing culturally from the Alaska Natives, there was also a large difference between whether the restrictions applied to commercial harvests or subsistence pursuits.
37. Eben Hopson, statement, Bowhead Whale Conference, Anchorage, January 16, 1979; Rafferty and Zeh, "Estimated Bowhead Whale Population."
38. Roberts, "*Hopson v. Kreps*," 248.
39. Eben Hopson, Sr. v. Juanita Kreps, 622 F.2d 1375 (9th Cir. 1980).
40. Japan has long believed itself to be a second-class member of the IWC and wants to have its fair quota. At one point Japan proposed that the IWC put a ban on Alaska Native whale hunting until they were allowed to harvest forty Minke whales as subsistence also. In the end this did not work out for Japan. For more on this controversy, see Wohlforth, *Whale and the Computer*. Japan finally dropped out of the IWC in 2018 to resume commercial whaling.
41. Case and Voluck, *American Laws*, 314.
42. Alaska Native Commission. "Final Report," 3:38.
43. Case and Volluck, *American Laws*, 270.
44. Brewster, *Whales*, 7–9.
45. Brewster, *Whales*, 42.

9. WHEN THE RAVEN FLIES WITH THE DOVE

1. Berger, *Village Journey*, 36.
2. Durbin, *Tongass*, 139, 147.
3. M. Jackson, "Climate Warrior"; see also the Hoonah Indian Association statement on watershed concerns. Hoonah Indian Association statement, typewritten copy in author's possession.
4. Schroeder and Kookesh, "Subsistence Harvest."
5. D. Purvis, *Ragged Coast*.
6. The purse seine–gear type is so called because it has a net that catches fish and then closes up like the strings of an old-fashioned purse.
7. Naske and Slotnick, *Alaska*, 102, 169, 175, 19.
8. Piracy was almost a way of life on these waters during the 1930s and 1940s. See D. Purvis, *Ragged Coast*.
9. Steve Langdon, anthropologist with an emphasis on Alaska fisheries, interview with the author, Anchorage, November 1989; Jake White, interview with the author, Hoonah, July 1990.
10. White, interview, July 1990.
11. Levey, "Pink Salmon Caught," tape A.
12. The purpose of the Limited Entry Act was to limit entry into the commercial fisheries and to allow more direct management of the fish stocks, which are the property of the holder and may be sold, bought, and inherited.
13. Jaegar, *Limited Entry Collage*; Langdon, *Transfer Patterns*.
14. White, interview, July 1990; John Hinchman, interview with the author, Hoonah, July 1990.
15. Langdon, *Transfer Patterns*.
16. In the early 1970s there was a so-called oil crisis caused by the machinations of the OPEC nations.
17. Schroeder and Kookesh, "Subsistence Harvest."
18. Schroeder and Kookesh, "Subsistence Harvest."
19. While conducting field studies in Douglas, Alaska, I happened on the notation on papers inside the ADFG file cabinet.
20. "Board of Fisheries Report."
21. White, interview, July 1990; Hinchman, interview, July 1990.
22. While working on my thesis, I went through the files at the ADFG office at Douglas, Alaska, with permission. I found things they did not realize were there.
23. Southeast Alaska Seiners Association (SEAS), "SEAS Indicator Opening Proposal," 1990, in author's possession.

24. Folta, Haas, and Simmons, *Hearing on Claims*.
25. Folta, Haas, and Simmons, *Hearing on Claims*.
26. Hardin, "Tragedy of the Commons."
27. Not everyone wanted the Alaska territory to be converted into a state, but many voted for statehood because they were promised the abolishment of fish traps that kept the fisheries at an unhealthy level and allowed a monopoly to the industrial fishing companies. The people also felt these companies were controlling Alaska politically and wanted the ability to make their own decisions and gain a sense of autonomy.
28. D. Purvis, "Eagle and the Raven."
29. Levey, "Pink Salmon Caught," tape D.
30. Wanda Culp, interview with the author, Hoonah, 1990.
31. Jaeger, *Limited Entry Collage*, 63.
32. White, interview, July 1990.
33. Levey, "Pink Salmon Caught," tape 44-11.
34. The Tlingit-Haida Central Council was formed to fight for the Tlingit and Haida Jurisdictional Suit, beginning in 1935, with the final recompense awarded in 1968.
35. Citizen advisory boards were added on by the Alaska Department of Fish and Game to give involved citizens (fishers in this case) a voice in decisions.
36. Langdon, interview with the author, Anchorage, May 1990.
37. The dead salmon was due to the nearby clear-cutting of old-growth trees on the hills. With no anchors the erosion was at its maximum level. The elders had warned the young people in the village corporation this would occur, but the do-or-die nature of corporations was a great motivator at the time. I was there during one of these occurrences, and I have no words for the smell of the rotting fish carcasses.
38. Stoebner, "Alaska Native Water Rights."
39. Case and Voluck, *Alaska Natives*, 70.
40. The Alaska National Interest Lands Conservation Act passed in 1980. Some parts were not new, such as the Arctic Wildlife Refugee, which had been protected since the 1970s.
41. Langdon, "Communal Property."
42. Hinchman, interview, August 1990.
43. White, interview, July 1990; Hinchman, interview, July 1990; Lily White, interview with the author, Hoonah, July 1990; Vic Bean, interview with the author, Hoonah, July 1990.
44. Levey, "Pink Salmon Caught," tapes A, E.
45. Levey, "Pink Salmon Caught," tape F.
46. Don Ingeldue, personal communication, July 1990.

47. Jaeger, *Limited Entry Collage*; Langdon, *Transfer Patterns*.

48. Levey, "Pink Salmon Caught," tape I.

49. Culp, interview, July 1990.

50. Goodrich, "Charting a Course."

51. Cerveny, *Sociocultural Effects*.

10. THE DAY THE WATERS DIED

1. Meganak, "Day the Water Died." Much of this chapter comes from my personal experience. Not only did I hear detailed reports about the *Exxon Valdez* grounding, but I went down to the Prince William Sound at the time to check out the situation for myself. I returned to the area again in 1991 with the Alaska Fish and Game Department.

2. The Yup'ik language divisions include Central Yup'ik (southwest Alaska), Siberian Yupik (Saint Lawrence Island), and Alutiiq (south-central Alaska).

3. Handwerk, "Ancient DNA Reveals." The Eyak are located to the Prince William Sound from a more northerly direction. They have assumed many of the Tlingit customs. They are not related to the Alutiiq, who are more Unangan or Yup'ik. Many of the Unangan or Alutiiq are in the area because they were brought over by the Russians.

4. Donna Ranney Plat, personal communication, June 2019.

5. Ross, *Environmental Conflict in Alaska*, 169–70.

6. The Alaska Syndicate discouraged all other competitors and were ruthless in their endeavors. In one case they burned down a Native woman's house when she went out to collect firewood. Frederica de Laguna, discussion with the author, Juneau, October 1995.

7. Partnow, *Making History*, 254.

8. Crowell, *Looking Both Ways*, 138.

9. Crowell, *Looking Both Ways*, 69, 75.

10. Braund and Associates, *Exxon Valdez Oil Spill*, 58–59.

11. Braund and Associates, *Exxon Valdez Oil Spill*, 60.

12. Braund and Associates, *Exxon Valdez Oil Spill*.

13. Braund and Associates, *Exxon Valdez Oil Spill*, 68, 71

14. Braund and Associates, *Exxon Valdez Oil Spill*, 78

15. Braund and Associates, *Exxon Valdez Oil Spill*, 78.

16. Ott, *Not One Drop*, 11–12.

17. Keeble, *Out of the Channel*, 68.

18. Shirley Komkoff, interview with the author, Juneau, May 1991, March 2007.

19. Keeble, *Out of the Channel*, 161, 75, 76.

20. Keeble, *Out of the Channel*, 93.

21. Ott, "They Have No Ears."

22. "Settlement." To show all sides, Jim McDaniel, who was part of the Natural Resources Division for the Eyak Corporation, told me that both Tatitlek and Chenega corporations profited from the EVOS money that was used to buy land. Personal communication, May 25, 2012.

23. Ott, *Nor One Drop*, 98.

24. Naske and Slotnick, *Alaska*, 349.

25. Wolfe and Walker, "Subsistence Economies."

26. Legal trials were numerous and often working at cross-purposes. This chapter provides a broad summary, an essence, of the outcomes, to provide a basic understanding. If the reader has further questions or wants more details, there are numerous resources on the spill, the environmental damage, and the legal angle. A good source to start with is Holba, "*Exxon Valdez* Oil Spill."

27. This law highlights the emphasis of complete equality within the Alaska Constitution, which, unlike the U.S. Constitution, did not protect the minorities from the tyranny of the majority. The dichotomy between the Alaska and U.S. Constitutions had previously come up, and this dispute continued.

28. "*Exxon Valdez*."

29. Naske and Slotnick, *Alaska*, 349.

30. Fall, "Subsistence Use."

31. Wilkins and Deloria, *Legal Universe*, 366–67.

32. Adam Liptak, "Damages Cut against Exxon in Valdez Case," *New York Times*, June 26, 2008.

33. Fixico, *Invasion of Indian Country*, 205–6.

34. Ott, *Not One Drop*, 270, 272.

35. Sylvia Lange, personal communication, June 2012; "Prince William Sound Recovered"; "Review of Impacts"; "Ten Years after Alaska Spill, Environmental Scars Remain, Progress Made, Long Ways to Go," *Baltimore Sun*, March 7, 1999.

11. GRANDMOTHER TO WATER GUARDIAN

1. Fred John Jr., personal communication, May 2019.

2. Katie invoked the Indigenous system of determining access to resources, referred to as "Indian Law." Though never documented, the important body of knowledge is now being passed to the next generation, so future Mentasta leaders can guide the community with wisdom and in accord with tradition. Ainsworth, *Mentasta Remembers*, 78.

3. Ainsworth, *Mentasta Remembers*, 78.

4. *Subsistence* is a Western term used to quantify the Indigenous way of life. The word has no equivalent in any of the Alaska Native languages. The people, however, adopted the usage of the term for better communication between themselves and the Western regulators.

5. Mike Dunham, "Renowned Athabascan Elder Katie John Dies," *Anchorage Daily News,* June 1, 2013.

6. Fred John Jr., personal communication, June 2018.

7. Case and Voluck, *Alaska Natives.*

8. Mylius, "Alaska State Land."

9. See the Supreme Court rulings in the 1820s under Chief Justice John Marshall. These rulings are sometimes referred to as the Cherokee Trilogy.

10. McGee, "Subsistence Hunting," 17.

11. "Grandmother Katie Prevails." This headline is one of many in either the mainstream press or the Native publications.

12. Thomas Morehouse, opinion, Supreme Court of the State of Alaska, No. 3540, December 22, 1989.

13. Morehouse, opinion, Supreme Court of the State of Alaska, No. A92-531 Civil, October 6, 1992.

14. Morehouse, decision, U.S. District Court for the State of Alaska, No. A90-0484-CV, March 30, 1994, 23.

15. Morehouse, decision, U.S. District Court for the State of Alaska, No. A92-0264-CV, March 30, 1994.

16. Katie John, "Fighting for Fish," *Anchorage Daily News,* July 19, 1988; Ainsworth, *Mentasta Remembers,* 36.

17. Morehouse and Holleman, "When Values Conflict," 24.

18. Morehouse and Holleman, "When Values Conflict," 24, 25.

19. "Knowles Faces Katie John Pressure," *Anchorage Daily News,* June 17, 2001.

20. Heather Kendall-Miller, online interview with the author, May 2014.

21. "Knowles Faces Katie John Pressure."

22. Dunham, "Renowned Athabascan Elder," 1, A-10.

23. Dunham, "Renowned Athabascan Elder."

24. Dunham, "Renowned Athabascan Elder."

25. Homestead should be considered "Indian Country" and protected by the Homestead Act of 1906. In Indian Country, natural resource policy is determined by the legal residents.

26. The Alaska Native Allotment Act allowed 160 acres to every qualifying Alaska Native male on land that was not otherwise reserved or appropriated or that contained known minerals. The land and resources belonged to the family in perpetuity.

Unlike the non-Native Homestead Act, there was no stipulation that agriculture had to be pursued. Native Allotments, 43 CFR 2212, Circular 2185, Dept. of the Interior at 6.

27. *"Katie John v. Norton."*

28. A victory was established later that closed the case, but that is beyond the scope of this chapter.

29. Dunham, "Renowned Athabascan Elder."

12. FISHING FOR FINES

1. In the Yup'ik language, there is no word or tense indicating future. In fact, it is considered boastful to even contemplate the future.

2. Barker, *Always Getting Ready.*

3. When this treaty was broken, the tribes eventually went to court and were victorious.

4. American Friends Service Committee, *Uncommon Controversy,* 25.

5. Governor Stevens served as governor of the Washington Territory from 1853 to 1857. He was responsible for making and breaking treaties with the tribes as the Pacific Northwest embodiment of Manifest Destiny.

6. For more details, see Sohappy v. Smith, USDC D. Oregon No. 68-409, plus the Boldt and Belloni decisions.

7. English common law, which has been referred to on several occasions, was another carryover from Europe to Jamestown. The law is based on tribunal precedent—that is, if a similar case had been heard before the courts, the outcome would be used to judge the current case. Chief Justice John Marshall combined English common law with the "Discovery Doctrine," another European import, to define Indigenous ownership of land.

8. Kyle Hopkins, "Akiak Elders Told Families to Fish Despite Government Ban," *Anchorage Daily News,* June 22, 2012.

9. Mike Williams, Akiak leader, interview with the author, Akiak, June 2013.

10. Hopkins, "Akiak Elders Told Families."

11. Hopkins, "Akiak Elders Told Families."

12. Tribal Councils were an outgrowth of New Deal legislation that allowed organized Indian "tribes" to organize and create their own constitution under the auspices of the Bureau of Indian Affairs. An effective political tool, these councils are often modeled after traditional elders' councils.

13. Jill Burke, "Trial Justice Lawyer, Defendant in Courtroom," *Alaska Dispatch,* October 10, 2012.

14. Burke, "Trial Justice."

15. *Alaska Native Subsistence,* 151.

16. Mike Williams, personal communication, November 2012. This sports fishing lobby is powerful because of the money it brings into the state. That money often translates into political sway.

17. Williams, interview, June 2013.

18. Jill Burke, "Trio of Native Kuskokwim Salmon Fishermen in Trial Found Guilty," *Anchorage Daily News*, October 30, 2012, https://www.adn.com/alaska-news/article/trio-native-kuskokwim-salmon-fishermen-trial-found-guilty/2012/10/30/.

19. Burke, "Trio of Native Kuskokwim."

20. Burke, "Trio of Native Kuskokwim."

21. Rachel D'Oro, "Yup'ik Fishermen Appeal Convictions for Taking King Salmon," *Anchorage Daily News*, June 23, 2013. *Dominant culture* is an anthropological term that indicates power but is not meant to denigrate Indigenous cultures.

22. Rachel D'Oro, "State Files Appeal in Illegal Fishing on Kuskokwim Case," *Anchorage Daily News*, July 11, 2013.

23. D'Oro, "Yup'ik Fishermen Appeal Convictions."

24. Frank v. State, 604 P.2d 1068 (1979).

25. American Indian Religious Freedom Act, Pub. L. No. 95-341, 95th Cong., 92 Stat. 469 (1978). The Yup'ik are not Indians, but so many federal laws use the term that at times the Yup'ik, Aleut (Unangan), and Iñupiat have to abide by the term themselves.

26. "When Global Warming Kills Your God," *Atlantic*, June 8, 2014. See also Kawagley, *Yupiaq Worldview*; and Fienup-Riordan, *Eskimo Essays*, particularly the chapter on cosmology.

27. "When Global Warming Kills."

28. Fienup-Riordan, *Eskimo Essays*, 167–91.

29. Lisa Demer, "Kuskokwim Fish Wars Heat Up Again as Silvers Enter the River," *Alaska Dispatch*, July 23, 2014.

30. D'Oro, "State Files Appeal."

31. Kawagley, *Yupiaq Worldview*, 16, 81.

32. Fienup-Riordan, *Eskimo Essays*, 18, 189.

33. "Request to Stand Down."

34. Williams, personal communication, May 18, 2022.

EPILOGUE

1. Fitzgerald, *Native Women and Land*, 107, 108.

2. Mike Williams, personal communication, September 2020.

3. Haycox, *Alaska*, 268.

4. "Scientists Assess Damage." As tectonic and unstable as the Alaska landmass has been for thousands of years, playing around with nuclear fission appears to be foolish.

5. Krista Langlois, "Salmon Power," *High Country News,* July 25, 2016, https://www
.hcn.org/issues/48.12/salmon-power.

6. Alaska Eskimo Whaling Commission, "About Us."

7. See Wohlforth, *Whale and the Supercomputer.*

8. Ned Rozell, "Despite Changing and Uncertain Habitat, Alaska's Bowhead Whales Appear to Be on the Rebound," *Anchorage Daily News,* January 30, 2021.

9. Breanna Draxler, "Gwich'in Voices Speak Out against Oil Drilling in Alaska," *Yes Magazine,* September 7, 2020.

10. Bob Childers and Charlie Kairaiuak in Soren Wuerth, quoted in "AFN Endorses Drilling in Arctic Refuge," *Arctic Sounder,* October 26, 1995. Twenty-plus years later, the argument is ongoing, and the basis and divisions remain.

11. "We Are Caribou People."

12. Alaska Federation of Natives, "Fifty Years of ANCSA." Two major issues are occurring right now, with no quick answers. The first issue deals with the landless Tlingit in southeast Alaska, who were left out of the distribution and are not fully covered by a village corporation. The other issue centers on the relationship of the corporations with the federal government and their status as tribes.

13. Larry Merculieff, telephone interview with the author, November 2021.

14. C. Jones, "Impact of Sturgeon II."

15. The *Sturgeon v. Frost* case had nothing to do with subsistence. It was instead an access issue. For an excellent analysis of the proceedings and the sometimes fickle finger of the law, see C. Jones, "Impact of Sturgeon II."

16. Donna Platt, testimony to the Trustee Council, Anchorage, Alaska, September 16, 1993. Platt was an activist against the damage that had occurred because of the oil spill and is named as a key witness on several documents. The "Dust Bowl" comment was part of personal communication, January 2023.

17. Schwing, "FEMA Sent Unintelligible Disaster."

18. Rhodes, *Environmental Justice in America,* 192.

19. Fixico, *Invasion of Indian Country,* 206.

20. The Alaska Native Allotment Act of 1906 guaranteed possession of the land or other resources if the proper paperwork had been filed and approved. Unfortunately, there were always questions of what exactly the proper paperwork was, and there never seemed to be anyone in charge of approving these allocations.

21. Fred John Jr., personal communication, August 2, 2021.

BIBLIOGRAPHY

ARCHIVES AND MANUSCRIPT MATERIALS

"Alaska Natives and the Land." 1962. Federal Field Committee Notes for Development Planning in Alaska. Loussac Library, Anchorage.

"Alice Petrivelli Interview." 1991. Project Jukebox. University of Alaska, Fairbanks. https://jukebox.uaf.edu/.

"Board of Fisheries Report." 1984. Fish and Game Office, Douglas, Alaska.

Frank, Richard. Story and testimony. Project Jukebox. University of Alaska, Fairbanks. https://jukebox.uaf.edu/.

Joseph, Philip. "The History of Aukquon." Manuscripts, 1967. ASL-MS-0004-33-010. Alaska Historical Collections. Alaska State Library, Juneau.

Kennedy, John F. "Remarks of Senator John F. Kennedy at the Edgewater Hotel, Anchorage, Alaska, September 3, 1960." Pre-presidential Papers. Senate Files. Series 12. Speeches and Press. Box 910. John F. Kennedy Presidential Library and Museum, Boston.

Levey, Stephen B. "Pink Salmon Caught in Salt Water: The Southeast Alaska Salmon Fishery; A Guide to Interviews with Men and Women Engaged in Commercial Fisheries, 1913–1978." Alaska Historical Collections. Alaska State Library, Juneau.

Lipps, Oscar H. "Eskimo Villages along the Coast and on the Islands of the Bering Sea: A Report on Their Economic and Social Conditions." Bureau of Indian Affairs. Entry 797. RG 75. National Archives and Records Administration, Washington DC.

Nash, Roy. "Recommendations regarding the General Reindeer Superintendent for Alaska, November 11, 1933." File 9-1-93. Part 4. Records of the Office of Territories and Island Possessions. National Archives and Records Administration, Washington DC.

Olson, Clarence. Papers. September 8, 1942. Fish and Wildlife Service Records. National Archives and Records Administration, Washington DC.

Rainey, Froelich G. "Memorandum concerning Control and Ownership of Native Reindeer in Arctic, Alaska." Unpublished memorandum. Territorial Government files. Native Misc. Pacific Alaska Region. National Archives and Records Administration, Washington DC.

"Reindeer Herding: The Present and the Past." Project Jukebox. University of Alaska, Fairbanks. https://jukebox.uaf.edu/reindeer-herding.

Roosevelt, Theodore. Letters. Stanford University Archives, Stanford.

Wickersham, James. Diary 40. MS 107. Box 8. Alaska Historical Collections. Alaska State Library, Juneau.

PUBLISHED WORKS

Ainsworth, Cynthea. *Mentasta Remembers*. Toronto: University of Toronto Press, 2002.

Alaska Eskimo Whaling Commission. "About Us: Alaska Eskimo Whaling Commission." Accessed August 15, 2023. http://www.aewc-alaska.org/about-us.html.

Alaska Federation of Natives. "Fifty Years of ANCSA." *Alaska Native Quarterly*, Spring 2021.

Alaska Native Commission. "Final Report." Alaskool. 1994. http://www.alaskool.org/resources/anc_reports.htm.

Alaska Native Subsistence and Fishing Rights: Hearing before the Committee on Indian Affairs. 107th Cong., 2nd sess. (2002) (to receive testimony on subsistence hunting and fishing by the Native Alaskans).

Aleut Evacuation: The Untold War Story. Gaff Rigged/Aleut Pribilof Islands Association, 1992. DVD.

Aleutian Pribilof Islands Association. *The Aleut Relocation and Internment during World War II: A Preliminary Examination*. Department of Community and Regional Affairs, 1981.

"Alice Petrivelli: Leader and Champion of the Aleut People and Life." Aleut Foundation. June 23, 2020. https://www.facebook.com/www.thealeutfoundation.org/videos/2549057455408471/.

American Friends Service Committee. *Uncommon Controversy: Fishing Rights of the Muckleshoot, Puyallup, and Nisqually Indians*. Seattle: University of Washington Press, 1970.

Andrews, Clarence Leroy. *The Eskimo and His Reindeer in Alaska*. New York: Caxton, 1938.

Atwood, Evangeline. *Frontier Politics: Alaska's James Wickersham*. Portland OR: Binford and Mort, 1979.

Auke Bay Breakwater and Related Marine Development: Final Environmental Impact Study. Washington DC: U.S. Army Corp of Engineers, 1985.

Banner, Stuart. *How the Indians Lost Their Land: Law and Power on the Frontier*. Cambridge MA: Belknap Press of Harvard University Press, 2005.

Barker, James. *Always Getting Ready: Upterrlainarluta; Yup'ik Eskimo Subsistence in Southwest Alaska*. Seattle: University of Washington Press, 1993.

"Barry Commoner and Paul Sears on Project Chariot: Epiphany, Ecology and the Atomic Energy Commission." University of Chicago Press. Accessed August 15, 2023. https://www.journals.uchicago.edu/doi/10.1086/701650.

Beach, Hugh. *The Saami of Lapland*. Finland: Minority Rights Group, 1988.

Beech, Mary L. "Refugees from the Pribilofs." *Alaska Life, the Territorial Magazine* 7, no. 8 (August 1944): 20–21.

Berger, Thomas R. *Village Journey: The Report of the Alaska Native Review Commission*. New York: Hill and Wang, 1985.

Berry, Mary Clay. *The Alaska Pipeline: The Politics of Oil and Native Land Claims*. Bloomington: Indiana University Press, 1975.

Black, Lydia. *Russians in Alaska, 1732–1867*. Fairbanks: University of Alaska Press, 2004.

Blackman, Margaret R. *Sadie Brower Neakok, an Inupiaq Woman*. Seattle: University of Washington Press, 1989.

Bockstoce, John. "A Preliminary Estimate of the Reduction of the Western Arctic Bowhead Whale by Pelagic Whaling, 1848–1915." *Marine Fisheries Review*, September 1980.

———. *Whales, Ice, and Men: The History of Whaling in the Western Arctic*. Seattle: University of Washington Press, 1986.

Boeri, David. *People of the Ice Whale: Eskimos, White Men, and the Whale*. New York: Harvard Brace, 1983.

Bordner, Autumn S., Danielle A. Crosswell, Ainsley O. Katz, Jill T. Shah, Catherine R. Zhang, Ivana Nikolic-Hughes, Emlyn W. Hughes, and Malvin A. Ruderman. "Measurement of Background Gamma Radiation in the Northern Marshall Islands." *Proceedings of the National Academy of Sciences of the United States of America* 113, no. 25 (2016).

Braund, Stephen R., and Associates. *Effects of the Exxon Valdez Oil Spill on Alutiiq Culture and People*. Anchorage: Braund and Associates, 1993.

Breu, Mary. *Last Letters from Attu: The True Story of Etta Jones, Alaska Pioneer and Japanese Prisoner of War*. Anchorage: Alaska Northwest Books, 2009.

Brewster, Karen, ed. *The Whales, They Give Themselves: Conversations with Harry Brower, Sr.* Fairbanks: University of Alaska Press, 2004.

Brinkley, Douglas. *The Quiet World, Saving Alaska's Wilderness Kingdom, 1879–1960*. New York: HarperCollins Books, 2012.

Brooks, Maria, dir. *The Reindeer Queen: The Story of Sinrock Mary*. Watertown MA: Documentary Education Resources, 2005.

Brooks, Paul H., and Joseph Foote. "The Disturbing Story of Project Chariot." *Harper's*, April 1962, 60–67.

Brower, Charles D. *Fifty Years below Zero: A Lifetime of Adventure in the Far North.* Fairbanks: University of Alaska Press, 1994.

Burch, Ernest. *Inupiaq Eskimo Nations of Northwest Alaska.* Fairbanks: University of Alaska Press, 1998.

Camacho, David E., ed. *Environmental Injustices, Political Struggles: Race, Class, and the Environment.* Durham: Duke University Press, 1998.

Carter, Erik. "Aleut Relocation." Master's thesis, Alaska Pacific University, 1992.

Case, David S. *American Laws, Alaska Natives.* Fairbanks: University of Alaska Press, 1980.

Case, David S., and David A. Voluck. *Alaska Natives and American Laws.* 2nd ed. Fairbanks: University of Alaska Press, 2002.

Cerveny, Lee K. *Sociocultural Effects of Tourism in Hoonah.* General Technical Report, PNW-GTR-734. Washington DC: U.S. Department of Agriculture, 1994.

Chance, Norman. *The Eskimo of North Alaska.* New York: Holt, Rinehart, and Winston, 1966.

———. *The Inupiat and Arctic Alaska.* Fort Worth: Holt, Rinehart, and Winston, 1994.

Churchill, Frank C. *Reports on the Condition of Educational and School Service and Management of Reindeer Service in Alaska for 1906.* Washington DC: Government Printing Office, 1906.

Coates, Peter A. *The Trans-Alaska Pipeline Controversy: Technology, Conservation, and the Frontier.* Fairbanks: University of Alaska Press, 1993.

Cohen, Fay. *Treaties on Trail: The Continuing Controversy over Northwest Indian Fishing Rights.* Seattle: University of Washington Press, 1986.

Cohen, Felix. *Handbook of Federal Indian Law.* Washington DC: Government Printing Office, 1941.

Commission on Wartime Relocation and Internment of Civilians. *Personal Justice Denied.* Seattle: University of Washington Press, 1983.

Committee of Territories. *To Provide for Administration of National Property and the Interests of the Territory of Alaska.* Washington DC: Government Printing Office, 1921.

Crowell, Aron. *Looking Both Ways: Heritage and Identity of the Alutiiq People.* Fairbanks: University of Alaska Press, 2001.

Cueva, Christopher. "America's Territory: The Aleut Evacuation; A Grave Injustice." Alaska History and Cultural Studies. October 1, 1998. https://akhistory.lpsd.com/articles/article.php?artID=215.

Daley, Patrick J., and Beverly A. James. *Cultural Politics and Mass Media: Alaska Native Voices.* Urbana: University of Illinois Press, 2004.

Dauenhauer, Nora Marks, and Richard Dauenhauer, eds. *Haa Kusteeyí, Our Culture: Tlingit Life Stories*. Seattle: University of Washington Press; Sealaska Heritage Foundation, 1994.

Deloria, Vine, Jr., and Clifford L Lytle. *American Indians, American Justice*. Austin: University of Texas Press, 1983.

Demuth, Bathsheba. "More Things on Heaven and Earth: Modernism and Reindeer in the Bering Strait." PhD diss., University of California, 2012.

Dorsey, Kurkpatrick. *Whales and Nations: Environmental Diplomacy on the High Seas*. Seattle: University of Washington Press, 2013.

Durbin, Kathie. *Tongass: Pulp Politics and the Fight for the Alaska Rain Forest*. Corvallis: Oregon State University Press, 2005.

Echo-Hawk, Walter R. *In the Courts of the Conqueror: The 10 Worst Indian Law Cases Ever Decided*. Colorado: Fulcrum, 2010.

Etok [Charlie Edwardsen Jr.]. *The Bitter Root of Truth: The Russian-American Occupation of a Sovereign People*. Anchorage: Alaska Federation of Natives, 1991.

"*Exxon Valdez: Alaska Native Class v. Exxon*." Lewis and Clark Law School's Environmental Law. Accessed October 6, 2013. http://www.elawreview.org/summaries/natural_resources/native_american_issues/in_re_exxon_.

Fall, James A. "Subsistence Use of Fish and Wildlife and EVOS." *Arctic Issues Digest*, October 1991, 12–15.

"Feds Recognize Indian Point as Historic Place." Sealaska Heritage. August 16, 2016. https://www.sealaskaheritage.org/node/293.

Fienup-Riordan, Ann. *Eskimo Essays: Yup'ik Lives and How We See Them*. New Brunswick: Rutgers University Press, 1990.

Fitzgerald, Stephanie J. *Native Women and Land: Narratives of Dispossession and Resurgence*. Albuquerque: University of New Mexico Press, 2015.

Fixico, Donald L. *The Invasion of Indian Country in the Twentieth Century: American Capitalism and Tribal Natural Resources*. Boulder: University of Colorado Press, 1998.

Fjeld, Faith. "The Alaska Sami: A Reindeer Story." Vesterheim. Accessed July 18, 2023. http://saamibaiki.org/contentConnections/Vesterheim-A%20reindeer%20story.pdf.

Flory, Charles. *United States of America v. Wm. E. Murphy Miles, Edward Murphy, Elsie Murphy Jones, Mabel Murphy Nelson, et al.* 1931. No. 3201-A. District 1 of the Territory of Alaska, Division 1.

Folta, George W., Theodore H. Haas, and Kenneth R. L. Simmons. *Hearing on Claims of Natives of the Towns of Hydaburg, Klawock, and Kake, Alaska, Pursuant to the Provisions of Section 201, 21b of the Regulation for Protection of the Commercial Fisheries of Alaska, 1944, Brief Proposed Findings of Fact, Conclusions of Law and Recommendation of the Petitioners 22*. Washington DC: Government Printing Office, 1944.

Forsyth, James. *A History of the Peoples of Siberia: Russia's North Asian Colony, 1587–1990*. Cambridge: Cambridge University Press, 1992.

Fortuine, Robert. *Chills and Fever: Health and Disease in the Early History of Alaska*. Fairbanks: University of Alaska Press, 1989.

Fouberg, Erin H., Alexander B. Murphy, and H. J. de Blij. *Human Geography: People, Place, and Culture*. 9th ed. New York: Wiley and Sons, 2009.

Freeman, Milton M. R. "Political Issues with Regard to Contemporary Whaling." In *Who's Afraid of Compromise*, edited by Simon Ward. Tokyo: Institute of Cetacean Research, 1990.

The Fur Seal of Alaska. Report No. 1425. Washington DC: Committee of Expenditures, Department of Commerce and Labor, 1913.

Gallagher, Hugh Gregory. *Etok: A Story of Eskimo Power*. Florida: Vandamere, 2001.

Garfield, Brian Wynne. *The Thousand-Mile War*. New York: Doubleday, 1960.

Gedicks, Al. *The New Resource Wars: Native and Environmental Struggles against Multinational Corporations*. Boston: South End, 1993.

Gewalt, Dinah. "Attu, a Lost Village of the Aleutians." National Park Service. Accessed August 16, 2023. https://www.nps.gov/articles/featured_stories_aleu.htm.

Gilio-Whitaker, Dina. *As Long as Grass Grows: The Indigenous Fight for Environmental Justice from Colonization to Standing Rock*. Boston: Beacon, 2019.

Glass, Henry. *Cruising in Alaska Waters, October 11, 1880, to June 8, 1881*. Pt. 1 of *Report for the U.S. Naval Officers Crossing Alaska Waters*. H. Ex. Doc 81, 47th Cong., 1st Sess. (1881) at 18–27.

Goldschmidt, Walter R., and Theodore H. Haas. *Haa Aani, Our Land: Tlingit and Haida Land Rights and Use*. Edited by Thomas Thornton. Seattle: University of Washington Press, 1998.

Golodoff, Nick. *Attu Boy: A Young Alaskan's World War II Memoir*. Edited by Rachel Mason. Fairbanks: University of Alaska Press, 2015.

Goodrich, Bethany. "Charting a Course for Prosperity in Isolated Rural Alaska." Alaska Business. March 22, 2018. https://www.akbizmag.com/industry/small-business/charting-a-course-for-prosperity-in-isolated-rural-alaska/.

Grabinska, Kornelia. "History of Events Leading Up to the Alaska Native Claims Settlement Act." Alaskool. January 1983. http://www.alaskool.org/projects/ancsa/tcc2/tananachiefs.html.

"Grandmother Katie Prevails over State of Alaska on Subsistence Fishing Rights." U.S. Department of the Interior. May 17, 1996. https://www.indianaffairs.gov/as-ia/opa/online-press-release/grandmother-katie-prevails-over-state-alaska-subsistence-fishing.

Gregg, Sheila. "Teller Misled Alaskans on Project Chariot." In *Authentic Alaska: Voices of Its Native Writers*, by Susan B. Andrews and John Creed, 96–98. Lincoln: University of Nebraska Press, 1998.

Gruening, Ernest. *Many Battles: The Autobiography of Ernest Gruening*. New York: Liveright, 1973.

Hadleigh-West, Frederick. *Project Chariot, Final Report: Archaeological Survey of Excavations at Ogoturuk Creek, Northwest Alaska*. Fairbanks: University of Alaska, 1961.

Handwerk, Brian. "Ancient DNA Reveals Complex Story of Human Migration between Siberia and North America." *Smithsonian Magazine*. June 5, 2019. https://www .smithsonianmag.com/science-nature/ancient-dna-reveals-complex-story-human -migration-between-siberia-and-north-america-180972356/.

Hardin, Garrett. "The Tragedy of the Commons." *Science* 162 (December 13, 1968): 1243–48.

Harring, Sid L. *Crow Dog's Case: American Indian Sovereignty, Tribal Law, and United States Law in the Nineteenth Century*. Cambridge: Cambridge University Press, 1994.

"Has Prince William Sound Recovered from the Spill?" NOAA Office of Response and Restoration. March 17, 2019. https://response.restoration.noaa.gov/oil-and -chemical-spills/significant-incidents/exxon-valdez-oil-spill/prince-william-sound -recovered.html#:~:text=Click%20on%20infographic%20to%20view,recovery %20has%20not%20taken%20place.

Haycox, Stephen. *Alaska, an American Colony*. Seattle: University of Washington Press, 2002.

———. *Frigid Embrace: Politics, Economics, and Environment in Alaska*. Corvallis: Oregon State University Press, 2002.

Haycox, Stephen W., and Mary Childers Mangusso. *An Alaska Anthology: Interpreting the Past*. Seattle: University of Washington Press, 1996.

Hearings of the Reindeer Committee in Washington D.C. Vol. 1. Washington DC: U.S. Department of the Interior, 1931.

Hensley, William L. Iggragurk. *Fifty Miles from Tomorrow: A Memoir of Alaska and the Real People*. New York: Crichton Books, 2009.

Hess, Bill. *The Gift of the Whale: The Inupiat Bowhead Hunt, a Sacred Tradition*. Seattle: Sasquatch Books, 1999.

Hickel, Walter J. *Who Owns America?* New York: Paperback Library, 1971.

Higginson, Ella. *Alaska, the Great Country*. New York: Macmillan, 1923.

Hoffman, Sarah, and Weonjin Kim. "Science or Slaughter?" Stanford Law School. November 20, 2015. https://law.stanford.edu/2015/11/20/science-slaughter-whaling -debate-continues/.

Holba, Carrie, comp. "*Exxon Valdez* Oil Spill." Alaska Resources Library and Information Services. March 22, 2019. https://www.arlis.org/docs/vol2/a/EVOS_FAQs.pdf.

Hopson, Eben. "Eben Hopson: An American Story." Bowhead Whale Conference. January 16, 1979. http://www.ebenhopson.com/papers/1979/Bowhead.html.

"*Hopson v. Kreps*: Bowhead Whales, Alaskan Eskimos, and the Political Question Doctrine." *Hastings Constitutional Law Quarterly* 9, no. 23 (Fall 1981): 231–56.

"Hunting and Fishing Rights (*Katie John v. Norton*)." Native American Rights Fund. Accessed August 15, 2023. https://narf.org/cases/katie-john-v-norton/.

Huntington, Henry P., and Lori T. Quankenbush. "Walrus Near Point Hope." State of Alaska. November 13, 2013. https://www.adfg.alaska.gov/static/research/programs/marinemammals/pdfs/2013_traditional_knowledge_point_hope.pdf.

"International Fur Seal Treaty Negotiated 50 Years Ago." U.S. Department of the Interior. July 2, 1963. https://fws.gov/sites/default/files/documents/historic-news-releases/1961/19610702.PDF.

Inupiat Paitot. "The Statement and Policy and Recommendations Adopted by the Point Barrow Conference on Native Rights." Barrow, Alaska, November 17, 1961.

Jackson, Matt. "Climate Warrior: Wanda Culp Stands up for Native Sovereignty." Southeast Alaska Conservation Council. March 12, 2020. https://www.seacc.org/climate-warrior-wanda-culp.

Jackson, Sheldon. *Fourth Reindeer Report, 1895*. Washington DC: Government Printing Office, 1896.

———. "Report of the General Education Agent to the Secretary of the Interior." In *The Department of Education Report from the General Agent of Education in the Years, 1889–1890*. Washington DC: Government Printing Office, 1890.

———. "Report on Education in Alaska, 1890–1891." In *Report of the Commissioner of Education, 1890–1891*. Washington DC: Government Printing Office, 1891.

———. *Report on Education in Alaska, Senate, 49th Congress, Ex. Doc. No. 85*. Washington DC: Government Printing Office, 1886.

———. *Report on the Introduction of Domestic Reindeer into Alaska*. Washington DC: Government Printing Office, 1893.

Jaeger, Sig. *A Limited Entry Collage*. Seattle: North Pacific Fish Vessel Owner's Association, 1975.

Johnshoy, Walter J. *Apaurak in Alaska: Social Pioneering among the Eskimos*. Translated and compiled from the records of the Reverend T. L. Brevig. Philadelphia: Dorrance, 1944.

Jones, Craig. "The Impact of Sturgeon II on Alaska Subsistence Management: A Chance for Peace in the Jurisdiction Wars." *Alaska Law Review* 36, no. 2 (2019): 221–49.

Jones, Dorothy Knee. *A Century of Servitude: Pribilof Aleuts under U.S. Rule*. Maryland: University Press of America, 1980.

Jones, Dorothy M. *Aleut in Transition: A Comparison of Two Villages*. Seattle: University of Washington Press, 1976.

Kawagley, A. Oscar. *A Yupiaq Worldview: A Pathway to Ecology and Spirit*. Prospect Heights IL: Waveland, 1995.

Keeble, John. *Out of the Channel: The Exxon Valdez Oil Spill in Prince William Sound*. New York: HarperCollins, 1991.

Krause, Aurel. *The Tlingit Indians: Results of a Trip to the Northwest Coast of America and the Bering Straits*. Translated by Erna Gunther. Seattle: University of Washington Press, 1956.

Krech, Shepard, III. *The Ecological Indian*. New York: Norton, 1999.

LaDuke, Winona. *All Our Relations: Native Struggles for Land and Life*. Cambridge MA: South End, 1999.

Laguna, Frederica de. *Under Mt. Saint Elias*. Washington DC: Smithsonian Institution, 1972.

Langdon, Steve. "From Communal Property to Common Property to Limited Entry: Historical Ironies in the Management of Southeast Alaska Salmon." In *A Sea of Small Boats*, edited by John Cordell. New York: Cultural Survival, 1989.

———. *Transfer Patterns in Alaskan Limited Entry Fisheries: Final Report to the Limited Entry Study Group of the Alaska State Legislature*. Juneau: Legislature, 1980.

Lantis, Margaret. "The Reindeer Industry in Alaska." *Arctic* 3, no. 1 (1953): 32.

Laughlin, William S. *Aleuts: Survivors of the Bering Land Bridge*. New York: Holt, Rinehart, Winston, 1980.

Leslie, Jacques. *Deep Water: The Epic Struggle over Dams, Displaced People, and the Environment*. New York: Farrar, Straus, and Giroux, 2005.

Limerick, Patricia Nelson. *Legacy of Conquest: The Unbroken Past of the American West*. New York: Norton, 1987.

———. *Something in the Soil: Legacies and Reckonings in the New West*. New York: Norton, 2000.

Lomen, Carl J. *Fifty Years in Alaska*. New York: McKay, 1954.

Lopp, William T. "Lapps and Finns Coming." *Eskimo Bulletin*. 1898. http://www.alaska .net/ahs/eskimo.htm.

———. *Report on the Reindeer Industry in Northern Alaska*. Washington DC: U.S. Bureau of Education, 1912.

———. *White Sox: The Story of Reindeer in Alaska*. New York: World Book, 1924.

Mangusso, Mary Childers. "Anthony J. Dimond and the Politics of Integrity." In Haycox and Mangusso, *Alaska Anthology*, 246–66.

Marks, Paula Mitchell. *In a Barren Land: American Indian Dispossession and Survival.* New York: Morrow, 1998.

Mason, Milo. "The Bowhead Whale Controversy: Background and Aftermath of *Adams v. Vance.*" *Harvard Environmental Law Review* 2 (1981): 363, 371.

Mason, Rachel, and Ray Hudson. *Lost Villages of the Eastern Aleutians: Biorka, Kashega, Makushin.* Washington DC: National Park Service, 1987.

McGee, Jack B. "Subsistence Hunting and Fishing in Alaska: Does ANILCA's Rural Subsistence Priority Really Conflict with the Alaska Constitution." *Alaska Law Review* 27, no. 221 (December 2010): 17.

Meganak, Walter. "The Day the Water Died." Project Jukebox. University of Alaska, Fairbanks. Accessed August 22, 2023. https://jukebox.uaf.edu/speech-written -chief-walter-meganack.

Meinhardt, Robert, ed. *The Legacy of Project Chariot.* Washington DC: Department of the Interior, n.d.

Merculieff, Ilarion "Larry." *Wisdom Keepers: One Man's Journey to Honor the Untold History of the Unangan People.* Berkeley: North Atlantic Books, 2016.

Miller, Robert J. *Native America, Discovered and Conquered: Thomas Jefferson, Lewis and Clark, and Manifest Destiny.* Lincoln: University of Nebraska Press, 2008.

Mitchell, Donald Craig. *Sold American: The Story of Alaska Natives and Their Land, 1867–1959.* Hanover: University Press of New England, 1997.

———. *Take My Land, Take My Life: The Story of Congress's Historic Settlement of Alaska Native Land Claims, 1960–1971.* Fairbanks: University of Alaska Press, 2001.

Mitchell, Edward, and Randall R. Reeves. "The Alaska Bowhead Problem: A Comment and Argument." *Arctic* 33, no. 4 (1980): 686–723.

Mobeley, Charles. *World War II: Southeast Alaska Internment Camps.* Washington DC: National Park Service, 2011.

Morehouse, Thomas A., and Marybeth Holleman. "When Values Conflict: Accommodating Alaska Native Subsistence." Occasional Paper 22. Anchorage: Institute of Social and Economic Research, 1994.

Morgan, Lael. *Art and Eskimo Power: The Life and Times of Alaskan Howard Rock.* Fairbanks: Epicenter, 1988.

Mowat, Farley. *The Siberians.* Baltimore: Penguin Books, 1972.

Muir, John. *Travels in Alaska.* Boston: Houghton Mifflin, 1915.

Mylius, Dick. "Alaska State Land, History and Federal Land Issues for Citizens Advisory Commission on Federal Areas." Alaska Department of Natural Resources. August 2013. http://dnr.alaska.gov/commis/cacfa/documents/FOSDocuments/ MyliusPresentation.pdf.

Nalder, Eric. *Tanker Full of Trouble.* New York: Grove, 1994.

Naske, Claus-M., and Herman E. Slotnick. *Alaska: A History of the 49th State*. Norman: University of Oklahoma Press, 1987.

Nelson, Edward William. *The Eskimo about Bering Strait*. Eighteenth Annual Report to the American Ethnology to the Secretary of the Smithsonian Institution. Washington DC: Government Printing Office, 1899.

Nelson, Richard. *Make Prayers to the Raven: A Koyukon View of the Northern Forest*. Chicago: University of Chicago Press, 1983.

New Study: Bowhead Whale Population Greater. Fairbanks: Alaska Offshore SOHIO Petroleum, 1982.

Newton, David E. *Environmental Justice: A Reference Handbook*. Santa Barbara CA: Contemporary World Issues, 1996.

NOAA (National Oceanic and Atmospheric Administration). "Subsistence Taking of Northern Fur Seal on the Pribilof Islands." *Federal Register*. October 2019. https://www.federalregister.gov/documents/2019/10/02/2019-21450/subsistence-taking-of-northern-fur-seals-on-the-pribilof-islands.

Norwood, Gus. "Rampart Dam at Perspective." *Alaska Construction*, July–August 1966, 18–20.

Olson, Dean F. *Alaska Reindeer Herdsman: A Study of Native Management in Transition*. Fairbanks: University of Alaska Press, 1969.

O'Neill, Dan. *The Firecracker Boys: H-Bombs, Inupiat Eskimos, and the Roots of the Environmental Movement*. New York: St. Martin's Press, 1994.

Ott, Riki. *Not One Drop: Betrayal and Courage in the Wake of the Exxon Valdez Oil Spill*. Vermont: Chelsea Green, 2008.

———. "They Have No Ears." In *Arctic Voices: Resistance at the Tipping Point*, edited by Subhankar Banerjee, 53–65. New York: Seven Stories, 2012.

Partnow, Patricia. *Making History: Alutiiq/Sugpiaq Life on the Alaska Peninsula*. Fairbanks: University of Alaska Press, 2002.

Paul, Fred. *Then Fight for It*. Victoria: Trafford, 2003.

Paul, Joel Richard. *Without Precedent: Chief Justice John Marshall and His Times*. New York: Riverhead Books, 2018.

"People of the Whale: A Fight for Survival." *Indian Affairs*, December 1979, 7.

Porter, Joy. *Native American Environmentalism: Land, Spirit, and the Idea of Wilderness*. Lincoln: University of Nebraska Press, 2012.

Purvis, Diane J. *The Drive of Civilization: The Stikine Forest versus Americanism*. South Carolina: CreateSpace Independent, 2016.

———. *Ragged Coast, Rugged Coves: Labor, Culture, and Politics in Southeast Alaska Canneries*. Lincoln: University of Nebraska Press, 2021.

————. "When the Eagle and the Raven Fly with the Dove: Hoonah's Purse Seine Fleet." Master's thesis, Alaska Pacific University, 1990.

Purvis, Thomas L. *Colonial America to 1763*. New York: Facts on File, 1999.

"Q and A with Rosita Worl: Indian Point, a Sacred Site." Sealaska Heritage. Accessed July 17, 2023. https://www.sealaskaheritage.org/node/621.

Rafferty, Adrian, and Judith E. Zeh. "Estimated Bowhead Whale Population Size and Rate of Increase from the 1993 Census." *Journal of Statistical Research* 93, no. 44 (June 1993): 451–63.

Rakestraw, Laurence. "A History of the United States Forest Service in Alaska." USDA Forest Service. 2002. https://foresthistory.org/wp_contents/uploads/2017/A -History-of-the-US-Forest-Service-in-Alaska.pdf.

Ray, Dorothy Jean. *The Eskimos of Bering Strait, 1650–1898*. Seattle: University of Washington Press, 1975.

————. "The Making of a Legend: Charlie and Mary Antisarlook's Reindeer Herd." In *Ethnohistory in the Arctic: The Bering Strait Eskimo*, edited by Richard A. Pierce, 132–40. Kingston ON: Limestone, 1983.

"Request to Stand Down during June 2022 Openers to Ensure Escapement of AYK Bound Salmon." Bering Sea Fisherman. June 13, 2022. https://deltadiscovery.com/ request-to-stand-down-during-june-2022-openers-to-ensure-escapement-of-ayk -bound-chum-salmon/.

"A Review of Impacts on Environmental Livelihoods, Space, Governance." *Energy Research and Social Science* 75 (2021).

Rhodes, Edwardo Lao. *Environmental Justice in America: A New Paradigm*. Bloomington: Indiana University Press, 2003.

Robbins, Paul. *Political Ecology: A Critical Introduction*. Boston: Blackwell, 2004.

Roberts, Sally A. "*Hopson v. Kreps*: Bowhead Whales, Alaskan Eskimos, and the Political Doctrine." *Hastings Constitutional Law Quarterly* 9, no. 1 (Fall 1981): 231–48.

Robertson, Lindsay G. *Conquest by Law: How the Discovery of America Dispossessed Indigenous Peoples of Their Lands*. New York: Oxford University Press, 2005.

Rogers, George. *An Economic Analysis of the Pribilof Islands, 1870–1947*. Fairbanks: University of Alaska Institute of Social, Economic, and Government Research, 1976.

Ross, Ken. *Environmental Conflict in Alaska*. Boulder: University of Colorado Press, 2002.

Saunt, Claudio. *Unworthy Republic: The Dispossession of Native Americans and the Road to Indian Territory*. New York: Norton, 2020.

"School Desegregation and Civil Rights Stories: Ketchikan, Alaska." National Archives. Accessed July 17, 2023. https://www.archives.gov/education/lessons/desegregation/ ketchikan.html.

Schroeder, Robert F., and Matthew Kookesh. "Subsistence Harvest and Use of Fish and Wildlife Resources and the Effects of Forest Management in Hoonah, Alaska." Technical Paper 142. Juneau: Alaska Department of Fish and Game, 1990.

Schwing, Emily. "FEMA Sent Unintelligible Disaster Relief Information to Alaska Native People after Typhoon Merbok." KYUK-Bethel. January 9, 2023. https://www.ktoo .org/2023/01/09/fema-sent-unintelligible-disaster-relief-information-to-alaska -native-people-after-typhoon-merbok/.

"Scientists Assess Damage Caused by Earthquake Near Amchitka." Office of Legacy Management. October 14, 2014. https://www.energy.gov/lm/articles/scientists -assess-damage-caused-by-earthquake-near-amchitka.

Segall, Peter. "Bill to Preserve Unangax̂ Gravesite Passes House." *Juneau Empire*. April 9, 2021. https://www.juneauempire.com/news/bill-to-preserve-aleut-cemetery -passes-house/.

Senate Hearing on Environmental Justice. C-SPAN. July 22, 2021. https://www.c-span.org/ video/?513610-1/senate-hearing-environmental-justice.

"Settlement." *Exxon Valdez* Oil Spill Trustee Council. Accessed July 21, 2023. https:// evostc.state.ak.us/oil-spill-facts/settlement/.

Sheador, L. R. L. "The Abandoned North." February 18, 2017. https://canonrose.net/ 2017/02/18/the-abandoned-north-part-iv-adak-island-unexploded-ordnance/.

Shields, Walter C. "Superintendent's Report: Bureau of Education for Alaska." *Bulletin Issue*, nos. 40–50 (1918): 21–23.

Sloan, Cliff, and David McKean. *The Great Decision: Jefferson, Adams, Marshall, and the Battle for the Supreme Court*. New York: Public Affairs Press, 2009.

Spencer, Robert F. *The North Alaskan Eskimo: A Study in Ecology and Society*. New York: Dover, 1988.

Spurr, Stephen H. *Rampart Dam and Economic Development of Alaska*. Ann Arbor: University of Michigan, 1966.

Stephanson, Anders. *Manifest Destiny: American Expansion and the Empire of Right*. New York: Hill and Wang, 1995.

Stern, Richard O., Edward L. Arobio, Larry L. Naylor, and Wayne C. Thomas. *Eskimos, Reindeer, and Land*. Fairbanks: University of Alaska, School of Agriculture, 1980.

Stoebner, Kerry. "Alaska Native Water Rights as Affected by ANCSA." *American Indian Journal* 4 (1978): 1–26.

Swanton, John R. *Social Conditions, Beliefs, Linguistics Relationship of the Tlingit Indians*. Washington DC: Government Printing Office, 1908.

Taliaferro, John. *In a Far Country: The True Story of a Mission, a Marriage, a Murder, and the Remarkable Reindeer Reserve of 1989*. New York: Public Affairs, 2006.

Taylor, Alan. *American Colonies: The Settling of North America.* Vol. 1. New York: Penguin Books, 2002.

"Teddy Roosevelt and the Indians." Native American Net Roots. Accessed August 15, 2023. http://nativeamericannetroots.net/diary/1093.

Thornton, Thomas F. *Haa Leelk'w Has Aani Saaxu/Our Grandparents' Names on the Land.* Seattle: University of Washington Press, 2012.

Torrey, Barbara. *Slaves of the Harvest: The Story of the Pribilof Aleut.* Anchorage: TDX Reprints, 1985.

Turner, Edith. "Native Reaction to Nuclear Contaminants: The Social Aspects." Paper presented at the Alaska Anthropological Association, April 1993.

Ulrich, Roberta. *Empty Nets: Indians, Dams, and the Columbia River.* Corvallis: Oregon State University Press, 2007.

U.S. Bureau of Education. *Report on the First Reindeer Fair.* Washington DC: U.S. Government Printing Office, 1917.

U.S. Congress. *Senate Compilation of the Acts of Congress and Treaties Relating to Alaska from March 30, 1867 to March 3, 1905.* Washington DC: Government Printing Office, 1906.

U.S. House of Representatives. *Congressional Record.* Washington DC: Government Printing Office, 1937.

——— . *Enhance the Effectiveness of International Fisheries Conservation Programs.* 181st Cong., House Rpt. 02-468 (1971).

——— . *Water Transportation Report, Alaska.* Washington DC: Government Printing Office, 1891.

Usner, Daniel H. "A Savage Feast They Made of It: John Adams and the Paradoxical Origins of Federal Indian Law Policy." *Journal of Early Republic* 33 (Winter 2013): 607–41.

"U.S. Pays Restitution, Apologizes to Unangan (Aleut) for WWII Internment." Native Voices. Accessed July 17, 2023. https://www.nlm.nih.gov/nativevoices/timeline/635.html.

Veltre, Douglas W., and Allen P. McCartney. "Russian Exploitation of Aleuts and Fur Seals: The Archaeology of Eighteenth and Early Nineteenth Century Settlements in the Pribilof Islands, Alaska." *Historical Archaeology* 36, no. 3 (2008): 8–17.

Veniaminov, Ivan. *Journals of the Priest Ioann Veniaminov in Alaska, 1823–1836.* Translated by Jerome Kissilinger. Fairbanks: University of Alaska Press, 1993.

Vorren, Ornulv. *Saami, Reindeer, and Gold in Alaska: The Emigration of Saami from Norway to Alaska.* Prospect Heights IL: Wayland, 1994.

"We Are Caribou People: Gwichin Leaders in Washington Push for ANWR Protection." CBC News. March 26, 2019. https://www.cbc.ca/news/canada/north/gwichin-washington-anwr-congress-1.5072215.

Wenz, Peter S. *Environmental Justice*. New York: State University of New York Press, 1988.

Whale and Dolphin Conservation. "Whaling in Greenland." Accessed August 15, 2023. http://us.whales.org/wdc-in-action/whaling-in-greenland.

White, Richard. *It's Your Misfortune and None of My Own: A New History of the American West*. Norman: University of Oklahoma Press, 1991.

Wilkins, David E., and Vine Deloria Jr. *The Legal Universe: Observations on the Foundations of American Law*. Golden CO: Fulcrum, 2011.

Williams, Gerald O. *The Bering Sea Fur Seal Dispute*. Eugene OR: Alaska Maritime, 1984.

Willis, Roxanne. *Alaska's Place in the West: From Lost Frontier to the Last Frontier*. Lawrence: University of Kansas Press, 2010.

———. "A New Game in the North: Alaska Reindeer Herding, 1890–1940." *Western Historical Quarterly* 37 (Autumn 2006): 278–82.

Wohlforth, Charles. *The Whale and the Supercomputer: On the Northern Front of Climate Change*. New York: North Point Books, 2004.

Wolfe, Robert J., and Robert J. Walker. "Subsistence Economies in Alaska: Productivity, Geography, and Development Impacts." *Arctic Anthropology* 24 (1987): 56–81.

Wolfe, Robert J., Joseph J. Crowe, Steven J. Langdon, John Wright, George K. Shrod, Linda J. Ellan, Valerie Sumida, and Peter Usher. "Subsistence-Based Economies in Coast Communities of Southwest Alaska." Technical Paper 95. Social and Economic Studies Program. Juneau: Alaska Department of Fish and Game, 1984.

Wooley, Christopher B. "Alutiiq Culture before and after the Exxon Valdez Oil Spill." *American Indian Culture and Research Journal* 19, no. 4 (1995): 125–53.

Yukon Flats National Wildlife Refuge. Washington DC: U.S. Fish and Wildlife Service, 1978.

INDEX

Adams, John, 9
Ahtna, 187, 188, 189, 192, 198
Akiak, 200, 204, 212
Alaska Conservation Society (ACS), 96,
    98, 217, 240n17
Alaska Constitution, 183, 192, 209, 251n27
Alaska Department of Fish and Game
    (ADFG), 54, 158, 160, 165, 166, 169–70,
    188–89, 201, 202, 206
Alaska Eskimo Whaling Commission
    (AEWC), 140–41, 145, 146, 147, 217
Alaska Federation of Natives (AFN),
    122, 197
Alaska-Juneau Mining Company, 18, 24
Alaska National Interest Lands
    Conservation Act (ANILCA), 166,
    191, 192, 194, 195, 197, 207, 208, 249n40
Alaska Native Brotherhood (ANB), 52,
    112, 165, 237n57
Alaska Native Claims Settlement Act
    (ANCSA), 82, 121, 129, 132, 153, 210,
    219–20

Alaska Organic Act (1884), 18, 21, 26, 29,
    63, 130
Alaska Reindeer Service (ARS), 71
Alaska Statehood Act (1959), 107
Alaska Syndicate, 175, 250n6
Aleut, 3, 4. See also Unangan (Aleut)
Aleutian Campaign (World War II), 41, 71
Aleutian Chain, 31, 32, 37
Aleutian-Pribilof Islands Association
    (APIA), 40, 60
Alutiiq, 4, 173, 174, 177
American Indian Freedom of Religion
    Act (1978), 210, 254n25
Antisarlook, Charlie, 65
Antisarlook, Mary Palasha Makrikoff,
    65–66
Arctic Slope Native Association
    (ASNA), 120, 121, 122, 123, 128, 129
Army Corps of Engineers, 102, 107, 113, 114
Athabascan (Dené), 3, 74, 104, 114, 115
Atomic Energy Commission (AEC), 86, 87,
    88, 90, 91, 92, 93, 94, 95, 96, 98, 99, 100

273